The New
Southern Cook

ALSO BY JOHN MARTIN TAYLOR

Hoppin' John's Lowcountry Cooking

The New Southern Cook

•

*Two Hundred Recipes
from the South's
Best Chefs and Home Cooks*

•

John Martin Taylor

with

WINE RECOMMENDATIONS BY

Debbie Marlowe

FOREWORD BY

Lee Bailey

BANTAM BOOKS
NEW YORK · TORONTO · LONDON · SYDNEY · AUCKLAND

THE NEW SOUTHERN COOK

A Bantam Book/ July 1995

Portions of this book have appeared in somewhat different form in *The New York Times Magazine*.

The words *Hoppin' John's* and the portrayal of a chef carrying a tray of books are the trademark of John Martin Taylor, registered in the U.S. Patent and Trademark Office.

Library of Congress Cataloging-in-Publication Data

Taylor, John Martin, 1949–
The new southern cook : 200 recipes from the South's best chefs
and home cooks / John Martin Taylor.
p.   cm.
Includes bibliographical references and index.
ISBN 0-553-09417-3
1. Cookery, American—Southern style.   2. Wine lists.   I. Title.
TX715.2.S68T392   1995
641.5975—dc20   94-41863
                                                            CIP

Published simultaneously in the United States and Canada

PRINTED IN THE UNITED STATES OF AMERICA

FFG   10 9 8 7 6 5 4 3 2 1

For Sue

Contents

7
Fresh Relishes and Salads

8
Breads

9
Sweets

Acknowledgments

Assembling a cookbook can be a lonely affair. Much of the work is pure lab work, developing recipes by testing formulas and codifying results. The process of writing always comes down to one person and a blank piece of paper—even if there's a computer between them. Before I could write this book, however, I depended on scores of people for advice, opinions, recipes, and connections. I slept in their homes and interviewed them at work. I read their books and ate in their restaurants. I used their produce and drew on their expertise as if they were public servants. This book is theirs, too.

The New Southern Cook evolved from an idea that Doe Coover, my agent, gave to me. She and Fran McCullough, my editor, bring much-needed professionalism and laughter to my work. The book is not the travelogue through the New South that they envisioned, but I did travel extensively in researching it. I have listed here those people who opened their homes and lives to me as I worked on this project.

As a social animal I know that there will always be a handful of people without whom I could not survive. I certainly would never have found the time or focus necessary to put this book together without, foremost, the help of my sister Sue Highfield. When she came to work with me, I left my bookstore—and the books—in her hands. The mutual love and trust were not only inspirational but also a boon to Hoppin' John's. We owe a big thanks to our regular customers, too.

Mikel Herrington and Debbie Marlowe were constantly loving and supportive even as I hid to write. Mikel tasted not only the recipes in this collection but the ones that didn't make it, too—and always with a smile. Debbie offered not only the consumer-friendly wine recommendations but also her skills at the grill.

JoAnn Yaeger, Adrianne Massey, Sally Stafford, Dana Downs, and Richard Little continue, year after year, to hear me out and to provide me with wonderful conversation, ideas, and friendship. My father and step-mother, Lila, have always shown a genuine interest in my work; his critical reading of my manuscripts is more akin to the work of a copy editor, and he has caught many syntactical and practical errors.

Karen Hess has inspired a certain quality in my work that is only vaguely related to hers. I have never found a factual error in her work, and she is often the ultimate source on questions of culinary history. She continues to share freely her vast knowledge with me; more important, I hold her friendship dear.

Mary Taylor, Andy Gowder, and my nephew Duke Highfield have provided me with good—and often free—legal and financial counsel. And my good friend Bessie Hanahan, who *should* be practicing law, knows just when to call to get me out of the kitchen. Thank you all.

In addition, my heartfelt thanks to all of the following, who have helped make this book possible:

In South Carolina: Shari Hutchinson, Pete Wyrick, Donna Florio and Bonnie Caracciolo, Richard Perry, Bubba and Mary Ann Foy, Jack and Lee Early, Veda Godwin, Cassandra McGee, Frank Lee, Bill and Kim-Anh Huebner, Connie Hawkins, Donna Skill, Rob Ennis, Philip Bardin, Steve Jackson, Ben Cramer, Roger Cooper, Scott and Ruth Fales, Dick and Tricia Schulze, Alice Marks, Mary Edna Fraser, Cheryl Van Landingham, Gilson Capilouto, Billie Burn, Marion Sullivan, Mark Gray, Rosemary and Sergio Franco, Christine Homer, all the great folks at Crosby's Seafood, Libby Ambrose, Tony Barwicke, Andrea and Jack Limehouse, Caroline and Pete Madsen, Nan Mahone of the Charleston Farmers Market, and the farmers Louise Bennett, York Washington, Dan and Karen Kennerty, Bokay Murray, Juanita Hammond, and Pink Brown.

In Georgia: Terrell Vermont, Emma Edmunds, Kate Bennett, George and Cecilia Holland, George Wearn, Damon Fowler, Gerard Krewer, J. B. Jones, Howell Boone, and Boo and DeNean Stafford.

In North Carolina: Lederman Rupp, Matt Neal, Bill and Catherine Diehl, Sam McGann, Jimmy Noble, Jenny and Keebe Fitch, Jeanne Voltz, and Ben and Karen Barker.

In Kentucky: Camille Glenn and Bill Hughes.

In Tennessee: Ginny Whitt of White Lily Foods.

In Alabama: Robert and Gertrude Hunter, Frank Stitt, and Chris Hastings.

In Virginia: Jamie and Rachel Nicoll, Kyle Strohman and Richard Pla-Silva, Charlie Jenkins, Jimmy and Stacey Sneed, and Scot Hinson.

In Louisiana: Lawrence Stanback, Tom Cowman and JoAnn Clevenger of Upperline, and Patrick Dunne.

In Florida: Bob and Debbie Wallace, Fish Skipper and Leila Bakkum,

Mark McDonough, Sam and Anne Salem and their mother, Farideh, Joe and Louise Assi, and Bob Merendino.

Also, thanks to Philadelphia's Judy Faye of the Book and the Cook and Michael and Terry McNally at London Grill; in New York, thanks to Elizabeth Schneider, Lee Bailey, and Jeff Steingarten; and in Italy, thanks to Gianni Martini and Alberto Ronchetti.

Foreword

Several years ago I was scheduled to spend a few weeks photographing in and around Charleston, South Carolina. Before leaving I asked around among my acquaintances in hopes of locating a Charlestonian whom I might speak to about the cooking and history of the area. The one name that seemed to crop up over and over again was "John Taylor," who happened to be winding up a tour promoting his own first book. When we finally connected, I found John not only to have a wealth of knowledge of the history and food of the region but also to have a lively sense of humor about the customs, preferences, and foibles of the local residents—himself included. In short, John was god-sent, and we became fast friends. His invaluable insights always proved to be right on the button.

So, as prejudiced as I admit to being, I'm pleased and flattered to have the opportunity to recommend this, his latest effort, to you. Quite simply I think you'll love it—and while I'm at it, congratulations to you, John!

My unscientific way of judging a new cookbook is to leaf through it and see how many things pique my interest. By that measure, THE NEW SOUTHERN COOK rates close to the top for me and when I came across a recipe for Green Tomato soup—being a confirmed soup and tomato nut— I was really hooked. Take my word for it, there's good fishing here.

Lee Bailey

Introduction

Who is the new southern cook? You might be surprised. But you might also be surprised by *where* the South is. I'm not sure that I could honestly describe the boundaries of the South or if any southerner could, though we certainly have profound opinions about where it *isn't*. I get out a map of the United States and take a good look at the southeastern quadrant. The Mississippi and Ohio rivers basically describe the western boundaries of what I think of as the South, but southerners in Texas, Louisiana, and Arkansas would beg to differ.

It should go without saying that the South is comprised of the states of the Confederacy, but today's South bears little political or demographic resemblance to the region's nineteenth-century agrarian society. And today's residents of the border states such as Kentucky and Arkansas are decidedly *southern*—just ask them. Eastern Texas and northern Florida are as southern as Alabama. Few consider northern Virginia truly southern, though I know some West Virginians who would be insulted if I called them anything but.

The southerner's much ballyhooed sense of place seems to define where the South is as much as anything else; that is, the South is more idea than area, more emotion than nation. It is "home" in the minds of those people who consider themselves southerners. And those people may no longer live here. When I lived in New York and asked people where they were from, I noticed that even if they had been living in the city for two decades they would name the state or country of their birth. When I ask the same question of someone who may have moved to the South just two months ago, the answer is likely to be Hilton Head or Atlanta or Charlotte.

For the purposes of this book, I have not attempted to define the South geographically. If people think of themselves as living in the South, then I think of them as southerners. And if people think of themselves as southerners, then they must be from the South. But the South is also where grits are automatically served with breakfast.

Which brings us to restaurants. I don't know of many honest, traditional southern restaurants that exist anywhere—outside the South or within it. Traditional southern cooking has rarely been available except in private homes. There are exceptions, of course, such as Mrs. Wilkes' in

Savannah, Dooky Chase in New Orleans, Dip's in Chapel Hill, and numerous fried fish and barbecue houses from the Ozarks to Jacksonville. But traditional southern cooking is rarely being cooked on a daily basis, however passionate we are about our food.

In what was forever a matriarchal society, women in the South now work at jobs outside the home, just as they do in the rest of the country. We watch the same TV, shop at the same malls, and share the same health crazes as midwesterners. We've embraced pizza and sushi just like New Yorkers. Trendy California-style bistro fare is cooked not only in our restaurants but also in our homes. We are no longer a separate nation and no longer rural, but we still start talking about supper before we've finished lunch. It's perhaps this passion for food that sets us apart.

The passion coupled with the climate. The hottest part of the summer and the coldest part of the winter seldom last more than a few weeks in the South; snow is rare in much of the area. Well-known southern hospitality is due at least partially to the warm weather. Dining is a far more casual—and often spontaneous—affair. Dropping by is not considered rude, even at suppertime, and your southern friends might even be offended if you were in the neighborhood and *didn't* call. A real friend is one who tells you, "If there's any good okra at the Farmers' Market, bring it over tonight. I've got some good tomatoes, and my crab trap is full."

The climate affords the South two tomato and corn crops, green vegetables throughout the year, and a seemingly endless supply of seafood. We spend a lot of time outdoors on our patios, in our boats, on our beaches, and in our forests. Much of the cooking is done outside. My back porch—really just a covered patio—has four coolers, an electric smoker, a charcoal grill, a gas grill, a two-burner propane camp stove, and a 240,000-BTU gas burner. I usually take some of the equipment in the back of my pickup when I go to the beach for a long weekend, but I also take it with me on the road when I'm researching so that I can have my pot of espresso even in the backwoods of Georgia.

It's not just the hunters and fishermen who cook with cast-iron skillets and who deep-fry turkeys in 10-gallon pots. As Jeff Steingarten wrote in *Vogue,* "In the South, everybody, I think, has a rusty old propane burner in the backyard." I know more than a few southern cooks whose backyards are better equipped than their kitchens, where toasters and mixers are second and third generation. Heritage still accounts for many of the flavors of the South, but when I use my grandmother's wooden spoon in her cast-iron skillet, I'm probably sautéing in olive oil, not frying bacon. I usually do my frying outdoors and invite a bunch of friends over.

Air-conditioning cannot be a grand success in the South for the reason that the honest natives of the region recognize the natural summer heat as a welcome ally in that it makes the inside of houses and offices agreeably uninviting, if not actually prohibited territory.

Clarence Cason, *90° in the Shade* (1935)

Clarence Cason was wrong. Air-conditioning did finally come, and the area embraced it. The Atlantic and Gulf coasts were forever changed. The Sea Islands that hug the Carolina and Georgia shores, once the sites of vast cotton plantations, had been transformed into exclusive resorts for the nation's first millionaires after the Civil War. But as European travel became easier and more popular, those luxurious Sea Island "cottages" were abandoned for more temperate travel. It was air-conditioning, golf, and marketing after World War II that effected the repopulation of those once-pristine subtropical islands. They again became the playgrounds of the wealthy, then later, as more and more resorts and housing developments (often called "plantations") were built, the destinations of thousands of midwestern and northeastern travelers and retirees. Chefs there began calling nontraditional dishes and ingredients "local." New tastes emerged.

Southern cities were similarly changed. Office parks went up along interstates that cut through former farmland. Atlanta, then Charlotte, then the "Triangle" (Raleigh–Durham–Chapel Hill) became the centers of commerce, stealing the limelight from the venerable old port cities like Charleston and New Orleans. Every Fortune 500 company opened an office in Atlanta. Geneticists flocked to North Carolina the way computer scientists had to Silicon Valley. Jacksonville, Florida, became a home base to major insurance companies. Miami became the port of entry for thousands and thousands of immigrants from the Caribbean, Central and Latin America, and Asia; these former aliens moved to Atlanta and Dallas and became citizens. Many began to consider themselves southern.

From these burgeoning Latin and Asian populations to African-Americans' return from northern cities to their roots in the South, the demographics of the region have changed dramatically in the last twenty or thirty years. The "New South" I often hear about has little to do with the Old. Southerners may have clung desperately to some of the most obvious symbols of the culture of the Old South, such as the architecture (Charleston, South Carolina, led the nation's preservationist movement), but they have often lost touch with the land and the way it works. (The same state saw more than 1,000 farms go out of business in 1990.)

The South is often air-conditioned, industrialized, and urban, however pastoral the countryside. It is international, and it is the new melting pot. We southerners are often misunderstood by our northern siblings, but we are as often misunderstood by ourselves. Some of us have been so wrapped up in change that we haven't noticed who has moved in next door. I imagine that most southerners would be amazed, for example, to hear that Jacksonville has the largest percentage of Middle Easterners of any American city. Northerners would be equally surprised to know that Atlanta's famed Chamblee Drive is now often referred to as "Chambodia," a name given to the street by the food writer Terrell Vermont, whose cross-cultural recipes are among those featured in this volume.

Today's southerner may be black, white, Yankee, Cuban, Middle Eastern, or Vietnamese; industrialist, oncologist, or clam farmer. Few of us still live on the farms that once were the southern norm; even fewer are the cooks that characterized the region just twenty years ago. When I was growing up in South Carolina, my mother stayed home and put three meals on the table every day (except on Sunday, when she cooked but two); in those days most women here were home during the day. Her constant "Don't slam the screen door!" was as much a plea to save her cake in the oven as it was a call for peace and quiet. Today I know only a handful of friends who still bake at home; none are without air-conditioning. What you'll find in our cupboards and refrigerators has changed as well. An early advocate of and participant in Charleston's revived Farmers Market, I have watched with wonder as markets have reappeared throughout the South's newly awakened urban areas. Beautiful local produce is once again widely available, but I see the bags of mesclun, the cilantro, and the Japanese eggplant selling as quickly as the collards and butter beans; tuna steaks as fast as the crabs. More than 150 languages are spoken in one of Atlanta's markets, where you can buy just about any ingredient you could possibly want. Clearly, what's cooking from Richmond to Dallas is something other than hog meat and hoecakes.

It amazes me how many weird ideas persist about the South and our cooking, even as our novelists and rock 'n' roll bands are best-sellers, and our population increases at twice the national rate. Fresh lard is next to impossible to find in the South, for example, yet outsiders think southerners cook everything in it.

Jamie and Rachel Nicoll raise the finest, free-ranging, milk-fed veal and lamb in the foothills of Virginia. They cook on open fires of oak and eschew traditional, heavier preparations of those meats. Scientific researchers from around the world have settled in North Carolina's "Triangle." Asian cooks work with the local greens, and young American chefs add lemongrass to traditional southern soups. Lederman Rupp, a clothing manufacturer from Ohio, has moved to Charlotte, near the South Carolina border, to be closer to cotton mills. From warehouses filled with camel hair he also distributes his natural lump charcoal—his grandfather's fifty-year-old product whose time has finally come—and over which he cooks "everything."

Farmers are growing mayhaws and pecans as commercial crops in the state of Georgia. Mayhaw is an indigenous plant whose fruits were once used by only the most traditional farm cooks; pecans were imported from the Mississippi Delta. The groves now produce the bonus of valuable truffles. New southern dairies are producing a variety of specialty and farmstead cheeses from both cow's and goat's milk. Recipes calling for fresh cream cheese and chèvre are now common south of the Mason-Dixon line.

Down on the coast, Howell Boone is a third-generation shrimper in idyllic Darien who harvests 600-pound Atlantic sturgeons, then processes caviar "the Russian way"—the only person doing so in America. His malossal caviar is as fine as any from the Baltic. From a deeply responsible fishing family, his father is the inventor of the highly publicized (and often controversial) "Georgia Jumper"—the Turtle Excluder Device certified for shrimp nets by the National Marine Fisheries Service.

The coal mines of Appalachia, sultry Tara-like oak alleys, and white sand beaches are just three small parts of the huge area I call the South in this book. Inland, beyond the low-lying coastal plain, much of the South is hilly; limestone and clay caverns are common. Former cotton plantations are still large tracts of land, but they are often managed as hunting plantations. Just outside the entrance to the one where his father cooked for sixty years (and just across the highway from where his grandmother, as a slave, bore her white owner twelve children), James Benjamin Jones serves some of the finest barbecue in the South. Right where Highway 319 crosses the state line into Georgia from Tallahassee, JB's Bar-B-Que and Grill is the favorite of everyone from many miles afar (and of the locals, such as neighboring plantation squire Jimmy Buffet). Jones is among the growing number of blacks who are returning south, reversing a fifty-year trend.

About the Recipes

The South is a vast region that changes character—and diet—even as you cross county lines. Appalachian cooks who learned to bake quick breads in coal-burning stoves know little of the rice cookery of the South Carolina and Georgia Lowcountry. The tidewater cuisine of Virginia is elegant and understated; the Creole cooking of the Mississippi Delta is anything but subtle. Mexican influences appear in most Texas kitchens, but neighboring Louisiana cooks with a profound French accent. They may fry chicken in Louisville the same way they do in Mobile, but horse people in Kentucky eat few of the same foods as African-Americans in the Deep South, and their cultures rarely mix.

In this collection you will see recipes that reflect the Sephardic, West African, Indian, Native American, German, Vietnamese, and Middle Eastern —to name but a few—influences that have shaped what's cooking down South. There are several fritter batters—it's true, southerners *can* fry—but there is no salmon, nor are there macadamia nuts, which have nothing to do with the area. There are recipes from some of the area's best chefs, but almost without exception those chefs are native southerners whose cooking is based in tradition. When I was submitted a recipe for something called Hoppin' John Risotto, I simply tossed it out: hoppin' john, my namesake, is a pilau; the pot must never be stirred, and each long grain of rice must stand separately. Risotto is made with the shorter and stickier Arborio rice of Italy; the pot is stirred constantly until the dish is creamy.

I traveled from Louisiana to Virginia, Kentucky to Florida to research this book. I sent hundreds of letters and made dozens of phone calls to cooks, writers, farmers, food purveyors, and chefs throughout the region looking for foods to include. Many chefs who consider what they are serving in their restaurants to be southern simply sent me their menus—they are, at first glance, often mind-boggling in their complexity and seemingly daunting to the home cook. A closer, second look might reveal honest fare of locally raised ingredients simply prepared.

Whether a recipe came from an award-winning chef or a stranger in the grocery store, my rules for inclusion in this book were always the same: (1) It had to be honest food rooted in the area and in who the cook is. (2) It had to be something that the average housewife in Iowa could and would do. (3) It had to work *and* taste good.

All of these recipes have been tested by me several times in my minuscule (three by four feet!) kitchen. I have no cooking assistant. I do not own a dishwasher, a microwave, or a heavy-duty mixer or food processor. None of the recipes in this book requires that you go out and buy a Cuisinart, a KitchenAid, or a set of new knives. Several recipes *do* require a well-seasoned cast-iron skillet, but every kitchen should have one. If a recipe required too many pots and pans, rarely did I include it. For example, I decided not to include the increasingly popular coconut fried shrimp. Not only do you use a frying pan, but you also need a bowl for the shrimp, one for the flour, one for the egg wash, and one for the coconut—and if you don't use freshly grated coconut you may as well not bother. And so, after perfecting a recipe through a dozen trials (and many errors), I omitted it. The recipes are simple; there are no difficult techniques to master.

I purposely have not included hard-to-find ingredients. I make my chili from venison, but the recipe gives you options; I've tested every recipe with every substitute suggested. Nearly every recipe that I got from a chef called for country ham and shallots. Sometimes my grocer wouldn't have shallots, but I left them in the recipes anyway and hope that you will use common sense and substitute the whites of scallions. Country ham may not be readily available where you live, but the Ingredients and Sources section tells you where to get it and a few other southern specialties. None of these recipes are written in stone; think of them as blueprints.

I call myself a culinary preservationist—part historian, part practitioner, and part mover and shaker. The vast changes that the South has seen in the last hundred years inspired me to write my first book, *Hoppin' John's Lowcountry Cooking*, in which I sought to preserve culinary traditions that I saw disappearing. The Select Bibliography includes basic reference books and books on the South and its cooking that I have found useful through the years. In this book I have embraced the changes and tried to sort out the best of the new and the old in today's southern kitchens.

In the acknowledgments of *The Cooking of South-West France*, Paula Wolfert said that she wanted to write a "living cookbook, a book that encompassed the traditional recipes of the region as well as the new ones adapted from the old." I don't pretend that this book should be compared to Paula's (or the American South to the Pays d'Oc), but I do take heed of her note on the attribution of recipes. These recipes are my written versions of ideas that seem to be recurrent in southern kitchens today. I don't think anyone *invented* them, but if there was a chef or home cook whose version was particularly exciting—or easy to prepare or readily adaptable to home kitchens across the land—I gave credit where it was due. I don't trust cooks who won't give out recipes, because no two people will have the same results with the same recipes. I've tried to make these recipes—even those from fancy restaurants—as easy as possible without sacrificing the integrity of the dish or of the region. I think they are honest statements about the South.

Some of the southern stereotypes are, of course, true. We are an eccentric bunch in a land where eccentricities are fostered and cherished: You have only to look at our representatives in Washington to understand that southern truth. Our passion for food and eating is just another of those eccentricities that has added to the popularity of our novelists, songwriters, and playwrights. When I called a friend whose father had died and asked her what food I could send, she told me, "Honey, you know Daddy wasn't dead five hours and there were already three hams here. I've got a freezer full of pound cakes, and we've started giving them away. One of them was pink!"

If some southern classics such as iced tea and candied yams seem conspicuous in their absence here, it may be because I have already given what I consider to be the best recipes in my first book. Or it may be that I find they are no longer the norm. This collection is admittedly a very personal one. I rarely drink iced tea, though at Pinckney Cafe and Espresso across the street from me in Charleston I often order the delicious Red Zinger Tea and Apple Juice combination because it truly quenches thirst. If there seems to be an inordinate amount of grilled food in this book, it is because there seems to be an awful lot of grilling going on down South. I've not put words in the mouths of southern cooks; what follows are quotes, not inventions.

Some of the food is surprisingly rich; some of it is as light as a mimosa blossom. The common ground seems to be the proverbial joy of cooking—a spark that ignites a passion for food in even the newest southerners. You find all kinds of folks eating at the barbecue shacks and grilling in their backyards down South—whether an elegant New Orleans courtyard or a dusty trailer park. But you also find good ol' boys dressed in silk shirts, dining out, and ordering wines from the South of France and dishes made with so-called exotic mushrooms. You're also likely to find those mushrooms in the Piggly Wiggly, the Winn Dixie, and Publix—southern grocery stores—and those wines in our home cellars. You're going to be surprised by the new southern cook.

People are often amazed to hear me say that I grew up in a small southern town and that we had a wine cellar. Indeed, I was brought up in a home where wine was part of the meal. I asked my dear friend Debbie Marlowe, whose wine knowledge has become instinctual, to offer suggestions for a choice of beverage with many of the recipes included. Her notes on those choices follow this Introduction.

"Hoppin'" John Taylor
Charleston, 1994

A Note About the Wine Recommendations

The right wine? There are so many! My recommendations are not the only wines that will properly accompany these recipes. You must take your own palate and mood into consideration. In recommending the beverages to accompany these foods, I have not specified vintage years because these recipes are timeless; wine has more variables. I have occasionally noted particular producers whose styles are timeless, but the harvest really dictates the final style. The region, grape variety, and winemaking technique have been my guidelines in making the suggestions. If I suggest an inexpensive Médoc, go ahead and buy a young château-bottled red Graves from an off year or ask your dealer to lead you to a Médoc-style wine from another region.

Find a wine merchant you trust and ask for details; he or she should be able to take my general recommendations and point out specific bottles for these meals. If I have recommended, for example, an earthy red Bordeaux, specify your price range and follow the merchant's suggestion. Share your wine experiences and let the merchant guide you accordingly, but if you find the advice not in tune with your palate, choose another merchant—this is not divorce, just another part of your wine education.

Not every wine style or every wine-producing country is represented in this book. In fact some of the wines that John and I often drink are not mentioned. I chose wines whose characteristics best complement this food. Sauvignon Blanc is a grape seldom seen in John's cellar, but it works well with the acidic sauces that are popular in the South today. In the winter we still eat some of the traditional meat dishes that call for a big, tannic Bordeaux, yet you seldom see it called for in this collection, which features some lighter preparations.

Perhaps you already have some wine in your cellar that you've been meaning to drink. Use our Wine Index at the back of the book to look up the wine, then find the dish(es) that I have recommended it accompany. It may be just what you wanted to cook.

The general guidelines I have used aren't always foolproof. I don't know of a perfect match year in and year out—except Champagne when you're happy and Champagne when you're sad.

Debbie Marlowe
Charleston, 1994

CHAPTER
1

Soups and Stews

Though traditional southern meals were rarely divided into a series of courses in the French manner, a soup as a first dish has been common since colonial days. The she-crab soup of Charleston, the turtle soup of Maryland, and delicate consommés in Virginia have begun many meals over the years.

More common, though, are the hearty one-pot meals such as gumbo and chili with roots much deeper than Europe. West African stews and Indian curries have enjoyed a popularity in the South as long as fried chicken. Many such meals are served over bowls of steaming white rice and with crusty golden corn bread cooked in a cast-iron skillet. In the winter months I often make dinner of a big pot of greens (with plenty of pot likker and corn bread to sop it up!).

These recipes include both the traditional and the newest of the South's many soups and stews. You'll want to make some of them for a crowd of hearty eaters and others as elegant first courses. Some of the soups make excellent lunch or supper fare by themselves.

Light Tomato Soup

I first had this delightful soup at the table of Bessie Hanahan, whose cook, Lucille Grant, is considered one of Charleston's best. Bessie first saw a version of the recipe in the Ft. Lauderdale Junior League cookbook, but it has become our own.

This is a thin, delicate soup that makes a perfect first course in summer. I puree the leftovers with a Cucumber–Yogurt Salad (Chapter 7) and serve it cold.

1 cup chopped onion, about 1 medium
½ cup finely diced carrot, about ½ large
¼ cup finely diced celery
4 tablespoons butter, ½ stick
6 medium vine-ripened tomatoes, cut into wedges,
   about 5 cups
2½ tablespoons tomato paste
1 garlic clove, minced
1 teaspoon salt
several parsley sprigs
1 fresh thyme sprig
1 bay leaf
1 quart chicken stock
freshly ground white pepper to taste
½ cup sour cream or crème fraîche, optional
fresh chives for garnish, optional

Sauté the onion, carrot, and celery in the butter in a large sauté pan over medium heat until the vegetables are soft, about 10 minutes. Add the tomatoes, tomato paste, garlic, salt, and herbs. Bring to a boil, stirring occasionally, reduce the heat, cover the pan, and simmer for 20 minutes. Strain well.

Add the stock to the sauté pan, then add the strained tomato mixture. Simmer for another 15 minutes, then correct the seasoning with white pepper. Strain a second time if desired. Serve warm, garnished if desired with a dollop of sour cream or crème fraîche and a few chives.
Serves 6

WINE:
Bordeaux Blanc Appellation Contrôlée

Green Tomato Soup

TO BE SERVED HOT OR COLD

This recipe came to me from Ben Barker, who, with his pastry chef wife, Karen, is the chef-owner of the Magnolia Grill in Durham, North Carolina. Durham lies at the center of the "Triangle" formed with Raleigh and Chapel Hill, one of the country's most progressive scientific research communities and home to NC State, UNC, and Duke. Academic types mix with good ol' boys, and nowhere are the results more evident than in the kitchen. This newfangled soup of Ben's is both hearty and refined; it bears witness to what sociologists are calling the New South. It's delicious and easy, too.

FOR THE SOUP:

    1 medium onion, thinly sliced

    2 to 3 tablespoons olive oil, vegetable oil, bacon drippings, or renderings from country ham

    4 to 6 garlic cloves to taste

    2 bay leaves

2 jalapeño chilies, seeded and sliced

2 Anaheim chilies, seeded and sliced

2 pounds green tomatoes, cut into eighths

3 cups chicken or shrimp stock or water

3 to 4 tablespoons capers to taste, chopped (see note)

1 to 2 tablespoons fresh lemon juice to taste

salt and freshly ground black pepper to taste

Tabasco or other hot pepper sauce to taste

FOR THE GARNISH:

thin julienne of cooked country ham or chicken

cooked crabmeat, boiled shrimp, or pickled shrimp

sour cream or crème fraîche

Corn and Crab Pudding (Chapter 2)

chopped ripe tomato or diced green tomato

chopped scallion and diced red bell pepper

In a large saucepan over medium heat, cook the onion in fat until soft but not colored, about 5 to 10 minutes. Add the garlic, bay leaves, and chilies and cook for another 5 minutes.

Add the tomatoes and stock, raise the heat, and bring to a boil. Reduce the heat and simmer for about 15 minutes or until the tomatoes are thoroughly softened.

Remove the bay leaves from the mixture and puree the soup in a blender, working in batches. Season with capers, lemon juice, salt, pepper, and Tabasco. Serve hot or cold with the garnishes of your choice. Ben says, "We typically serve it cold with crabmeat or pickled shrimp and crème fraîche or hot with country ham, boiled shrimp, and sour cream . . . but any variation works." His preferred stock is shrimp.

I like to unmold the Corn and Crab Pudding into a pasta bowl and ring it with this soup, served cold.

Serves 4 to 6

NOTE:

Capers come in a variety of sizes, usually pickled in a vinegar brine. They are also available packed in salt. Whichever type you use, be sure to rinse them well first or add them first and taste the soup before adding lemon juice or salt.

WINE:

A very crisp but not overly acidic wine such as St. Supéry Sauvignon Blanc

Smoked Tomato Soup with Basil Sorbet

I developed this recipe as a combination of several good ideas for a summer soup. Jenny Fitch's excellent *The Fearrington House Cookbook* includes a recipe for chilled cream of tomato soup with a basil sorbet, the recipe for which follows. Fearrington, near Chapel Hill, has been developed as a country village on the site of an eighteenth-century farm. The Fitch family has overseen the project that now includes a bookstore run by Jenny's daughter Keebe, a pottery shop, a garden shop, a gourmet market, beautiful herb and flower gardens, and the highly acclaimed restaurant and inn.

Fearrington Village is also home to the charming and redoubtable food writer Jeanne Voltz, whose work includes excellent books on barbecue and Florida.

This recipe is closer to an Andalusian gazpacho than a cooked soup, but the smoked vegetables add an intensity of flavor that welcomes the refreshing basil sorbet. Serve it as a first course before roast turkey.

FOR THE SORBET:

        ½ cup sugar

        1½ cups water

        ½ cup parsley leaves

        1½ cups fresh basil leaves plus a few for garnish

        2 lemons—1 tablespoon grated zest and ⅓ cup juice

FOR THE SOUP:

>2 pounds large vine-ripened tomatoes, about 6
>
>1 medium Spanish onion
>
>1 small head of garlic or about ½ large head, cloves still connected
>
>1 small jalapeño chili
>
>1 large cucumber
>
>2 cups fresh white bread crumbs, preferably from French or Italian bread, crusts removed
>
>1 cup water, chicken or vegetable stock, or chopped fresh tomatoes
>
>2 tablespoons olive oil
>
>salt and freshly ground black pepper to taste
>
>red wine or balsamic vinegar to taste

For the sorbet, make a syrup by dissolving the sugar in the water and bringing it to a boil. Cool.

Put the parsley and basil in a blender and chop fine. Add the syrup, lemon zest and juice and process until well mixed. Put the mixture in the refrigerator to cool, then freeze in your ice cream maker according to the manufacturer's instructions or simply put the mixture in a metal bowl or tray in the freezer. When it's partially frozen, stir it a bit with a wooden spoon. When it's totally frozen, beat it with a wooden spoon until it reaches the desired consistency. However you make it, after it's frozen you may want to return it to a processor or blender for a finer consistency.

For the soup, slice the tomatoes and onion in half. Rub the grates of a smoker with oil and put the halved tomatoes and onion, cut side up, in the smoker with the head of garlic and the chili. Smoke for about an hour.

Transfer the vegetables to a platter, cut side down. You may wear rubber gloves and continue with the recipe at this point or wait for the vegetables to cool. Lift the skins off the tomatoes. The blossom ends will lift

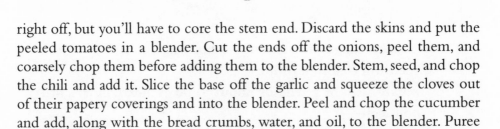

right off, but you'll have to core the stem end. Discard the skins and put the peeled tomatoes in a blender. Cut the ends off the onions, peel them, and coarsely chop them before adding them to the blender. Stem, seed, and chop the chili and add it. Slice the base off the garlic and squeeze the cloves out of their papery coverings and into the blender. Peel and chop the cucumber and add, along with the bread crumbs, water, and oil, to the blender. Puree on high speed.

Taste the soup and correct the seasoning with salt, pepper, and vinegar. Chill the soup well and serve in bowls with a scoop of sorbet and a garnish of fresh basil.
Serves 6 (This amount should exactly fill your blender.)

WINE:
Dry Riesling, especially Trimbach

Duck Soup with Turnips and Parsnips

This delicious soup of turnip greens bolstered with root vegetables is welcome in fall and winter, when greens appear throughout the South. It is very easy to make, cooks in a half hour, and is a heartier alternative to traditional boiled greens.

2½ quarts duck stock (Chapter 4)
2 dozen young 1- to 1½-inch turnips with about 12 inches
    of greens attached, 2 pounds cleaned greens
2 tablespoons hot pepper vinegar (see note)
1 tablespoon salt
1 pound parsnips

Begin heating the duck stock in a large pot over high heat while you clean the turnip greens. Discard any wilted or blemished leaves, tear out the tough stems, and put the greens in a large basin filled with water. Shake them around in the water until they are free of all grit, changing the water several times if necessary. You should have about 12 cups of cleaned greens.

Chop the greens well, adding them to the pot as you go. Add the vinegar and salt as well. When all of the greens are in the pot, simmer uncovered for 10 minutes. In the meantime, peel the turnips and parsnips and dice them into bite-size pieces.

Add the root vegetables, cover the pot, and simmer for 15 minutes. Serve with corn bread (Chapter 8) or a crusty European-style bread.
Serves 8 to 12

NOTE:
If you can't find hot pepper vinegar, you can make it by pouring boiling white or cider vinegar over fresh hot peppers in a jar. Cap the jar and allow to cure for at least a week before using.

WINE:
An earthy red Bordeaux

Peanut Soup

Why this recipe caught on in Virginia and not in Georgia, the South's other great peanut producer, is anyone's guess. The soup is traditional in several West African countries, where it is often made with guinea fowl and served with a starch such as rice or yams as a complete meal. Both the hot pepper and the peanuts are New World plants that found their way back to America via the slave trade. You can make this soup with a fish stock, as they do in Nigeria, and pour it thick over grilled shrimp; you can also serve it with any number of garnishes such as okra, tomatoes, or mashed yams, as in Ghana. This recipe is traditional Virginia style.

3 tablespoons butter

1 medium onion, chopped

2 large celery ribs, chopped

2 garlic cloves, minced

2 tablespoons unbleached all-purpose flour

5½ to 6 cups chicken, veal, or fish stock (see note)

1 cup creamy natural peanut butter (see note)

½ teaspoon hot red pepper flakes

½ cup whipping cream, optional

salt to taste

fresh chives and roasted peanuts for garnish

In a large heavy sauté pan over medium heat, melt the butter. Add the onion and celery and cook until wilted, about 10 minutes. Add the garlic and stir for about 30 seconds, then add the flour and whisk in well until all the vegetables are coated. Cook for a minute or two, but do not let the flour brown.

Turn up the heat to high and gradually add about half of the stock, whisking constantly so that the flour and vegetables are blended in well. In a mixing bowl off the heat, add the remaining stock to the peanut butter and, using a heavy whisk, blend the two together well. Add the peanut butter mixture to the pan, whisking constantly until the soup is well mixed and has come to a boil.

Add the pepper flakes and stir in, reduce the heat, and simmer for 20 minutes. Taste for seasoning (see note), stir in cream if desired, and serve at once, garnished with chives and roasted peanuts.
Serves 6

Note:
You can use canned chicken broth, but be sure to buy broth with lowered salt content. You will probably need to use unsalted natural peanut butter, or the soup may be too salty.

Wine:
A two- to four-year-old white Graves

Peach Soup

Don't think sweet here—this is a very old-fashioned potage that I developed from a sixteenth-century recipe for blancmange (literally, white food, thickened with almonds and bread crumbs)—really as much chicken soup as white sauce. The almonds pair well with the peaches, to whom they are closely related. This soup, typical of the almond-enriched fare of Georgia's early settlers, can be served either warm or chilled. It is delightful garnished with some spicy boiled shrimp or with nasturtium blossoms.

1 tablespoon butter

1 shallot, minced

1 quart chicken stock

3 cups (about 1¼ pounds) peeled and sliced fresh or
   frozen peaches

1 large lemon thyme sprig

½ cup raw almonds

1 thick slice of day-old hearty white bread, crust removed

½ cup whipping cream

salt and freshly ground white pepper to taste, optional

¼ teaspoon almond extract or a little peach schnapps or
   peach brandy

Melt the butter in a saucepan over medium heat and add the shallot. Sauté until limp, about 5 minutes. Add the stock, peaches, and thyme, increase the heat, and bring to a boil. Reduce the heat and simmer for 30 minutes.

Meanwhile, blanch the almonds: Bring a pot of water to a boil. Put the almonds in a sieve that will fit down in the pot and plunge it into the water so that the almonds are covered. Turn off the heat. Lift the sieve occasionally and check the almonds to see if the skins are loosened. It will take only a few minutes. As soon as they can be skinned easily, lift the sieve from the hot water to the sink and run cold water over them. Peel the almonds by rubbing them between thumb and forefinger. Discard the skins. Put about a dozen aside for garnishes.

Tear the bread into pieces. You should have about a cup. Remove the thyme sprig from the soup, add the almonds and the bread, and allow to sit until the bread is totally soaked in the soup. Puree the mixture thoroughly in a blender. Return the soup to the pot over low heat, add the cream (see note), and stir well. Season to taste with salt and pepper if desired.

Cut the almonds for garnish into several slivers and toss them in a frying pan until toasted lightly. Add almond extract or a splash of peach schnapps or peach brandy to the soup before serving, then garnish with the toasted almonds.

Serves 6 to 8

NOTE:
If you prefer to serve the soup cold, leave the cream out and refrigerate the soup at this point. Whip the cream with the almond extract or peach liquor and garnish the chilled soup with the whipped cream and toasted almonds.

WINE:
Sauvignon Blanc that has hints of melon or one that's made in the light, herbaceous style

Cream of Fresh Shiitake Mushrooms

Jimmy Sneed is a well-known Virginia chef who cites his tutelage under the great French chef Jean-Louis Palladin as his major influence. It's in their use of the finest—often local—produce that his dishes perhaps resemble Palladin's most.

Not far from Sneed's Richmond restaurant, Art Ensley has spored more than 3,000 white and chestnut oak logs with shiitake mushrooms. The mature king and queen shiitakes are often featured on the menu in dishes such as this luscious soup. Serve it as the first course of a long, leisurely meal.

FOR THE CREAM BASE:

- 1 large onion, diced
- 4 shallots, sliced
- 1 tablespoon extra-virgin olive oil
- 1 cup dry white wine
- 2 cups chicken stock
- 3 cups heavy cream

FOR THE SOUP:

- 3 pounds fresh shiitake mushrooms
- extra-virgin olive oil
- sea salt and freshly ground black pepper to taste
- 2 garlic cloves, diced
- 2 shallots, diced
- 2¼ cups rich chicken stock or bouillon

For the cream base, in a large sauté pan over medium heat, cook the onion and shallots in the olive oil until transparent, 5 to 10 minutes. Add the wine and boil to reduce until almost dry. Add the stock and boil to reduce until almost dry. Add the cream, turn down the heat, and reduce slowly for 10 minutes. Strain well and set aside.

Stem and slice the mushrooms. Heat a large heavy skillet or sauté pan, preferably cast iron, over medium-high heat and add ¼ inch of olive oil. Add the mushrooms and stir. Season with salt and pepper. Add the garlic and shallots and continue to cook over medium-high heat, stirring so that the mushrooms sizzle as they cook. When the mushrooms are almost soft, after about 2 minutes, add ½ cup of the stock to stop the cooking. Puree in a blender or food processor, then mix with the cream base and adjust the consistency with the rest of the stock. Adjust the seasoning before serving.

Serves 6

WINE:
Meursault or a good St-Véran

Celeriac and Fennel Soup with Sausage

From fall to spring, knobby celery roots now appear in your grocer's produce section alongside better-known fennel, which is often maddeningly marketed as anise (whose bittersweet, seedlike fruits only vaguely compare in flavor to the crisp celerylike sweetness of fennel). Celeriac and fennel are both delicious raw in salads and slaws or briefly cooked in acidic liquids, but they also marry well in this soup with Italian sausage, which should include some fennel seeds.

1 pound Italian sausage in casings
vegetable oil or bacon grease, optional
2 cups sliced fennel bulb, about 1 large or 2 small
¾ to 1 pound celeriac, peeled and cubed, 2 to 3 cups
6 cups chicken stock
1 tablespoon hot pepper vinegar (see note in recipe for
    Duck Soup with Turnips and Parsnips)
1 large leek, white part only, or 1 large red onion, chopped
1 pound (3 medium) white potatoes, peeled and diced
2 teaspoons salt

Cut the sausage into 1-inch slices and in a large sauté pan over medium-high heat, sauté until browned and cooked thoroughly, about 7 minutes, adding oil or fat to the pan if necessary. Remove the sausage and set aside. Add the fennel, celeriac, 2 cups of the stock, the hot pepper vinegar, and the leek to the pot and simmer until the vegetables are becoming transparent, about 10 minutes.

Add the remaining stock, the potatoes, and the salt and simmer for 45 minutes. Transfer in batches to a food processor or blender and puree. When all of the soup is pureed, return to the pot. Just before serving, add the sausage and stir to make sure that everything is warm, reheating gently if necessary.
Serves 6 to 8

WINE:
Fumé Blanc from Dry Creek Valley

Chicken and Vegetable Curry

Curry has been popular in the South since colonial days, when the spice and slave trade brought ships laden with exotica. Chicken Country Captain, a curried chicken dish with tomatoes and currants, is a perennial favorite. This recipe, with its sweet potatoes and lemongrass, is closer to Vietnamese versions. It makes a large meal that will feed eight people.

Many Vietnamese have come to the American South since the war, some as wives of U.S. servicemen. My friend Kim-Anh Huebner has had restaurants in both Saigon and South Carolina. She grows much of her food in her suburban Charleston backyard, including several kinds of fish! Along one of her fences there's a long row of lemongrass plants.

I first had this style of curry at Kim-Anh's table. A variety of curry powders are available in Vietnam; I use my own blend, roasted and ground just before I begin the dish. Measuring out all the ingredients before you begin will make the recipe go smoothly.

Serve this hearty dish as a one-pot meal, then follow it with fresh fruit.

FOR THE CHICKEN AND STOCK:

1 3¹/₂- to 4-pound chicken

3 quarts water

2 to 3 celery ribs, broken into pieces

1 large onion, quartered

2 bay leaves

2 carrots, broken into pieces

a few thyme and other fresh herb sprigs of your choice

FOR THE CURRY MIX:

1 tablespoon whole coriander seeds

2 teaspoons whole cumin seeds or 1¹/₂ teaspoons ground

2 teaspoons hot red pepper flakes or 1 large dried pod or 1¹/₂ teaspoons cayenne pepper

2 teaspoons ground turmeric

1 teaspoon black peppercorns

a 2-inch piece of fresh lemongrass (see note), crushed and chopped

FOR THE FINISHED DISH:

> ¹/₂ cup slivered blanched almonds
>
> ¹/₃ cup peanut oil
>
> 2 medium white potatoes and 2 medium sweet potatoes, peeled and cut into 2-inch pieces
>
> 1 large onion, chopped
>
> 4 garlic cloves, minced
>
> 2 tablespoons peeled and minced or grated fresh ginger
>
> 2 carrots, cut into 2-inch pieces
>
> 1 medium cauliflower, about 2 pounds, cut into 2-inch pieces
>
> 1 medium eggplant, about 1 pound, cut into 1-inch cubes
>
> 1³/₄ cups coconut milk or a 13¹/₂-ounce can
>
> salt to taste
>
> cilantro, scallions, or chives for garnish

Rinse the chicken well, put it in a large stockpot, and cover with the water. Add the neck and other giblets (except the liver) if they are included. Add the celery, onion, bay leaves, carrots, and herbs, bring almost to a boil, reduce the heat, and simmer until the meat is cooked evenly, about 1 hour.

Remove the chicken and allow to cool. Strain the remaining solids out of the stock and discard. Allow the stock to cool, then refrigerate it. Remove any fat from the surface of the stock before using. Freeze all but 3 cups.

When the chicken is cool enough to handle, remove the skin and discard. Pull the meat off the bones. You should have about a pound, or 4 cups, of meat. Discard the bones.

To make the curry, roast the coriander and cumin seeds in a heavy Dutch oven over medium heat, stirring constantly, until they begin to darken, 2 to 3 minutes. If you're using ground cumin, add it about a minute after the coriander. Transfer to a spice mill or blender. Add the rest of the dried spices and the lemongrass and grind thoroughly. Do not clean the pot.

Add the almonds to the Dutch oven and roast, stirring constantly, until browned evenly, about 5 minutes. Remove and set aside.

Add the oil to the pot and increase the heat to medium-high. Add the white and sweet potatoes and fry until lightly browned, about 10 minutes. Remove with a slotted spoon and set aside. Pour off all but about 3 tablespoons of the oil.

Add the onion to the pot and lower the heat to medium. Cook, stirring often, for about 10 minutes or until the onions are becoming transparent. Add the garlic and ginger and cook for about 2 minutes, stirring constantly. Do not let them brown.

Add the reserved stock and carrots and simmer for about 10 minutes, then add the curry mix and fried potatoes, the cauliflower, eggplant, and coconut milk. Stir together well, raise the heat, bring almost to a boil, then lower the heat and simmer for 30 minutes or until the vegetables are cooked.

Cut the reserved chicken meat into uniform pieces and add to the pot, stirring well. Taste and correct the seasoning with salt. Cover the pot and remove from the heat. Allow to sit until the chicken is warmed through.

Serve in pasta bowls garnished with fresh cilantro, scallions, or chives along with the reserved toasted almonds.

Serves 8

NOTE:

Lemongrass is now widely available in supermarkets; if you can't find it, try an Asian market. Remove the tough outer leaves and cut away the base. Cut the portion you need, then crush it with a heavy object such as a can or the flat side of a cleaver. Chop as finely as possible.

WINE:

California Chardonnay with lots of tropical fruit flavor and a bit of residual sugar

Chicken Chili

Most southerners do not regard the Southwest as part of their region; in the Deep South even Texas is considered foreign soil. But Texans think of themselves as being as southern as Alabamans, and Tex–Mex flavors have been revered across the region since long before the national restaurant trend of the eighties. Chili is made with everything from venison—a very popular version—to mere vegetables, southern chili gardens spicing the stews with a great variety of peppers.

In this version, with beans, chicken bolsters the pot; homemade stock intensifies the flavor. The chili is best when allowed to mellow slowly for hours, but the preparation is simplicity itself. The chicken can be poached in the chili or while making the stock in advance (see preceding recipe).

³/₄ pound dried beans such as pinto or kidney, 1¹/₂ cups, soaked at least an hour, rinsed well, and drained

2 quarts chicken stock

3 large carrots, peeled

2 large onions, unpeeled, cut in half

1 bay leaf

1 fresh thyme sprig or ¹/₂ teaspoon dried

1 dried ancho or mulato chili

1 28-ounce can crushed tomatoes

3 cups cut-up poached chicken meat or 2 to 3 large raw chicken breasts on the bone

salt, freshly ground black pepper, and Tabasco or other hot pepper sauce to taste

Preheat the oven (I use a toaster oven) to 350°. Place the beans, stock, carrots, onions, and herbs in a large stockpot and bring to a simmer. Seed and stem the chili, place it on a baking pan, and roast for 10 minutes, turning once. Do not let it burn or char. There should be a chocolaty aroma but no whiffs of smoke. Remove from the oven, immediately add to the stockpot, and simmer for 45 minutes, stirring occasionally so that the beans do not stick to the bottom of the pot.

Remove the carrots, onions, and chili and set aside to cool. Remove a cup of the beans, add them and the chili to a blender or food processor, and puree. Add the puree and crushed tomatoes to the pot and bring to a simmer again, stirring occasionally. If you're using raw chicken, add it to the pot now.

After about an hour, test the beans and chicken. If the chicken is cooked through, remove from the pot and remove the skin and bones, discarding both.

Cut up the chicken and carrots and add them to the pot (if you're using precooked chicken, add it now). Peel and cut up the onions and add them. Season to taste with salt, pepper, and hot pepper sauce. Cover the pot and continue to cook over very low heat until the beans are done to your liking. Serve with cornsticks and a green salad.
Serves 8

BEVERAGE:
Beer

Chili

This is a hearty winter chili, full of lean meat bolstered by oxtails. Oxtails are deliciously fatty, but the chili is totally degreased before serving. It has no beans but can be served alongside Black Beans and Rice (Chapter 6) if desired. I prefer to use the lean ground venison that my hunter friends bring me, but you can use any cubed or ground lean meat. Some butchers automatically add a little fat to ground venison. You shouldn't have to add any oil to the pot unless the meat you are using is fat-free.

Chili is best when allowed to mellow for a couple of days or at least overnight. The instructions allow for personal touches: choose the chilies and/or chili powders to suit your own palate.

1½ to 1¾ pounds oxtails cut into 2-inch lengths

3 to 4 pounds ground or cubed lean meat such as venison,
    veal, lamb, or beef

3 tablespoons vegetable oil if needed

2 cups chopped onion, about 2 medium

4 to 6 garlic cloves to taste, minced

1 green bell pepper, seeded and chopped

1 cup mixed fresh or canned chilies to taste, such as red
    frying peppers (Italian or cubanelle), Anaheims,
    jalapeños, and chipotles

¼ cup masa harina or corn flour (see Ingredients and
    Sources, Corn Products)

1 quart beef stock

6 vine-ripened tomatoes, about 2 pounds, peeled and
    chopped, or a 28-ounce can peeled tomatoes with their juice

2 tablespoons fresh oregano leaves or 1 tablespoon dried (see note)

1 teaspoon cumin seeds

2 tablespoons pure hot (New Mexican) chili powder

2 tablespoons pure mild (Californian) chili powder

1 bay leaf

2 teaspoons salt

Place the oxtail pieces, fatty sides down, in a 5- to 6-quart heavy pot over medium-high heat. Brown them on all the fatty sides first, then brown the exposed meaty areas. Remove from the pan and set aside. If the meat you're using is very lean, such as cubed venison, add the oil to the pan and allow to heat before adding the meat in batches, browning it evenly, and removing it from the pan with a slotted spoon, setting aside with the oxtails.

Add the onion, garlic, and bell pepper and chilies to the pot and continue to cook over medium-high heat, stirring occasionally, until the onion is limp and translucent, about 10 minutes. Add the masa harina or corn flour and stir in until the vegetables are evenly coated, then gradually add the stock, stirring constantly. Add the tomatoes, browned oxtails, and meat and stir together well.

Add ¼ cup commercial chili powder or grind the oregano and cumin seeds together in a mortar and pestle, blender, or spice mill, then add to the pot along with the pure chili powders, bay leaf, and salt.

Simmer the chili for 2 hours, occasionally skimming any fat or scum from the surface. Remove the chili from the heat, bring it to room temperature, then remove the bay leaf and oxtails. Pick the meat from the oxtails and add it to the pot. Discard the bay leaf and any bones, gristle, or fat from the oxtails. Refrigerate the chili overnight. The next day (or before serving), remove any grease that has congealed on the surface and place the pot on the stove to reheat. Serve with the accompaniments of your choice: corn bread (Chapter 8), chopped cilantro, grated mild cheese such as Cheddar or Monterey Jack, sour cream or crumbled goat cheese, chopped onions, cooked pinto or kidney beans, or black beans and rice.
Serves 10 to 12

NOTE:

You can substitute ¼ cup commercial chili powder for the oregano, cumin, and pure chili powder, but be forewarned that the commercial mixes lose their punch quickly and vary greatly in flavor and spiciness.

WINE:

Beer is best, but if you must have wine, try a medium-dry California Riesling such as Trefethen's White Riesling

Oyster Stew

Bill Neal's untimely death saddened the food world, especially in the South, where he had spearheaded the return of traditional southern cooking to restaurants. He helped repopularize many old favorites such as shrimp and grits, oyster stew, and hoppin' john, and his modern adaptations never seemed contrived because they were rooted in a lifetime of southern cooking.

His beautifully written first book, *Bill Neal's Southern Cooking,* noted: "A basic southern oyster stew highlights the simplest ingredients: 3 parts milk, 1 part heavy cream, heated, with 2 parts shucked oysters added and poached lightly, seasoned only with fresh black pepper and whole butter—salted crackers the only accompaniment." A more elaborate version used not only different proportions but also onion, celery, chicken stock, watercress, and scallions.

Bill Neal loved North Carolina's Outer Banks, where chef Sam McGann cooks, and I'm sure he would have loved this rendition of Sam's, too. "The key to a good oyster stew," claims Sam, "is the liquor that comes from the freshly shucked oyster—and I prefer the Eastern Shore oyster."

Serve this soup as a first course or as a late-night supper.

1 pint freshly shucked oysters and their liquor, about 4
    dozen oysters

1½ to 2 cups heavy cream

1½ to 2 cups half-and-half

Tabasco sauce

Worcestershire sauce

salt if needed

butter, optional

2 or 3 slices of bacon, preferably an old-fashioned cure
    such as those from Surry or Smithfield, Virginia,
    cooked and crumbled

about ¾ cup finely diced or julienned mixed vegetables
    such as cucumbers, carrots, celery, leeks, and fennel

Drain the oysters and reserve the liquor. Taste this juice for salt. Many oysters are very salty and will need no further salting. Measure the oyster liquor and add an equal quantity of cream and half-and-half. Season very slightly with Tabasco and Worcestershire. Add salt only if necessary.

Simmer the stew for 3 to 4 minutes or until the oysters are plump and the edges begin to curl.

To serve, Sam says, "A dollop of sweet butter and fresh snipped dill would add a little elegance, but a purist might beg to differ. Divide into small bowls and finish with crumbled bacon and some thinly cut vegetables." *Serves 4 generously*

WINE:
Pouilly-Fumé or a Chardonnay from Monterey, Sonoma, or Santa Barbara

Hearty Fish Stew

I love fish stews, and this is a basic recipe for a really hearty one. Buy a whole large nonbony lean fish that has firm white flesh; avoid oily or delicate fish. Many of the perchlike fish from the *Perciformes* genus—grouper, sea bass, wreckfish, porgy, sheepshead, tile—work just fine.

Get your fishmonger to scale, gut, and fillet the fish. Have him remove the gills from the head, but take the head and backbone home to make the stock. You will need a fish weighing about 7 pounds before it is cleaned.

>   a 7-pound fish, cleaned and filleted, or 3 pounds firm,
>   thick fish fillets plus 2 pounds fish head and bones with
>   no blood, guts, or gills
>   1 quart water
>   3 celery ribs
>   2 large onions

a handful of fresh herbs, including parsley and thyme
  and others such as marjoram, basil, and savory
2 cups dry white wine
½ cup olive oil
2 carrots, chopped
1 large green bell pepper, seeded and chopped
1 jalapeño chili, seeded and chopped
3 garlic cloves, minced
6 vine-ripened tomatoes, about 2 pounds, peeled and
  chopped, or a 28-ounce can peeled tomatoes with their juice
3 long white potatoes, peeled and diced
salt and freshly ground black pepper to taste

Combine the fish head and bones with the water in a stockpot. Add one of the celery ribs, one of the onions, quartered, and the herbs and bring to a boil. Reduce the heat and simmer for 15 minutes, skimming off any foam that rises to the surface. Add the wine and continue to simmer for 30 minutes. Strain out the solids and discard. Strain again and set aside. You should have about 1 quart.

In a large pot or Dutch oven, over medium heat, heat the oil. Add the remaining celery and onion, chopped, and the carrots, pepper, and chili. Cook until the vegetables are wilted, about 10 to 15 minutes. Add the garlic and tomatoes and cook until most of their liquid has cooked out, another 10 minutes or so. Add the reserved stock, increase the heat, and bring to a boil. Add the potatoes and simmer for 10 minutes.

Skim the soup and add the fish fillets, cut into 2-inch cubes. Correct the seasoning with salt and pepper. Cook at a bare simmer until the fish is just done, about 8 minutes. Serve with corn bread (Chapter 8) and a green salad.
Serves 8 to 10

WINE:
Pinot Blanc from Alsace or California

Gumbo

*Gumbo exists in countless forms throughout the South. . . .
The origin of the word is not clear . . . [but] in the South,
gumbo means "all together" or "all at once," as in the phrase
"gumbo ya-ya," meaning everybody talking at once. It also
means a potpourri of turkey, chicken, rabbit, squirrel, fish, crab,
oyster, shrimp or almost any available ingredients; or a thick
kind of stew that is a close cousin to bouillabaisse, Italian fish
soup, couscous or other mixed-ingredient dishes of the
Mediterranean and North Africa.*

EUGENE WALTER

Claimed by South Carolinians, Cajuns, Creoles, African-Americans, and Choctaw Indians, gumbo is the very hodgepodge that is our culture. It has been likened to jazz, with its multicultural history and improvisational nature, but its roots run even deeper than those of that distinctly American music.

Some people say that New Orleans okra gumbo developed among the great port city's wealthy merchants and planters who entertained with their slave cooks at the hearths. Based on a French roux (a cooked paste of flour and fat), a Spanish-Caribbean sofrito (onions, peppers, garlic, tomatoes, and seasonings), and the African vegetable (okra is called "gumbo" in several West African languages), it is one of the great dishes of the world—truly Creole, or born in the New World to a mixed heritage.

Filé gumbo, on the other hand, is said to have evolved at the hands of backwoods Cajuns (descendants of a group of exiled Acadians who settled in Louisiana in the eighteenth century), who had been shown by the Choctaw Indians how to thicken soups and stews with filé, or powdered sassafras leaves. Eighteenth-century naturalists often noted Native

Americans' use of powdered roots and leaves as thickening agents, but only in Louisiana, with its great culinary traditions, has this bit of Native American fare survived.

A New Orleans gumbo thickened with a roux and either okra or filé is often thought of as the definitive version today, but this was not always the case. Louisiana's poorly recorded history offers us few surviving written recipes prior to the late nineteenth century. Sarah Rutledge of Charleston included a recipe for New Orleans gumbo in her *Carolina Housewife* of 1847. Made with turkey, beef, and oysters, the recipe called for the cook to "Season to taste; and just before taking up the soup, stir in until it becomes mucilaginous two spoonsful of pulverized sassafras-leaves." By then the mucilaginous quality of okra had become the defining characteristic of the dish, even though the dish needn't include its namesake ingredient.

Today's Charleston gumbo is more of a soup, reflecting the palates of the West Africans from rice- and okra-growing lands who had been brought to South Carolina plantations as slaves years before Louisiana was settled by the French. Miss Rutledge also included in her collection recipes for okra soup and "okra à la daube," both closer to current Charleston versions of gumbo with West African roots.

It seems silly to compare the dozens of versions that range from mere sautés of okra and tomatoes to 30-ingredient seafood gumbos, especially since they all start with a roux and end up served over mounds of steamed white rice, for 200 years a staple crop in Carolina and still grown in Louisiana. Most culinary scholars agree with the down-home wisdom of Mobile's redoubtable and self-proclaimed Renaissance man Eugene Walter and place gumbo among the many one-pot dishes—burgoo, Brunswick stew, cioppino, jambalaya, clam chowder, beef stew—that are rooted in the traditions of our ancestors but are very American in their current form.

It is quite possible, for example, that the English masters of those Carolina slaves were already familiar with okra as a thickener, for its use is common in India. Pickled okra, another old Indian favorite, appears throughout the modern-day South, virtually unchanged for several hundred years. Gumbo, though, seems to change timbre even as you cross county lines.

Coastal versions naturally include the shrimp, crab, and oysters of the marshes. Inland, sausage, fowl, and game are common. Charleston and Savannah, with their ties to England, developed gumbos that are hearty soups. New Orleans gumbo is a New World French sauce, and there every gumbo recipe begins with the line "First you make a roux." The easiest way to make a roux—a cooked flour paste used to thicken the gumbo—is to use the oven, rather than stirring a pot for an hour. Since the slightest burned speck of flour will destroy the delicate nutty flavor of a properly cooked roux, it is much easier to bake it, which frees you to start chopping the "Holy Trinity," as Cajuns call the onions, peppers, and celery that add zest to the gumbo.

Mix equal parts of melted fat (vegetable oil, lard, duck fat, or any combination) and flour in a sheet pan and bake in a preheated 350° oven until the desired color is achieved, stirring the mixture every 10 or 15 minutes so that it does not scorch. Cook the roux until it reaches a rich mahogany color. Remove some from the pan and allow the rest to reach an intense chocolate color. The darker roux goes into seafood gumbos. Freeze what you don't use immediately in $1/2$-cup quantities.

The real secret to any successful gumbo, whether soup or sauce style, is good homemade stock. A simmering pot of bones and aromatic vegetables changes a house into a home; homemade stocks similarly enrich gumbo. Flavors are simmered to mingle in a stock. Ingredients are then added to the stock; the flavor of each should be discernible.

The following recipe for shrimp gumbo is one of the easiest gumbos you can make; it is absolutely delicious.

Easy Shrimp Gumbo

This gumbo will take about three hours from the making of the roux to serving your table of eight, but most of the work is unattended and simple.

FOR THE STOCK:

    3 pounds shrimp

    1 large or 2 small carrots

    1 large onion, quartered

    2 celery ribs

    a handful of fresh herbs such as parsley, oregano, thyme, and savory

    1 bay leaf

    1 gallon water

FOR THE GUMBO:

    ¼ cup dark roux (see page 25)

    ½ cup chopped onion, about ½ medium

    ½ cup chopped celery, about 1 large rib

    ¼ cup chopped green bell pepper

    1 pound okra, trimmed and cut into ½-inch pieces

    6 vine-ripened tomatoes, about 2 pounds, peeled and chopped, or a 28-ounce can peeled tomatoes with their juice

    2 fresh jalapeño or other hot chilies

    3 cups cooked long-grain white rice

Peel the shrimp, dropping the shells into an enameled or stainless-steel stockpot. Cover the shrimp with plastic wrap and store in the refrigerator to use later.

Add the rest of the stock ingredients to the pot and cook at a low boil until the onion is transparent, the carrots are soft, and the stock is pleasantly infused with a shrimp flavor—about an hour. The liquid will be reduced to about 3 quarts. Strain out and discard the solids, reserving the stock. If you do not have roux on hand, make it while the stock is cooking.

To make the gumbo, heat the roux in a large stockpot over medium heat. Add the onion, celery, and bell pepper and cook until the onion is becoming transparent, stirring constantly, about 10 minutes. Add the okra and cook, stirring often, until all the ropiness is gone, about 20 minutes. Add the tomatoes and simmer for 10 minutes. Add the chilies and reserved stock and simmer for about an hour.

Five minutes before serving, add the reserved shrimp to the gumbo. Serve in large bowls over fluffy white rice. Follow this one-pot meal with a fresh green salad.

Serves 8

WINE:
A well-chilled Marsanne Blanc

Fish and Shellfish

I grew up fishing, and only when I went away to college did I realize that people actually *pay* for fish! The rivers, ponds, lakes, streams, swamps, marshes, bays, ocean, and gulf have always provided me—and most southerners—with a seemingly endless supply of fish, shrimp, crabs, and oysters. I have a photograph of me with my first fish dangling from a string attached to a stick—it was taken a week after my third birthday in Key West. I have vivid memories of my first marlin, my first tuna, my first eel, and my first sea urchin.

I barely give the cooking of fish and shellfish a second thought. All of my fish and shellfish preparations are similar in that the meat is cooked quickly—whether steamed, fried, baked, or grilled. All else is garnish. If you look closely at these recipes, you will see that they are all variations on the main theme of not overcooking the fish. Most of the fish recipes do not specify a particular species, because these recipes will work with any number of fish. It matters not whether you are baking, grilling, or steaming a snapper or tilefish with lemon, carambola, or pomegranate—the cooking will be done when the flesh just flakes moistly from the bone. That one rule of fish cookery is really all that you need to know to prepare elegant, delicious fish dishes—as long as the fish is fresh.

You need not live on the coast as I do to find fresh fish. Much of the fish that I buy has been shipped into Charleston from brokers in Chicago—even fish caught in our waters. The important thing is how the fish is kept. Find a fishmonger you like and buy from him regularly. Buying fish that is fresh is simple. Look for bright red gills and clear eyes (if you can buy whole fish) and firm flesh, with a fresh smell of the water—*not* "fishy."

The recipes that follow (and those in Chapter 1) cover the main types of fish cookery. I urge you to use what you have on hand and, if nowhere else in your cooking, keep the preparation of fish simple. I have included two recipes inspired by Chef Jamie Shannon of Commander's Palace in New Orleans. They are admittedly a little more complicated than what most southern fish cooks prepare in their homes, but they are delicious and they demonstrate some of the new ideas evolving in southern cooking.

These are some of my favorite recipes in this book, not only because I love fish, but also because they show off some of our best foodstuffs. You will find no cream with the fish or mushrooms with the shellfish; I find that those flavors compete too heavily with the delicacy of these "fruits of the sea."

Grilled Fish with Sorrel

Sorrel is common again in the South, and I keep a couple of plants in my yard to provide me with the tart leaves for soups, salads, and omelets and to top fish. The slightest amount of heat wilts sorrel to a puree; it is usually then whipped into cream to sauce vegetables and fish.

Young chefs in the South are following the lead of New York's Jean-Georges Vongerichten and infusing oils with the intense flavors of herbs and spices, but sorrel has the disadvantage of turning a drab olive color when it's heated. This classic white wine reduction rubbed into butter is a better use of sorrel.

I use a big fish fillet for this dish—muscular fighters like dolphin from the Gulf Stream. Use any large-flaked white fish fillet. Accompany the dish with potatoes and glazed carrots.

FOR THE SORREL BUTTER:

> 1 shallot, minced
> ½ cup dry white wine, preferably the one you will drink
>   with dinner
> 2 cups loosely packed sorrel leaves, deribbed and chopped
> 4 tablespoons butter, ½ stick, at room temperature
> salt, freshly ground black pepper, and fresh lemon
>   juice to taste

FOR THE FISH:

> salt and freshly ground black pepper to taste
> 4 1-inch-thick fish fillets, about 2 pounds
> olive oil

Put the shallot and wine in a sauté pan over high heat and reduce to about 2 or 3 tablespoons. Add the sorrel all at once and wilt thoroughly; it will take only a moment or two. Dump the mixture out onto a plate and set aside to cool (in the refrigerator is fine).

When the sorrel has cooled thoroughly, put it and the butter in a small bowl and mix well together with a wooden spoon. Season with salt, pepper, and lemon juice.

Build a charcoal fire or preheat a gas grill to medium-high. Salt and pepper the fish, and when the grill is hot, oil the grill racks and the fillets. Grill for about 4 minutes on each side. Spread with the sorrel butter and serve.
Serves 4

WINE:
A medium-bodied Bordeaux Blanc

Fish with
Tropical and Exotic Fruit

Fish has forever been paired with lemon or lime, but it also marries well with other citrus and brightly flavored tropical and exotic fruits. The coastal plain of South Carolina, Georgia, and the Gulf States is subtropical; many dooryards sport banana and pomegranate trees. In south Florida and Texas, citrus, mangoes, and star fruit are common in both inner city and suburban yards.

If I am grilling a lightly flavored fish, I'll take a banana, oil the skin, and toss it on the fire, too. Sliced lengthwise and served with hot sauce, the grilled banana makes a quick Caribbean- or Indian-inspired chutneylike accompaniment. The Mango Relish in Chapter 7 also goes well with grilled fish.

Southerners are fond of grilled grapefruit. Before interstates were built in the South, old southern motels and hotels often served a dish of grapefruit halves topped with honey and broiled; it was called "Georgia grapefruit." These days I just quarter a grapefruit and add it to the grilling basket or baking dish with either lean or oily fish. I serve Grapefruit Relish (Chapter 7) alongside the grilled fish and grapefruit with a plate of rice. The next time you have an oily fish, squeeze some grapefruit juice on it instead of lemon before you cook it.

You can also put whole carambolas (star fruit) in the grilling basket with fish, but their elusive flavor is shown off better when sliced and added to the top of a whole fish in a steamer. Star fruits come sweet and very sour, and it's nearly impossible to tell which you are buying. Cooked with fish, it won't matter; both the sweet and the tart work well. If you can buy fish only as fillets, season them with salt and white pepper, put them in a buttered baking dish, top with carambola slices and some lime juice to taste, and bake in a 450° oven for about 8 minutes. That recipe comes from Elizabeth Schneider's brilliant *Uncommon Fruits and Vegetables: A Commonsense Guide,* which every cook should own.

Though still uncommon in some parts of the United States, pomegranates have enjoyed regional popularity across the South. Elizabeth attributes the pomegranate's popularity in other cultures to the fact that other peoples are less in a rush than most Americans. Perhaps that is why we southerners, who are also known for our leisurely eating, are among the country's few pomegranate eaters. It is said that it takes incredible patience to appreciate the pomegranate because the fruit is so difficult to clean, but it's easy compared to the hickory nuts and black walnuts my grandmother used to make us clean!

Pomegranates appear in the fall just when the mackerel and bluefish are running. The fruit's leathery skin covers a mass of seeds, each encased in clear, ruby-colored flesh that is both sweet and tart. Pomegranate juice can be used with fish just like lemon juice. Removing the seeds from the extremely bitter white pith is laborious but worth the effort. Lightly score the outer skin in several places down to, but not into, the pith. Peel away the skin, then carefully separate the seeds from the pith. Place the seeds in a sieve, reserving a few for garnish. Cook your fish simply, then, just before serving, press the seeds firmly in the sieve to release their juice; sprinkle it over the fish.

WINE:
With any of these fish dishes prepared with tart fruits, serve a Sauvignon Blanc.

Poached Fish with
Ginger and Rosemary

Karen Hess all but invented culinary history, and while her work covers continents and centuries, it is based mostly on her study of southern food in the eighteenth and nineteenth centuries. This recipe appears in *Martha Washington's Booke of Cookery,* which Karen copiously annotated in a facsimile edition published by Columbia University Press in 1981. It is a bible of sorts for those of us interested in the larger picture—not just what to buy and how to prepare it but the wheres and whys and hows of what we eat.

This "delightful recipe" (Karen's words) appears to have been lifted from a modern southern restaurant menu. In fact, by the time Mrs. Washington was given the cookbook, it was long a family heirloom; the recipes date from Elizabethan and Jacobean England.

Ask your fishmonger to gut the fish through the gills for this recipe; it will keep its shape better. You need not have a fish poacher among your kitchen pots, but you will need a heatproof dish large enough to hold your fish.

The original manuscript recipe called for trout, but you can use just about any fish you want—left whole, cut into steaks, or filleted. Just don't overcook the fish or let the water boil. I buy two 1-pound whole fish such as sea trout (weakfish), gut them through the gills, and place them upright in a heavy sauté pan, curled around to fit in the pan. The poached fish then fit nicely on dinner plates.

Rosemary and ginger are strongly flavored, so be sure to use a fish that takes well to seasoning. Obviously, the choices of fish and wine will alter the taste of the dish, as will the freshness of the seasonings. The amounts of ginger and rosemary are arbitrary on my part. Use this recipe as a guide to develop your own version.

2 cups dry white wine, preferably the one you will drink
  with dinner

2 small fresh rosemary sprigs, about 4 inches long

a 1-inch piece of fresh ginger, peeled and thinly sliced

2 tablespoons butter at room temperature

2 whole fish such as sea trout weighing 1 pound each,
  scaled, gills removed, and gutted

salt and freshly ground black pepper to taste

Preheat the oven to its lowest setting and place 2 dinner plates in it to warm.

Place the wine, rosemary, ginger, and butter in a heavy wide sauté pan or fish poacher over high heat. Bring to a boil. Meanwhile, season the fish to taste with salt and pepper.

As soon as the wine boils, lower the heat and place the fish upright (bellies down) in the wine, curving them around to fit in the pan and placing them on the rosemary and ginger to hold them up off the bottom of the pot (or place them on the rack in a poacher). Cover the pan and cook at a bare simmer until the flesh is opaque and just flakes from the bone when pried with a fork, about 10 minutes. If you are poaching in a pot without a lid, fashion one of aluminum foil and seal it tightly.

Carefully lift the fish out of the poaching liquid onto the warmed plates with 2 metal spatulas, returning them to the oven to keep them warm.

Increase the heat to high and reduce the liquid to a thick sauce. Strain and pour over the poached fish. Serve immediately with boiled potatoes and creamed peas (Chapter 6).

Serves 2

Wine:
Spanish white, such as Rioja or Viña Sol

Benne Fried Sea Bass

Chicken notwithstanding, nothing could be more southern than fried fish. From the Ozarks to Florida, from Galveston Island to the Chesapeake Bay, you can't go far without finding a fried fish house. When a bunch of my friends gather after a day of offshore fishing, we're liable to take turns at the fryer, cooking 2-inch cubes of dolphin fish dusted with a little seasoned corn flour in a large pot of hot oil. The frying is usually done outdoors over a gas burner made specifically for this sort of affair. When prepared properly (clean oil heated to 365° and the fish not crowded in the pot), the fish will be crispy on the outside, moist on the inside, cooked just to the point of flaking, and not at all greasy.

Black sea bass ranges from Canada to Florida. Its firm white flesh is well suited to frying, and it is widely available in fish markets across the country. If you frequent Asian or Italian restaurants anywhere in the eastern United States, you will recognize this as the fish often served fried or steamed whole. If you live on the West Coast, you can use sea bream or porgy (which is what those Asian and Italian cooks are used to at home). Small whole snappers will do, but they are so lightly flavored as to be overpowered by the strong flavors of this dish.

Benne is a West African word for "sesame." We have cooked with it in the South Carolina Lowcountry for 300 years. In this updated southern classic the fish are panfried with a crusty coating of benne, then served with hot sauce. This is one of my favorite new dishes. Serve with green beans or spinach, which are also complemented by the sesame.

I prefer the intense flavor of the sesame oil. If you have a really fiery palate, use the chili sesame oil.

Small whole gutted fish or fillets with the skin work well in this dish.

1 1/2 to 2 pounds fish fillets or 4 small whole fish less than
   1 pound each, dressed
salt and freshly ground black pepper to taste
1/4 cup unbleached all-purpose flour
1/4 cup benne (sesame) seeds
2 eggs
1 tablespoon peanut, sesame, or chili sesame oil
1/4 to 1/2 cup peanut oil for frying
Tabasco or other hot pepper sauce

Pat the fish dry and season with salt and pepper. Spread the flour out on a piece of wax paper. Place each fillet or whole fish down in the flour and make sure the fish is covered in it. Dust off any excess. Add the benne seeds to the remaining flour and mix well.

In a large shallow container, beat the eggs with the tablespoon of oil. Dip each piece of fish in the egg wash, then place in the flour-benne mix. Coat each fish well, then put them on a platter. When all of the fish are coated, put them in the refrigerator for about 10 minutes.

Cover the bottom of a large heavy skillet or sauté pan with peanut oil and heat over medium-high heat until very hot but not smoking. Just as the surface begins to ripple, take the fish out of the refrigerator and place them flesh side down in the oil. Fry the fish until golden brown, about 3 minutes on each side.

You may have to cook the fish in batches. If so, preheat the oven to its lowest temperature and put a rack over a sheet pan and 4 dinner plates in the oven to keep the fish warm.

Serve immediately, splashing the fish and plate with hot sauce.

Serves 4

WINE:
Pouilly-Fumé

Fresh Tuna Salad

Many of us who live on the coast have long known the superior quality of freshly caught tuna. The rich red flesh is more like steak than fish, and like beef it's shown off to best advantage when not overcooked; rare is preferred. This tuna salad bears little resemblance to those of canned tuna fish (I've always found it telling that only when canned does tuna become "fish") swimming in mayonnaise with sweet pickle and celery flotsam.

On the French Riviera, similar salads made with walnut oil contain raw vegetables such as fennel; indeed, an authentic salade Niçoise contains no cooked vegetable. In my version, the seared tuna is accompanied by boiled and grilled vegetables. The flavors and textures are complementary and bright. You needn't use expensive imported oil for this salad, but by all means use walnut oil; the nuttiness provides a rich base for the intense vegetable overtones.

½ cup walnut oil

1 large vine-ripened tomato, halved

½ large red onion, unpeeled

½ large red bell pepper, seeded and halved lengthwise

½ cup loosely packed basil leaves

1 pound fresh tuna, sliced 1½ inches thick

salt and freshly ground black pepper to taste

3 tablespoons fresh lemon juice

1 pound (about 3) medium white potatoes, boiled with
   their skins on, then peeled while hot

3 hard-cooked eggs, shelled

Prepare a charcoal fire or preheat a gas grill to high. Pour the walnut oil into a large mixing bowl. Place the cut side of the tomato and the onion and bell pepper halves down in the oil for just a second to coat them. Place them on a platter.

Put the basil leaves down in the oil. Remove any dark brown meat from the tuna, then place the fish down in the oil. Generously salt and pepper the tuna on one side, then turn it over and season it on the other.

Make sure the tuna is covered with oil and the basil leaves are both on it and under it. Set aside to marinate while you grill the vegetables.

Place the onion oiled side down and the tomato and pepper halves skin down on the hot grill. Cover the grill and cook for 5 to 10 minutes or until the tomato is blistered and bubbly. Turn the onion and tomato halves. If the pepper skin is charred, transfer it to a platter. Grill until the skin peels away from the tomato and the onion is starting to separate into rings. The pepper should be charred. Transfer all to the platter to cool.

Place a well-seasoned heavy cast-iron pan over high heat. When the pan is hot, remove the tuna from the marinade, scrape off any basil leaves stuck to it, and place in the hot skillet. Cook for exactly 1 minute on each side, then transfer to a wooden cutting board. Cut the tuna into pieces about 1 inch square. The edges should be firmed and white, but the center of each piece should be red and rare.

Place the tuna down in the marinade again and sprinkle the lemon juice all over the tuna. Let the tuna sit for a moment or two while you peel the tomato, onion, and pepper. Discard stems and skins.

Using both hands, reach down under all the tuna and lift it up carefully and turn it all over so that the tuna is well mixed with the lemon juice, oil, and basil leaves. Do not break up the tuna pieces.

Chop the peeled onion and slice the peeled pepper into strips. Scoop out the seeds from the tomatoes and discard; chop the tomato into bite-size pieces, then cut up the potatoes and eggs as well. Add all to the tuna and again toss together using both hands, careful not to break up the tuna. Correct the seasoning with salt and pepper and serve immediately over mixed salad greens or cover well and refrigerate to serve later.
Serves 6

WINE:
Bandol Rosé or any good Rosé from Provence or a California Rosé of Cabernet

Seared Tuna with Tomato-Basil Vinaigrette

This delicious dish appears on the menus of many restaurants throughout the South, where young chefs use the fine local ingredients—including Gulf Stream tuna and vine-ripened tomatoes—to show off their skills at the grill and as sauciers. Nothing could be easier to prepare. The tuna can be seared in a frying pan; grocers throughout the country now regularly stock fresh tuna and basil, and I'm able to get wonderful tomatoes throughout the winter now because they're shipped from south Florida in nonrefrigerated trucks. (What kills the flavor and texture of tomatoes are temperatures below 55°.)

> 1 pound tuna, trimmed of blood line and cut into 2
>   1-inch-thick steaks
> salt and freshly ground black pepper to taste
> 3 tablespoons extra-virgin olive oil
> 2 or 3 small or 1 large vine-ripened tomato, peeled,
>   seeded, and chopped
> about 8 large basil leaves, cut up
> dash of cayenne pepper
> 1 tablespoon sherry vinegar

Place the tuna steaks in a large flat nonreactive bowl and season one side with salt and pepper. Drizzle the olive oil over the steaks, then turn the steaks over. Salt and pepper the second side, then turn them over again to be sure they are well coated with oil. Let them sit for about 30 minutes.

In another bowl, mix the tomatoes, basil, cayenne, and vinegar with a little more salt and pepper.

Heat a well-seasoned cast-iron skillet over high heat until it begins to smoke and is very hot. Lift each tuna steak out of the oil and allow to drain of excess oil, then place them down in the skillet. Cook for 1½ minutes on each side.

Meanwhile, add the tomato mixture to the remaining olive oil and toss.

Remove the pan from the heat and dump the tomato-basil vinaigrette into the pan over the steaks. Shake the pan a little and allow some of the vinegar to evaporate. Serve immediately.

Serves 2

WINE:
Vineyard-designated Chianti—not a Chianti style that has Cabernet Sauvignon in the blend

Fried Flounder

The French do not care for *flet,* as they call the watery flounder of the Mediterranean and North Atlantic. But that fish has little to do with the delicious winter and summer flounders of the eastern American coast. This is one of my favorite dishes, flounder in the classic French preparation, à la meunière, or panfried in butter. It is truly a dish to be cooked with love for the object of your affection as part of an intimate dinner for two—not because of any complicated technique but because it is done most easily one fish at a time in a pan shaped roughly like the fish itself. I fry mine first, put it on a warmed plate in a low oven, then fry my guest's.

    6 tablespoons butter, ¾ stick
    2 ¾-pound flounders, dressed
    salt and freshly ground black pepper to taste
    ¼ cup unbleached all-purpose flour
    1 lemon, halved

Set the oven to the lowest setting and place two dinner plates in it to warm. In an oblong or 10-inch round skillet over medium-high heat, place 3 tablespoons of the butter.

Season the fish with salt and pepper, then dredge in the flour, dusting off any excess. When the butter has melted and stopped sputtering and hissing, add one of the fish to the pan, white side down. Fry for about 3 minutes on each side, until golden brown, then transfer to a warmed plate. Squeeze lemon juice all over the fish, then add the browned butter from the pan. Place the fish back in the oven, quickly wipe out the pan, and repeat with the second fish. Serve immediately.
Serves 2

WINE:
Dry Chenin Blanc or a young Sonoma Valley Chardonnay

Fish with a Potato Crust

Lyonnaise Fish with Potato Crust is a popular new menu item at the venerable Commander's Palace in New Orleans, where chef Jamie Shannon uses a thick crust of julienned potatoes rather than the thin slices of the French dish popularized by Paul Bocuse. The potatoes fry to a golden brown; the fish inside steams perfectly, and the whole is served with a lemon butter sauce.

Lee Bailey, a Louisiana native, assembled a cookbook with Ella Brennan, who is the owner, with her brother Dick, of not only Commander's, but also Mr. B's and The Palace Café. Lee serves his version, as I do mine, in summer with a quickly made sauce of fresh tomatoes and sweet local onions. Shari Hutchinson, a fellow South Carolinian who produces programs for National Public Radio, says that this is nothing more than an updated version of fish and chips with ketchup.

Assemble all the ingredients before beginning this recipe. Make the sauce first, then proceed quickly but methodically with the fish.

FOR THE SAUCE:

2 to 3 tablespoons olive oil

1 medium sweet onion, chopped

2 garlic cloves, finely minced

6 vine-ripened tomatoes, about 2 pounds, peeled, seeded, and chopped, or a 28-ounce can plus a 16-ounce can peeled tomatoes, seeded and chopped

1 teaspoon salt

freshly ground black pepper and fresh lemon juice to taste

FOR THE FISH:

4 medium baking potatoes

1 egg

½ cup milk

4 trout or other firm white-fleshed fish fillets, about ¼ pound each

1 teaspoon salt, plus more to taste

½ teaspoon freshly ground black pepper, plus more to taste

1 cup unbleached all-purpose flour

½ cup olive oil

1 lemon, quartered

Heat the olive oil in a nonreactive saucepan over medium heat. Add the onion and cook until it is becoming transparent, about 5 minutes. Add the garlic, tomatoes, salt, and pepper to taste. Cook for another 15 minutes or until the sauce has begun to thicken. Season with lemon juice, then transfer to a blender or processor and puree. Return to the pan off the heat, straining if necessary or desired.

Peel the potatoes and cut them into thin shoestring or julienne shapes, using a mandoline if you have one. Spread half of the potatoes out on a damp kitchen towel. Make an egg wash by beating the egg in a bowl with the milk. Set aside. Season the fillets on both sides with salt and pepper. Mix the teaspoon salt and the ¹/₂ teaspoon pepper with the flour. Dredge the fillets in the flour, then shake off any extra. Dip the fillets in the egg wash, then place them on top of the potatoes. Cover the fish with the remaining half of the potatoes. Cover with another kitchen towel and lightly but firmly press the potatoes onto the fillets.

Preheat the oven to its lowest setting and place a baking rack over a sheet pan in the oven. Heat the oil in a large skillet or sauté pan over medium-high heat, letting it approach the smoking point. Uncover the fish and place 2 of the potato-encrusted fish in the hot oil. Do not disturb the fish for several minutes. You want the potatoes to form a golden crust that releases itself from the bottom of the pan when the sugars caramelize. Turn down the heat if the potatoes appear to be cooking too rapidly—they should take about 6 minutes on each side.

After about 5 minutes, peek under the fish to see if the potatoes are fully browned. They should have loosened from the bottom of the pan. Use a knife or a sharp metal spatula to slice the 2 potato-encrusted fillets apart, then carefully turn each to cook on the other side, using 2 spatulas if necessary. Repeat the cooking process on the other side, then carefully remove each fillet from the pan, being sure to let any excess oil drain back into the sauté pan. Place the fillets on the rack in the oven. Turn off the oven and place 4 dinner plates inside to warm them. Remove any bits of potato from the oil while it reheats, then continue with the second batch of fish.

When the fish are finished cooking, place them on the rack in the oven to drain off excess oil. Remove the plates, add a pool of tomato sauce to each, then add a potato-encrusted fish to each.

Serve with lemon quarters.

Serves 4

WINE:
Washington State Fumé Blanc, full-flavored and medium-bodied

Crispy Steamed Fish

This "steamed" fish with a peppery crust is another recipe inspired by one that Chef Jamie Shannon of Commander's Palace taught at a culinary conference in New Orleans. It's served with a very light red wine fennel sauce that's a typically elaborate restaurant preparation but well worth the trouble.

Use a light, flaky fish for this recipe. Red snapper fillets with the skin on work well, as do butterflied trout. Serve with plain white rice.

FOR THE RED WINE FENNEL STOCK:

> 1 quart fish stock, not from an oily fish
>
> 1 cup red wine, preferably the one you will drink with the fish
>
> 1 fennel bulb with stalks and feathery leaves
>
> 3 to 4 vine-ripened tomatoes, chopped

FOR THE SAUCE:

> olive oil
>
> ⅛ cup diced red onion
>
> ⅛ cup diced carrot
>
> ⅛ cup diced celery
>
> ⅛ cup chopped tomato pulp
>
> several fresh tarragon leaves, finely chopped
>
> 1 tablespoon butter (optional)
>
> salt and freshly ground black pepper to taste

FOR THE FISH:

> ¼ cup black peppercorns
>
> ¼ cup cornstarch
>
> 1 cup unbleached all-purpose flour
>
> 1 small red onion, chopped
>
> 1 tablespoon salt
>
> 1 egg
>
> 1 cup milk
>
> ¼ cup olive oil
>
> 4 small trout, butterflied, with skin or 4 fish fillets with skin

Simmer all the stock ingredients in a stockpot until the liquid is reduced by half, about 30 to 45 minutes. Remove the fennel bulb, then strain out and discard the remaining solids. Core and trim the fennel bulb and set aside with the stock.

For the sauce, paint the bottom of a sauté pan with just enough oil to keep the onion, carrot, and celery from sticking. Sauté them until limp, then add the stock and warm through.

Just before cooking the fish, add the tomato, tarragon, and ¼ cup diced reserved fennel bulb. Increase the heat and, if desired, whisk in the butter. Season with salt and pepper. Remove from the heat but keep warm while you prepare the fish.

Put the peppercorns, cornstarch, flour, onion, and salt in a food processor or blender and grind for a moment or two. It will be chunky. Dump it out into a pasta bowl.

In another pasta bowl, mix the egg and milk together.

In a large sauté pan, heat the olive oil over medium-high heat.

Carefully lower each fish or fillet into the egg wash just enough to coat the skin side only. Let any extra drip off, then lower the fish into the pepper mixture, coating one side. Add to the sauté pan, skin side down, then repeat for each fish. As soon as all of the fish are in the pan, cover tightly with a lid, lower the heat, and allow to steam until the fish is just cooked, about 5 to 7 minutes.

Place a pool of the sauce on each plate and transfer a fish from the pan to each plate, crispy side up.

Serves 4

WINE:
Pinot Noir, but not one that's covered in oak

Shark en Brochette

Twenty years ago few southerners were eating tuna or squid, much less shark. Federal and state wildlife departments hired marketing experts about ten years ago to spark consumer interest in a variety of fishes. Many of them are excellent cooks, like Donna Florio in Charleston. She has often shared her recipes with me, among them this one for grilled shark.

Scallops are often skewered with bacon, but they're very rich. This lemon-soaked shark makes a much more appealing brochette.

2 pounds shark steaks

½ cup fresh lemon juice

¼ cup olive oil

2 tablespoons chopped parsley

1 teaspoon salt

½ teaspoon dried thyme, or 1 tablespoon fresh
 thyme leaves

¼ teaspoon freshly ground pepper

12 slices of bacon

2 cups cooked seasoned rice

If you use bamboo skewers, you will need to soak 6 of the long ones in water while the fish marinates. Cut the fish into 1–inch pieces and place in a shallow nonreactive container. Combine the lemon juice, olive oil, and seasonings and pour over the fish. Marinate for 30 minutes. Meanwhile, prepare a charcoal fire or preheat a gas grill to medium.

Fry the bacon until cooked but not crisp. Cut each slice into thirds. Alternate the fish and bacon on the skewers. They should all be filled. Cook about 4 inches from moderately hot coals for 5 minutes. Baste with marinade. Turn and cook for 5 to 7 minutes longer or until the bacon is crisp. Serve with rice.

Serves 6

WINE:
A Chardonnay with light body and crisp apple flavors—try a simple one from Sonoma or the North Coast

Grilled Squid

This dish can be served either warm or cold, as an appetizer or a main course. Cilantro and lemongrass flavor a similar salad of poached squid in Thailand. In Provence there's garlic, basil, and mint. Neapolitans add bell peppers and olives. Greeks use nothing but olive oil and lemon juice, then toss it with potatoes or pasta. My version, with grilled squid, calls for seasoning from my courtyard garden in downtown Charleston, typical of the new flavors of the South: lemongrass, basil, and hot peppers. You can make this hearty summer salad early in the day, then serve it for supper, or you can grill the squid at the last minute, warm the vinaigrette, and serve it over pasta. If you're serving the squid as an appetizer before another grilled item, this is a perfect way to appease hungry dinner guests while you wait for the coals to die down a bit.

To clean squid, pull the head away from the body. Most of the entrails will come out with the head. Squeeze the head to force out the chick-pea-size mouth and hard beak. Cut the tentacles from the head just in front of the eyes. Remove the plasticlike "quill" from the body and discard, then squeeze out any remaining viscera from the body and rinse well. Many books tell you to remove the outer purplish skin and fins, but I seldom do.

Squid will lose a third of their weight in cleaning. I often go down to the shrimp docks as the boats are pulling in to get three- or four-inch freshly caught squid.

You will need to use skewers—soak bamboo ones in water for about a half hour before grilling. Three pounds of small squid will fill about 20 foot-long skewers.

3 pounds fresh squid, 2 pounds cleaned

1 cup olive oil

salt and freshly ground black pepper to taste

⅓ cup fresh lime juice

2 large garlic cloves, minced

½ teaspoon hot red pepper flakes

1 tablespoon minced lemongrass

1 fresh hot chili, seeded and finely slivered, or hot pepper
    sauce of your choice to taste

fresh basil, cilantro, or mint leaves or a combination to taste

Build a charcoal fire or preheat a gas grill or your broiler to high. Cut the cleaned squid into ¹/₂-inch rings and skewer them, opening out the rings and leaving a little space between them, filling each skewer with as many rings as will fit (sizes of squid and skewers vary). As you fill the skewers, place them over a casserole dish or mixing bowl large enough to hold all of the squid. Continue until all of the squid rings are skewered. Skewer the tentacles as well, with a little space between sets.

Pour half the oil over the skewered squid, coating them all evenly, then salt and pepper them. Turn the skewers over and repeat with the remaining half of the oil. Salt and pepper the second side as well. If you're going to serve the squid hot over pasta, begin cooking the pasta at this point. Mix the remaining ingredients together.

Grill the squid quickly over high heat, about 1 minute per side depending on the size of the squid. While the squid is cooking, add the rest of the ingredients to the oil and mix well. To serve the dish warm, simply transfer the mixture to a pan and heat, then pour over the grilled squid. For a salad, transfer the squid from the skewers to the oil mixture and toss together, chilling it for a while—but not too much—before eating.
Serves 6 as a main course, 12 as an appetizer

WINE:
Whether you serve the squid warm or cold, Pinot Grigio

Shrimp

As far inland as Kentucky, southerners take shrimp for granted. Camille Glenn's excellent cookbook, *The Heritage of Southern Cooking,* includes 19 recipes for these delicious shellfish, and she hails from Louisville, just across the border from Indiana! Recipes throughout the region call for boiled shrimp, shrimp stock, and pickled shrimp as if every kitchen has shrimp on hand as a matter of course.

Shrimp are best when not allowed to boil: just dump them in boiling seasoned water and count one, two, or three minutes depending on their size, then take them out before the water returns to a boil. There is a standard recipe for stock in Chapter 1 with the Easy Shrimp Gumbo recipe, but here's a variation that gives you seasoned steamed shrimp as well as stock. It's a bit more involved but not difficult. If you're making the Green Tomato Soup in Chapter 1, follow these instructions for the shrimp and stock, then pickle the shrimp according to the recipe in Chapter 7.

Steamed Shrimp and Shrimp Stock

In addition to the ingredients, you'll need rubber gloves and a clean terry cloth towel.

FOR THE SHRIMP:

> 2 quarts water
> 2 pounds small to medium shrimp, 90 to 100
> 1 tablespoon commercial crab boil such as
>   Old Bay seasoning
> 2 tablespoons salt

FOR THE STOCK:

> 1 carrot
> 1 celery rib
> 1 small onion, unpeeled, quartered
> a few fresh herb sprigs

Fold the towel as small as you can get it and place it in the bottom of a stockpot. Put a colander over it.

In another pot on the stove, bring the water to a rolling boil. Add the shrimp and count 1 minute. Put on the rubber gloves.

Immediately dump the contents into the colander. Remove the colander with the shrimp from the pot and set aside. Save the shrimp water for the stock. Pick up the towel and wring out as much water as you can. Unfold the towel and lay it across a counter. Dump the shrimp onto the towel, then sprinkle with the spices and salt. Immediately fold the towel over the shrimp and roll it up to steam.

After 10 minutes, unroll the towel. The shrimp are ready to eat but will last for 2 weeks if you pickle them according to the directions in Chapter 7. Peel them for pickling, placing the shells in the reserved shrimp water.

Bring all the stock ingredients, including the reserved shells and water, to a boil, reduce the heat, and simmer until reduced to about 3 cups of liquid, about 30 minutes. Strain and discard the solids. Freeze what you don't plan to use immediately.

This recipe makes 3 cups of stock that will already be lightly seasoned because of the salt and spices that stick to the shells. Use it accordingly.

Two pounds of shrimp serve about 6 as a main course

Shrimp Awendaw with Kiwi

Chef Fran Freeberg has worked for the Smithsonian and as head chef for the Central Intelligence Agency in Bethesda, Maryland, near where she grew up. For several years she also worked in Charleston. Her recipe here is a variation on the Charleston classic of shrimp and grits, which we might eat for lunch or supper as well as breakfast.

Awendaw refers to the creamy whole-grain cooked grits so often used in the cooking of the Lowcountry, as the Carolina coastal plain is called. It is also the name of a fishing village about ten miles north of Charleston, where kiwifruit are now grown. This recipe, to be served over creamy grits (or pasta), shows Fran's signature on a Lowcountry classic.

> 1 tablespoon butter
> 1 tablespoon chopped shallot
> 2 tablespoons diced country ham
> 1 pound medium-large shrimp, 21 to 26, peeled
>   and deveined
> ½ cup dry white wine
> ½ cup heavy cream
> 1 kiwifruit, peeled and diced
> cooked grits (Chapter 6) or pasta

Heat the butter in a large skillet over medium-high heat. Add the shallot and ham and sauté for 1 minute. Add the shrimp, toss, then add the wine. Cook until the wine is almost completely evaporated, removing the shrimp as soon as they are cooked (just a few minutes).

Add the cream and the kiwifruit to the pan and cook until the sauce is thickened. Remove from the heat and stir in the shrimp, then serve immediately over pasta or creamy grits.

Serves 4 as an appetizer or 2 as a main course

WINE:
North Coast California Chardonnay

Shrimp Creole

From New Orleans and Charleston, this dish has spread throughout the country as one of the hallmarks of southern cooking. While similar dishes are served over pasta in the Mediterranean, the heritage of this rice dish is purely Caribbean.

1½ cups white rice

3 tablespoons olive oil

1 cup chopped onion, about 1 medium

½ cup chopped bell pepper, about ½ large

1 small jalapeño chili, seeded and chopped

½ cup chopped celery, about 1 large rib

1 teaspoon mixed dried herbs such as herbes de Provence or Italian seasoning, crushed

2 garlic cloves, minced

4 cups peeled and chopped tomatoes, about 7 medium

salt and freshly ground black pepper to taste

1½ pounds shrimp, peeled

fresh lemon juice if needed

Cook the rice so that each grain stands separately (see Chapter 6). Meanwhile, in a large skillet or sauté pan, warm the olive oil over medium-high heat and add the onion, peppers, celery, herbs, and garlic. Cook until the vegetables are soft and the onion is translucent, stirring occasionally, about 10 minutes.

Add the tomatoes and cook until all the flavors are well mingled and most of the tomato juice has cooked away, about 10 minutes. Adjust the seasoning with salt and pepper.

Add the shrimp, toss well with the mixture, and cook until the shrimp are just cooked through, no longer than 5 minutes. Do not overcook the shrimp. Taste again for seasoning, sprinkling with a little lemon juice if necessary. Serve immediately over the hot rice.
Serves 4

WINE:
Barbera d'Alba or a very fruity white, such as a dry Muscat from Portugal

Sautéed Oysters over Grits Cakes

Rob Ennis is southern to the bone, and his oceanfront eatery on Litchfield Beach at the southern end of South Carolina's Grand Strand is one of the state's best restaurants. For this recipe, Robby uses yellow grits, stone-ground for him a bit inland at Blackwell Mill in the hamlet of Johnsonville on the Lynches River.

> **1 recipe grits cakes (Chapter 6)**
> **20 shucked oysters with their liquor**
> **salt and freshly ground black pepper to taste**
> **¼ cup unbleached all-purpose flour**
> **¼ cup clarified butter or a blend of butter and peanut oil**
> **¼ cup cooked country ham, julienned**

3 shallots, julienned

1 garlic clove, minced

2 tablespoons dry sherry

1 tablespoon chopped fresh sage or 1 teaspoon dried

2 tablespoons butter at room temperature

Preheat the oven to its lowest setting. Place a rack over a sheet pan and place it in the oven along with 4 appetizer plates or 2 dinner plates. Prepare the grits cakes, transferring them to the wire rack in the oven to drain and keep warm while you prepare the oysters.

Just before sautéing the oysters, remove the grits cakes from the oven and divide them among the warmed plates.

Drain the oysters and reserve the liquor. Place them on a paper towel and pat dry. Season with salt and pepper, then roll in the flour. Sauté the oysters in the ¼ cup butter in a frying pan over medium-high heat until browned, a couple of minutes on each side. Place the cooked oysters on and around the grits cakes.

Reduce the heat and add the ham, shallots, and garlic to the pan. Sauté gently until barely browned, about 5 minutes. Add the sherry, increase the heat, and cook until most of the sherry has evaporated, stirring to loosen any bits stuck to the pan.

Add the oyster liquor and sage and reduce slightly. Turn off the heat and add the 2 tablespoons butter. Melt by gently swirling the pan. Correct the seasoning with salt and pepper, then pour over the oysters and grits cakes. Serve immediately.

Serves 4 as an appetizer or 2 as a main course

WINE:
Appellation Contrôlée Chablis or a Grand Cru when the budget permits

Pasta with Oysters, Leeks, and Country Ham

A few mild leeks and a little country ham added to an oyster cream reduction make a delicious sauce for fettuccine. Certainly not traditional, but dishes like this one featuring the area's finest foods appear regularly on southern restaurant menus—like the preceding recipe from Rob Ennis.

This recipe serves two but can easily be multiplied to feed more.

> ½ **pound dried pasta of your choice**
>
> 1 **cup shucked oysters and their liquor**
>
> 3 **tablespoons butter**
>
> 1 **leek, white and light green parts only,**
>   **well washed and chopped**
>
> **salt and freshly ground black pepper to taste**
>
> **dash of cayenne pepper**
>
> ¾ **cup whipping cream**
>
> 2 **ounces (¼ cup) country ham, diced**

While you cook the pasta, drain the oysters, reserving the liquor. Taste the liquor for salt so you can season accordingly.

Melt the butter in a sauté pan over medium-high heat and sauté the leeks for 1 or 2 minutes, until they wilt. Season with a little salt and pepper and the cayenne. Add the reserved oyster liquor and the cream and cook to reduce until the sauce is very thick. The pan will appear to be all bubbles.

Add the oysters and ham and cook until the oysters just begin to curl and the ham is softened, just a few minutes. The sauce will have thinned from the addition of the oysters. If it is not thickened when the oysters are plumped, remove the oysters and ham from the sauce with a slotted spoon and set aside while the sauce reduces to the desired consistency. Toss all together with the cooked pasta and serve immediately.

Serves 2

Wine:
Muscadet de Sèvre-et-Maine sur lie

Oyster Pie

In the Lowcountry surrounding Charleston and Savannah, no Thanksgiving dinner is complete without an oyster "pie"—really just scalloped oysters. To keep the oysters plump and juicy, wait until the last moment to prepare the dish and serve it right from the oven.

> **1 quart shucked oysters and their liquor**
> **½ cup cream, half-and-half, or milk**
> **2 cups crumbled saltines, about 40 or ¼ pound**
> **freshly ground black pepper to taste**
> **pinch of ground mace**
> **½ cup butter, 1 stick, melted**

Preheat the oven to 350°. Drain the oysters, reserving the liquor. Add the cream to the oyster liquor to make 1½ cups. Season the cracker crumbs with the pepper and mace. Pour the butter over the crumbs, mixing it in well.

Make a layer with a third of the crumbs in an 8-inch casserole dish, followed by a layer of oysters. Make another layer of crumbs and oysters, then pour the oyster liquor mixture over the pie and top with crumbs. Bake for 30 to 40 minutes until it sets, and serve at once.

Serves 6 to 8

WINE:
Although this dish is usually served as part of the Thanksgiving dinner, when an entirely different wine would be served, if offered as a course by itself it demands an estate-bottled Muscadet aged sur lie or Pinot Blanc.

Scallops with Fennel, Orange, and Red Onion

This recipe for seared jumbo sea scallops with a light orange vinaigrette is inspired by one from Sam McGann, whose upscale diner, The Blue Point Bar and Grill, is located in Upper Duck, on the Outer Banks of North Carolina. The Blue Point is noted for its excellent seafood and delicious local vegetables. Sam serves the scallops warm as an appetizer in the dead of winter when Florida oranges are in season, but I've had it chilled for lunch in the middle of summer, and it's just as delicious.

> 3 or 4 navel oranges
>
> 1 tablespoon fresh lime juice
>
> 2 tablespoons rice vinegar
>
> 1/2 cup peanut oil or olive oil, plus a little for the pan
>
> salt and freshly ground black pepper to taste
>
> 24 jumbo sea scallops, about 1 1/2 pounds
>
> salad greens
>
> 1/2 red onion, thinly sliced
>
> 1/2 fennel bulb, thinly sliced

Peel and section the oranges over a bowl. You will need about 30 orange sections for the garnish. Set aside. Make the vinaigrette by whisking a tablespoon of the juice from the oranges with the lime juice, vinegar, and oil. Season with salt and pepper. Set aside.

Season the scallops with salt and pepper. Brush a cast-iron skillet with oil and heat until the pan begins to smoke. Add the scallops to the pan and sear, about 30 seconds on each side. Remove the scallops from the pan, cover, and keep warm while you prepare the plates.

Arrange a bed of salad greens on each of 6 plates. Toss the onion and fennel in the vinaigrette. Divide the vegetables among the plates, top each salad with 4 scallops, and garnish with about 5 orange sections per plate.
Serves 6

WINE:
An Italian white such as Orvieto or, in summer, a Vouvray or cold Wente Brothers Le Blanc de Blanc

Crabs

The meat of the Atlantic blue crab is delicate and sweet, but it takes well to both fiery seasoning and heavy cream. As a child I loved nothing more than crabbing—probably because there is no food I love as much as crab. When I'm out west I eat Dungeness and king crabs, and when I'm in Miami I eat at Joe's, the world-renowned stone crab house. But blue crabs are a very important part of what defines the cooking—both new and old—of the South, and I never tire of them.

There are recipes here featuring the meat with cream and corn, with ham and sherry, and in crab cakes—all based in southern tradition. Use the crabmeat that you can find where you live to prepare these recipes. There's also a recipe for soft-shell crabs, one of the world's great culinary delicacies that unfortunately has no substitute.

Most coastal residents (and most southern states have a coastline) know that freshly steamed seasoned crabs are a treat by themselves. It's a messy meal, but it's delicious. Veda Godwin is considered by some to be the best cook on Edisto Island, South Carolina. She cleans her crabs live, covers them with water, adds some bacon drippings, salt, and pepper, and boils them, uncovered, till done, 7 to 10 minutes. "You can remove the crabs then if you want," she told me. "Thicken the stew with cornstarch and eat that on bread. You'll need plenty of napkins when you eat the crabs."

Crab with Country Ham and Sherry Vinaigrette

In coastal cities where fresh crabs are plentiful, they are most often still simply steamed or boiled and served on newspaper-covered tables. This recipe features the already picked meat in a simple chilled salad. Buy the freshest crabmeat you can and doctor it little. Serve as a first course on a bed of mixed young salad greens.

> **1 pound fresh lump crabmeat**
> **¼ pound country ham trimmed of all fat and cut into little pieces**
> **¼ cup fresh lemon juice**
> **¼ cup dry sherry**
> **½ cup finely chopped celery**
> **½ cup finely chopped sweet onion**
> **½ cup extra-virgin olive oil**
> **salt and freshly ground black pepper to taste**
> **2 tablespoons finely chopped fresh herbs of your choice**

In a nonreactive mixing bowl, pick over the crabmeat. Add the ham and sprinkle with the lemon juice. Add the remaining ingredients and toss together lightly so as not to break up the crab lumps. Chill well, but allow to warm up for a few minutes before serving over a bed of mixed greens.
Serves 6

WINE:
Provence Rosé

Crab Cakes

There are as many recipes for crab cakes as there are coastal villages in the South, but those with neither bread nor mayonnaise in them are, in my opinion, the best. Some chefs such as Jimmy Sneed just bind some crabmeat together with a little mustard and egg and bake them off, but I prefer the traditional fried cake. In any case, as Jimmy says, "The secret of the dish is in the quality of the crabmeat!"

Crab cakes are delicious for breakfast, lunch, or dinner. They are heavenly topped with a poached egg and napped with a mousseline sauce. They are equally at home with a down-home tartar sauce (see following recipe), with an elegant puree of roasted red peppers, or with a variety of relishes and sauces.

I like to serve these cakes on a warm pool of quick tomato puree (see Fish with a Potato Crust in this chapter) to which I have added a tea-spoon of hot red pepper flakes or bottled hot pepper sauce to taste. A good serving of black bean relish made with fresh dill (Chapter 7) and a handful of tortilla chips rounds out this delicious dish.

These are infinitely tastier if you use dried leftover rolls or baguettes and freshly grate them (I keep them in a paper bag).

 1 lemon
 1 pound fresh lump crabmeat
 1 heaped tablespoon coarse-grain mustard
 2 eggs, separated
 ½ cup butter, 1 stick
 2 tablespoons minced mild onion
 ½ cup chopped red bell pepper or ¼ cup green
 1 tablespoon sherry vinegar
 salt, freshly ground black pepper, and cayenne pepper
    to taste
 1 tablespoon finely chopped fresh herbs of your choice
 about 2 cups fine dry bread crumbs

Sprinkle the juice of half the lemon over the crabmeat in a bowl to freshen it. (If the lemon is not juicy, use the juice from the whole lemon.) In a separate small bowl, mix the mustard with the egg yolks.

Melt half the butter in a skillet over low heat and add the onion and bell pepper, cooking until the onion is becoming transparent, about 10 minutes. Add the vinegar, raise the heat, and cook until the vinegar has evaporated. Pour the mixture over the crabmeat, add the egg yolk mixture, and toss all together, being careful not to break up the big clumps of crabmeat. Season to taste with salt, pepper, cayenne, and the herbs.

Place the bread crumbs in another large mixing bowl. Just before cooking the crab cakes, heat the remaining butter in a large frying pan over medium heat. Beat the egg whites until stiff but not dry and fold into the crab mixture.

Reach down into the crab and fill your palm with a scoop of the mixture. Gently press it into a cake about 3 inches wide and about 1 inch thick. Place the cake down in the bread crumbs. Scoop up crumbs from around the cake and pour over the top of the cake. Do not mash the cake or press the crumbs into it: you want only a dusting of crumbs *on* the cake, not *in* it.

When the butter in the pan is foamy, gently pick up the first cake and put it in the pan. Continue making the cakes and placing them in the pan. You should have 6 cakes, which should just fit into the skillet. Cook until browned—about 3 minutes—on the first side, then carefully turn each cake so it does not split and cook on the other side.

When cooked, the cakes should resemble nothing more than seasoned crabmeat, slightly crisp on the outside.

Makes 6 cakes to serve 3 as a main course or 6 as an appetizer

WINE:
Alexander Valley Pinot Blanc

Fried Soft-Shell Crab and/or
Oyster Po' Boy

In New Orleans the oyster po' boy is called *la médiatrice,* "the peacemaker." The story goes that the husband who has been out carousing in the French Quarter all night long brings one home to his waiting, angry wife.

In this version, for two, I use fried soft-shell crabs with a *lagniappe* (Cajun for "something extra") of fried oysters. You can make the po' boy with just oysters if you prefer, but during the last of the season's oysters in spring, add the soft-shell crab, one of the great culinary delicacies of the South.

Of course, fried soft-shell crab and oysters are perfectly delicious by themselves or served with any number of sauces, but this sandwich garnished with homemade tartar sauce makes a wonderful spring lunch. The unique flavor of fresh chervil, slightly reminiscent of fennel, is an elegant addition if you can find it; if not, use parsley or dill.

FOR THE TARTAR SAUCE:

>   1 recipe homemade blender mayonnaise (see Pimiento Cheese recipe in Chapter 5)
>   1 tablespoon sweet pickle cubes, rinsed and drained
>   1 tablespoon capers, rinsed and drained
>   1 tablespoon minced onion or shallot
>   1 tablespoon minced fresh chervil, parsley, or dill
>   cayenne pepper to taste

FOR THE PO' BOYS:

>   1 loaf of French or Italian bread, about 15 inches long and 3 inches wide, or 2 hoagie loaves
>   2 live soft-shell crabs and ¹/₂ pint oysters or 1 pint oysters
>   ¹/₄ cup unbleached all-purpose flour
>   ¹/₃ cup Dijon mustard
>   ¹/₄ cup corn flour (see Ingredients and Sources) or unbleached all-purpose flour
>   vegetable oil for frying
>   lettuce

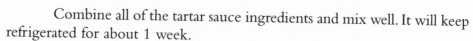

Combine all of the tartar sauce ingredients and mix well. It will keep refrigerated for about 1 week.

Preheat the oven to 200°. Put a metal rack on a baking sheet and put it in the oven.

Split the bread lengthwise and scoop out most of the fluffy center from the loaf or loaves. Place the bread in the oven.

If you have crabs, use scissors and cut off most of the mouth and eyes at an angle with one cut. Lift the pointed flaps on each side of the crabs and pull out the gills or "dead man's fingers." Turn the crab over and cut off the apron. (Virginia's chef Jimmy Sneed, who keeps his own soft-shell pens, notes, "A male's apron looks like the Washington Monument; a female's, the Capitol building.")

Pat the crabs and/or oysters dry. Put the flour, mustard, and corn flour in separate shallow bowls or plates. Preheat about ½ inch of oil to 365° in a deep skillet, sauté pan, or Dutch oven.

Use one hand to handle the food, the other to wield the tongs. Prepare one crab at a time, followed by oysters. Dredge the crabs and oysters in the flour, knocking off any extra. Place down in the mustard and use a pastry brush to distribute the mustard evenly all over the shellfish. Place the mustard-coated crabs and/or oysters down in the corn flour and dust all over. When the oil has reached 365°, add them to the oil and fry for a couple of minutes on each side, until golden brown all over. Be careful; they pop. Do not crowd the skillet. Two crabs and a couple of oysters or 6 to 8 oysters can be fried at the same time.

Transfer the crabs and/or oysters to the rack in the oven to drain. Remove the bread and spread thickly with tartar sauce, then cover with either lettuce leaves or shredded lettuce.

When the crabs and all of the oysters have been fried, add them to the sandwiches and serve immediately.
Serves 2

WINE:
Rully Blanc from the Côte Chalonnaise

Corn and Crab Pudding

Fresh corn and crabmeat belong together, and they are paired in soufflés, soups, chowders, bisques, casseroles, stir-fries, and salads from Texas to Maryland. This is the most elegant recipe I've tried: no eggs, no cheese, no butter, no flour, and no heavy seasonings. Serve these as an appetizer and you'll have your dinner guests crying for more!

> **1 cup fresh crabmeat**
>
> **½ lemon**
>
> **1 cup fresh corn, grated from the cob**
>
> **1 tablespoon cornmeal**
>
> **¾ cup heavy cream**
>
> **1 tablespoon finely grated onion**
>
> **salt, freshly ground black pepper, and cayenne**
>
>   **pepper to taste**

Preheat the oven to 350°. Grease four ½-cup ramekins or custard cups. Freshen the crabmeat with lemon juice and pick it over, discarding any bits of shell. Add the remaining ingredients and season to taste.

Divide the mixture among the ramekins and bake for 35 to 45 minutes or until the puddings firm up. Serve in the ramekins. These puddings are also delicious cold. I like to unmold them into pasta bowls and ring them with the green tomato soup, also cold, in Chapter 1.

Serves 4

WINE:
If served warm, direct but plump Monterey or Sonoma Chardonnay; served cold with the green tomato soup, a Sonoma County Sauvignon Blanc

Littleneck Clams in a Fennel and Tomato Court Bouillon

Court bouillon means quick stock in French, but in Louisiana, where it's pronounced "coobeeyon," it's a soup made by adding fish to the stock as it cooks. Neither the French nor French immigrants in Louisiana would dream of cooking shellfish or fennel in unseasoned water. The quick stock is made in a matter of minutes to provide an aromatic poaching liquid. Fennel is traditionally poached in a court bouillon and served cold as an hors d'oeuvre. For some reason this very French preparation is called *à la grecque* (in the Greek style).

Although I have been extremely disappointed by many farm-raised fish, I've also watched the development of the aquaculture of the most delicious, the cleanest, and the safest clams I've ever eaten (see Ingredients and Sources). Just outside Charleston on James Island, Atlantic LittleNeck ClamFarms began its operation in 1989. The clams are bred, grown, and nurtured for the world's most sophisticated palates. Grit-free and ready to use, whether live or frozen, these littlenecks are actually superior to clams from the wild.

1 small onion, chopped

2 tablespoons olive oil

2 cups water

1 cup dry vermouth or dry white wine

1 bay leaf

¼ teaspoon cayenne pepper

4 or 5 black peppercorns

1 fresh thyme sprig

juice of 1 lemon

1 garlic clove, unpeeled but crushed

2 fennel bulbs with stalks attached

2 medium vine-ripened tomatoes, peeled, seeded, and diced

4 dozen littleneck clams

Sauté the onion in the olive oil in a sauté pan over medium heat until it is transparent, 5 to 10 minutes. Add the water, wine, bay, cayenne, peppercorns, thyme, lemon juice, and garlic. Trim the stalks from the fennel bulbs and add the stalks, saving a few of the feathery leaves for garnish. Raise the heat, bring to a boil, reduce to a simmer, and cook, covered, for 20 minutes.

Strain the court bouillon and discard the solids. Cut the base from the fennel bulbs, but do not core them. Remove any discolored or damaged outer ribs and discard. Slice the fennel into 1/4- to 1/2-inch slices, about 6 per bulb. Place the fennel in a large sauté pan with the court bouillon, bring to a boil, reduce the heat, and simmer, covered, for 5 minutes.

Add the tomatoes to the pot, raise the heat to medium-high, and cook until the liquid is reduced by half, about 10 minutes. Stir occasionally as it cooks, breaking up the fennel clusters so that they cook evenly and mingle with the tomatoes.

Add the clams, cover the pot, and cook, shaking the pan occasionally, until all of the clams open, about 5 minutes.

Serve immediately as an appetizer in pasta bowls with crusty bread and a dipping dish of extra-virgin olive oil, or refrigerate immediately and serve chilled.

Serves 4

WINE:
An Italian Chardonnay/Pinot Grigio blend, such as Libaio

Meats

Pork is not the only meat in the South. Beef and veal, lamb and mutton, and game such as deer and rabbit are old southern favorites that continue to appear on restaurant menus and in southern kitchens in spite of a national trend toward vegetarianism. In this chapter you'll find traditional preparations such as eastern North Carolina–style barbecue and country-fried steak with mashed potatoes and gravy, but you'll also find the simple steaks and roasts, grilled chops, and veal dishes that are also southern standards.

In Charleston, where I live, there isn't even a vegetarian restaurant; my grocer stocks several different grades of beef, including cuts from increasingly popular naturally raised "free-range" cattle. In states where game sales are outlawed, mail-order brokers (see Ingredients and Sources, Meats) do booming business in farm-raised venison and other exotic meats. Rabbit is readily available in grocery stores throughout the region. I've included two recipes for it, one of which is grilled.

Summerfield Veal Rib Chops Grilled Over an Oak Fire

From their idyllic setting in the foothills of Virginia, Jamie and Rachel Nicoll send out glossy brochures for their Summerfield Farm products (see Ingredients and Sources, Meats), complete with color studio shots of dinner plates prepared by some of the nation's finest chefs. Jamie Stachowski's veal paillards and asparagus pinwheels, for example, are a kaleidoscopic view of colorful foodstuffs, artfully arranged around a vegetable puree and a perfectly clear sauce. These elegant photos belie the down-to-earth nature of both the farm and its owners, however, who admit to enjoying simpler preparations of their naturally raised veal and lamb. The recipes they send out with orders reflect their own home cooking: Tuscan vegetable soup (made with their excellent *glace de veau*), lamb shanks cooked in white wine with celery root and thyme, and several recipes for grilling, such as this one, which is a fancier version of what they would normally cook for themselves.

Though the Nicolls grill this over oak in the open hearth of their house, you can use a backyard charcoal or gas grill with good results. Aaron Schlabach's natural lump charcoal (see Ingredients and Sources) is an excellent natural product that produces incomparable results.

> 3 tablespoons virgin olive oil
> 1 shallot, minced
> 2 tablespoons dried rosemary leaves
> 4 garlic cloves, coarsely chopped
> ⅛ teaspoon ground star anise
> ½ teaspoon cracked black pepper
> 3 bay leaves
> 1 tablespoon balsamic vinegar
> ½ cup dry white wine
> 4 veal rib chops

Warm the olive oil in a small saucepan over medium heat, then add the shallot, rosemary, and garlic and let them sizzle gently for 2 minutes. Remove from the heat and add anise, pepper, bay leaves, vinegar, and wine, stirring well. Pour the marinade over the chops in a large baking dish; let stand at cool room temperature for 6 to 8 hours, spooning the marinade over the meat frequently as it stands.

Prepare a wood or charcoal fire and allow it to burn down to embers. Spread them out, then position a grill about 4 inches over the bed of coals. When you hold your hand over the grill, you should feel a penetrating warmth. Grill the chops for about 8 minutes per side, rotating the chops on each side to be sure that they brown evenly, brushing them occasionally with the marinade. Serve immediately with potatoes cooked in the coals.
Serves 4

WINE:
Côtes-du-Rhône

Braised Veal Shanks

This is one of Kentucky chef Bill Hughes's excellent meat recipes. Since the first time Bill came into my bookstore when he was a culinary student in Charleston, we've enjoyed stimulating conversations, always sharing recipes and cooking ideas. Bill suggests serving this dish on a bed of white rice cooked with lemon zest and adds that it's important to use a decent white wine.

Get the butcher to cut the steaks from the veal shanks.

> 1½ teaspoons dried oregano or 1 tablespoon fresh
>   oregano leaves
> 1½ teaspoons dried basil or 1 tablespoon fresh chopped
>   basil leaves
> 1½ teaspoons dried thyme or 1 tablespoon fresh chopped
>   thyme leaves
> 4 1½-inch-thick steaks cut from veal shanks

salt and freshly ground black pepper to taste

¼ cup unbleached all-purpose flour

2 tablespoons olive oil

2 garlic cloves, peeled

¾ cup chopped carrot, about 1 medium

¾ cup chopped onion, about 1 small

1 cup peeled and chopped tomatoes

2 bay leaves

1½ cups dry white wine

¾ cup veal or chicken stock

chopped parsley for garnish

freshly grated Parmesan cheese for garnish

Three hours before serving, preheat the oven to 325°. Grind the oregano, basil, and thyme in a spice mill or a mortar. Season the shank steaks with the ground herbs and salt and pepper, then dust with flour. In a skillet over medium-high heat, brown the steaks in the olive oil on both sides, then transfer them to a baking dish.

In the skillet, sauté the garlic, vegetables, bay leaves, and any remaining dried herbs over medium-high heat until the vegetables are soft, about 10 minutes, stirring occasionally and scraping up any browned bits of flour from the bottom of the pan. Add the wine and stock and simmer for 15 minutes. Taste again for seasoning, adding salt and pepper if necessary. Pour the mixture over the shanks and cover the pan very tightly with aluminum foil. Bake for 2½ hours.

Garnish the dish with parsley and Parmesan and serve with a side dish of your favorite green vegetable.
Serves 4

WINE:
A spicy wine with body and high alcohol content—a white Côtes-du-Rhône or for red a Barbera, Barbaresco, or Barolo

Veal Edistonian

Chef Philip Bardin continues to be one of South Carolina's most beloved chefs. His generous plates of wholesome, honest food are rooted in the southern classics that were popular in both homes and grand old southern hotels until our towns were fractured by the interstate highway system and the flight to suburbia.

Philip admits his favorite foods are those that he learned at his Aunt Min's side, but his customers demand his updated versions of the classics such as this pecan-crusted veal with mousseline sauce. In his Edisto Island restaurant Philip tops the veal with some shrimp or scallops (I've seen veal Edistonian on other restaurant menus with crabmeat), but when we eat this at home we never do. I have cooked this dish with a veal chop—longer and over a lower flame—as well as the cutlets.

If you have a good butcher, your cutlets and scallops will be cut so that traditional pounding is unnecessary. Nevertheless, you should at least flatten the meat so that it is an even thickness and will cook evenly. I put the cutlets between two sheets of wax paper and place a heavy skillet on top and press firmly. Philip adds a little lemon juice and vermouth to the sauté pan to "cut the swampy taste of veal," but I don't find it necessary.

Mousseline is hollandaise loosened with some cream. Make it first, then put it on the back of the stove to stay warm while you prepare the veal. Serve this dish as Philip does, with creamy grits and just-picked asparagus.

FOR THE MOUSSELINE SAUCE:

> **3 egg yolks**
>
> **2 tablespoons fresh lemon juice**
>
> **½ teaspoon salt**
>
> **½ cup butter, 1 stick, cut into pieces**
>
> **½ cup whipping cream**
>
> **cayenne pepper to taste**

FOR THE VEAL:

> **¼ cup clarified butter (see note)**
>
> **1⅓ pounds veal cutlets or scaloppine**

¼ **cup pecan pieces**
¼ **cup unbleached flour**
½ **teaspoon salt**

For the sauce, in a wide bowl that will fit snugly over a pan or in the top of a double boiler, whisk the yolks with 1 tablespoon of the lemon juice and the salt. Place the bowl over simmering water and, whisking continuously, add the butter bit by bit, making sure each bit of butter is well incorporated before adding another piece. Scrape the sides of the bowl as you whisk and be sure that the eggs don't scramble. If they do, pick up the bowl, get a spoonful of hot water from below, and whisk it in. Continue whisking until all the butter is mixed in and the sauce is velvety smooth.

Remove the double boiler from the heat, but leave the bowl over the water. Whisk in the cream, then adjust the seasoning with the remaining lemon juice and the cayenne. Set the double boiler with the sauce aside to stay warm while you prepare the veal. Whisk it occasionally so that it neither breaks nor forms a skin.

For the veal, put the butter in a large heavy sauté pan over medium heat. Flatten or pound the veal.

Put the pecans, flour, and salt in a food processor and pulse until you have a meal. Dump the mixture out onto a piece of wax paper and coat each cutlet well on both sides.

Increase the heat to medium-high and sauté the cutlets on each side for about 3 minutes. Transfer to warm plates and nap with the mousseline sauce. If you're adding scallops or shrimp to the dish, quickly cook them in the same pan as the veal, top the meat with the seafood, then add the sauce. Serve immediately.

Serves 4 (1¼ cups sauce)

NOTE:
You can add the milk solids from the clarified butter to the grits you're serving or whisk them into the mousseline.

WINE:
Château Greysac (a Cru Bourgeois Médoc) or a rich, elegant Chardonnay such as Arrowood

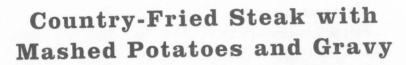

Country-Fried Steak with Mashed Potatoes and Gravy

Throughout the South this staple of the country table appears also as "chicken-fried" steak and "smothered" steak. It's a typical way of dealing with the tougher cuts, such as a round of beef, but it's also commonly prepared with deer meat. Sometimes grocers market already pounded—really machine-perforated—meats as "cube" steak. If you're going to pound the meat yourself, a pound of meat will feed three or four people.

FOR THE POTATOES:

4 baking potatoes, about ¾ pound each, peeled and cut into ½-inch wedges

2 teaspoons salt

1 cup whipping cream

FOR THE STEAKS AND GRAVY:

4 cube steaks or 4 steaks of beef or venison cut from 1 pound of meat and pounded with a mallet

salt and freshly ground pepper to taste

¼ cup peanut oil

¼ cup unbleached all-purpose flour

In a saucepan, cover the potatoes with water, add the salt, and bring to a boil. Cook for about 10 minutes. You can fry the steaks and make the gravy while you cook the potatoes. In the meantime, in another pot, bring the cream to a boil, then turn off the heat. When the potatoes are done, immediately pour off the water and mash them with a potato masher, adding the cream a little at a time. (I put the potatoes in a large stainless-steel mixing bowl and beat in the cream with a heavy wire whisk.)

Season the steaks with the salt and pepper. Heat the oil in a heavy skillet over medium-high heat. Dredge the steaks in the flour, then fry in the oil until well browned, a few minutes on each side. Transfer to a rack to drain.

To make the gravy, pour off the grease but leave the browned bits in the skillet. Reduce the heat and add the leftover flour (you should have 2 or 3 tablespoons) to the skillet, stirring constantly. Add a cup of water and continue stirring over medium-low heat until you have a rich gravy. Correct the seasoning with salt and pepper, then pour over the steaks and mashed potatoes.

WINE:
Any good red table wine

Grilled Flank Steak

Summers are so hot in the South that grilling has become more and more popular over the years. Gas grills sport additional burners for pots of side dishes, and many patios have portable camp stoves so that no cooking has to be done indoors. In the Carolina Lowcountry where I live, we carry out-door burners aboard when taking day trips to barrier islands, where we cook fresh-caught shrimp and crabs in creek water.

Even the lean, tough cuts of red meats are grilled outdoors, and I often carry a plastic bag of marinated meat on picnics to grill for sandwiches. This grilled flank steak is often called a London Broil. Some marinade recipes call for lemon juice, which breaks down the meat; I use red wine. Served with traditional sandwich garnishes, the meat is fine cold and left over as well. If you're taking the meat on a picnic, use Arabic bread. There's a recipe for homemade in Chapter 8.

2 to 2½ pounds flank or top round steak

¼ cup dry red wine, preferably the one you will drink with the meal

a few drops of Tabasco or other hot pepper sauce

2 garlic cloves, finely chopped

2 tablespoons chopped parsley

2 tablespoons fresh marjoram, thyme, and/or rosemary in any combination

½ cup olive oil

salt and freshly ground black pepper to taste

Place the meat in a nonreactive container or a 1-gallon Ziploc bag. Put the wine, hot sauce, garlic, and herbs in a small bowl, mix well, then whisk in the oil. Add salt and pepper. Pour the marinade over the meat, covering it well, cover the container or close the bag, and refrigerate overnight.

The next day, take the meat out of the marinade while you build a charcoal fire or preheat a gas grill to medium-high. Place the marinade in a stockpot and simmer for 10 minutes. Grill the meat over a medium fire for about 5 minutes per side, basting with the marinade. Let the meat rest for 5 minutes after it is cooked, then cut into thin slices across the grain on the bias. *Serves 8*

WINE:
Young California Cabernet Sauvignon with forward fruit flavors or a young inexpensive Bordeaux

Sliced Tenderloin with Three Sauces

When I want a steak, I always opt for more flavorful cuts, but the luxurious tenderloin is perfect for the buffet table, sliced and served with bread or rolls (try the Sally Lunn in Chapter 8) and a variety of sauces. Your guests will appreciate not only making their own sandwiches with their choice of sauces but also being able to eat the tender meat with one hand while standing. It is the quintessential heavy hors d'oeuvre, but the meat all but melts in your mouth. Preparing the meat for the table is simplicity itself. Make the sauces the night before and place them in the refrigerator.

FOR THE MUSHROOM PASTE AND BUTTER:

1½ cups butter, 3 sticks

2 pounds mushrooms, finely chopped (see note)

1 pound shallots, minced

½ cup Madeira

1 teaspoon mixed dried herbs, such as herbes de Provence
or Italian seasoning, crumbled

1 teaspoon salt

FOR THE WATERCRESS MAYONNAISE:

1 egg

¼ teaspoon salt

½ teaspoon dry mustard or 1 teaspoon prepared

1 cup olive oil

1 cup watercress leaves

1 tablespoon fresh lemon juice

FOR THE HORSERADISH SAUCE:

1 cup whipping cream

3 tablespoons grated horseradish (see note)

1 tablespoon fresh lemon juice

salt and freshly ground black pepper to taste

prepared mustard and/or Tabasco or other hot pepper
sauce to taste, optional

FOR THE MEAT:

1 trimmed whole beef tenderloin, 5 to 6 pounds, at room
temperature

salt and freshly ground black pepper to taste

For the mushroom paste and butter, allow one of the sticks of
butter to soften. Melt the other two in a heavy pan over medium heat, then
add the remaining ingredients and sauté until the mushrooms have given off

most of their liquid, about 30 minutes. Remove from the heat and cool to room temperature.

To make mushroom butter, beat the softened stick of butter until very light, then beat in some of the mushroom paste to taste. You may want to put the mushroom butter in a food processor for a finer texture. Serve alongside the tenderloin in a ramekin. Put the remaining paste aside.

NOTE:

Ordinary mushrooms will do, but I like a mix of varieties. Truffles are an elegant addition, and you can intensify the flavor with the addition of 2 tablespoons of truffle paste, sold in squeeze tubes.

For the watercress mayonnaise, put the egg, salt, and mustard in a blender and blend for about 20 seconds. Add the oil very slowly, in droplets at first, and blend until all of the oil has been bound with the egg mixture and the mayonnaise is thick and creamy. With the blender running, begin adding the watercress leaves a little at a time. Stop occasionally and scrape down the sides of the container with a rubber spatula, tasting the mayonnaise. You should continue adding the leaves and blending in until the mayonnaise has taken a cress flavor to suit your own palate (I use the entire cup). Add the lemon juice and blend briefly to incorporate.

For the horseradish sauce, whip the cream to soft peaks, then fold in the remaining ingredients, seasoning the sauce to taste.

NOTE:

You can use commercially prepared horseradish in this sauce if you must, but the flavor of freshly grated is much brighter.

Build a charcoal fire in a covered grill or preheat a gas grill to hot. The tenderloin should be trimmed of excess fat and the bluish-gray membrane called the *silver skin.* The fat-encased side strap should also be removed and cut up for use in stir-fries. When the fire is medium-hot, season the meat heavily with salt and pepper and place on the grill. Cover the grill and cook the meat until well seared on one side, about 10 minutes, then turn the meat over, cover the grill again, and cook until well seared on the second side, 10 to 12 minutes. The center cuts of the tenderloin should still be rare; when poked with a finger it should be soft, giving to the touch.

The smaller loin tip should be medium to well done, feeling firm to hard. Don't worry about undercooking the meat; there will be meat cooked to please every palate. (You can also roast a whole tenderloin in a 500° oven for 25 to 35 minutes, turning it every 10 minutes; rare meat will register 125° on a meat thermometer.)

Transfer to a platter and allow to cool for at least 15 minutes. You can slice and serve the meat at this point, but I like to pat the mushroom paste all over the tenderloin, refrigerate it overnight, slice it the next day while it is still chilled, then serve it at room temperature. Garnish the plate with watercress and serve with the mushroom butter, the watercress mayonnaise, and the horseradish cream sauce.

Serves 8 as a main dish or 16 as part of a buffet

WINE:
If roasted, Savigny-lès-Beaunes; if grilled, a soft Merlot

Bessie's Standing Rib Roast

Bessie Simpson Hanahan is Charleston's consummate hostess. Invitations to dine in her lovely eighteenth-century South Battery home and garden are much coveted. Her food is always delicious and often hearty and soul-satisfying, such as this classic standing rib beef roast.

Bessie says: "It's Gary Drake's recipe. He worked for the Simpson family of South Carolina for three generations, and he's really the one who reared me. Mammy Lula was the baker, but Gary Drake was the cook. He was from Little Rock, South Carolina, near Dillon."

I might serve this with Yorkshire pudding (popovers) and a horseradish sauce, but Bessie says Gary always served it with stuffed potatoes.

Tell the butcher you want a standing rib of beef, with the chine bone removed from the ribs to make carving much easier. Bessie also removes some of the fat from the roast, but she gets a roast that is "four ribs over to the fifth," with plenty of fat and bone to protect the meat while it's roasting.

1 4- or 5-rib beef roast, about 9 pounds

4 or 5 garlic cloves, split lengthwise

freshly ground black pepper to taste

Place the roast in a shallow roasting pan and bring it to room temperature. Preheat the oven to 450°. Slip a thin sharp knife into the meat next to the ribs in several places and poke the slivers of garlic into the slits, an inch or so deep. Coat the meat well with black pepper on the fat and bones but not on the flesh.

Place the roast in the oven and sear well all over, about 30 minutes. Turn the heat down to 400° and place a large piece of aluminum foil loosely over the meat. (Bessie says that Gary used a covered roasting pan with the lid "caterwhomper.") Roast for a total of 2 hours, or 14 minutes per pound. If you find the oven firing again during the cooking time, turn the heat down a little bit. Remove the roast from the oven, remove the aluminum foil, and allow to rest for at least 15 minutes before you carve it.
Serves 10 to 12

WINE:
This is the time to pull out the great red Burgundy you've been cellaring—especially Volnay!

Pan-Seared Steaks with Mushrooms

I prefer a pan-seared steak to a grilled one. The following recipe is, in my opinion, near perfect. Use tongs rather than a fork to turn the steaks; you don't want to pierce the meat. If you work quickly, the steaks will be perfectly rare and delicious. The recipe serves two, but you can multiply it for more people. I like this best served with the Panfried Potatoes in Chapter 6.

2 well-marbled boneless prime or choice strip steaks, each
about ½ pound and 1 inch thick
coarsely ground black pepper to taste
2 tablespoons butter
1 cup chopped onion, about 1 medium
¼ pound mushrooms, preferably shiitake, thickly sliced
or left whole if small
spicy young red Rhône wine such as Côtes-du-Rhône

Take the steaks out of the refrigerator at least 30 minutes before you
cook them to bring them to room temperature. Meanwhile, begin
preparing the Panfried Potatoes if you're serving them.

Preheat the oven to its lowest setting and place 2 dinner plates inside
to warm. Put a cast-iron skillet over high heat to get hot. Pepper the steaks
well on both sides, and as soon as the skillet is searingly hot, place them in
the skillet. Cook them for 1½ to 2 minutes, then shake the pan. They should
be seared enough to loosen. Turn down the heat a bit and turn the steaks to
the other side. Cook for 2 minutes on the second side, shake the pan again
to loosen the steaks, and transfer them to the warm plates in the oven.

Immediately put the butter, onions, and mushrooms in the pan and
cook, shaking the pan often, until the mushrooms have given off most of
their juice, about 3 to 5 minutes. Pour yourself a glass of wine, remove the
steaks on their plates from the oven, and splash some of the wine into the
pan to deglaze any bits of deliciousness that may have stuck to the pan. Stir
once or twice with a wooden spoon and serve immediately over the steaks,
with the Panfried Potatoes on the side.
Serves 2

WINE:
Guigal Côtes-du-Rhône

Blue Cheese Burgers

These are my favorite burgers. I started making them when I was in college. Serve them on English muffins, lightly toasted on the grill; they'll hold together and not stick to the roof of your mouth like ordinary, fluffy hamburger buns.

1 pound ground chuck, broken up with a fork
¼ pound blue cheese, crumbled

Toss the meat and cheese together. Make 4 patties from the mixture, *lightly* pressing them into shape. Bring them to room temperature while you build a charcoal fire or preheat a gas grill. Grill 3 or 4 inches over medium heat for about 2 or 3 minutes per side or to taste. Serve with the usual accompaniments.
Serves 4

WINE:
Gamay from California or Beaujolais Nouveau

Ham

Ham can mean a number of things in the South, but it usually refers to the hind leg of a pig. A *country ham* is one that is cured with salt (see Ingredients and Sources, Meats). It is often smoked as well. Virginia and Kentucky are rightfully well known for their excellent country hams, but I have eaten perfectly delicious ones from the Carolinas and Tennessee. The best ones are hung for a year after a dry salting and slow smoking. *Ninety-day wonders* are what I call hams injected with brine and sold as country hams after a mere three months, even though they may not have been smoked at all. They have nothing to do with the rich, aged flavor of a real country ham.

At Easter and during the warm spring and summer months, though, we prefer one of two types of hams—fresh hams, straight from the hog, or the pink partially cooked or smoked hams found in grocery stores. Slices appear on the dinner plate and stuffed into sandwiches; cubes are added to jambalayas and omelets. Try to avoid "water-added" hams; they are salty and pink, but you pay more for something that is neither cured nor fresh and simply cooked. Look for a fresh or "regular" (cooked to an internal temperature of 137°) whole ham not trimmed of all its fat. The butt end is more expensive and yields larger slices, but the shank end proves that the meat closer to the bone is tastier.

To cook a fresh ham, put it on a rack in a roasting pan and place it in a cold oven. Do not season it and do not cover it. Turn the oven to 325° and roast for 30 minutes per pound or until a meat thermometer inserted in the thickest part reads 160°. Remove from the oven and allow to rest for 20 minutes before carving.

To prepare a partially cooked or smoked ham for the table, follow the packager's instructions.

Debbie's Homemade Eastern North Carolina–Style Barbecue

Barbecue sauce changes hue and tone as you cross county lines in the South, but most aficionados agree that real southern (not Texan) barbecue is pork—preferably a whole hog pit-cooked with hardwoods. In North and South Carolina there are vinegar-, mustard-, and tomato-based sauces, infinitely varied, but the cooking is mostly the same. It's an all-night (or all-day) affair in the country that usually involves a bunch of good ol' boys and beer. Some people cook just the shoulders, some cook three shoulders to one ham, and traditionalists still insist on the whole hog cooked over a pit of smoldering hickory or oak coals. Some chop the meat, some pull it from the bone, and some shred it, but a Carolinian would never slice barbecued pork.

Some of the tastiest southern barbecue is found in the Carolinas, and many people think eastern North Carolina's is the best. My friend Debbie Marlowe (whom we call "Lady Merlot" for her vast oenological knowledge and whose wine recommendations add so much to this book) lived for many years in Roanoke Rapids, North Carolina. A genius at the grill, Debbie is not one to let men claim the province of barbecuing. Debbie has successfully duplicated eastern Carolina barbecue in this home version. It still takes all night, but you can smoke enough meat on two home smokers (and the electric ones require little attention) to feed a crowd of 50. Her buttery vinegar sauce may seem like gilding the lily, but it is absolutely delicious.

FOR THE MEAT:

> **30 to 35 pounds fresh pork, including a picnic shoulder or 2, a blade or butt roast, a loin, a ham, and 1 set of ribs**
> **several pounds hickory chunks, soaked in water for several hours or overnight**

FOR THE SAUCE:

> **1 cup butter, 2 sticks**

2 quarts white vinegar

2 cups apple cider vinegar

3 tablespoons hot red pepper flakes

juice of 1 large lemon

2 teaspoons salt

1 teaspoon freshly ground black pepper

Grease the racks of your smokers and set aside. Prepare the coals or preheat electric smokers. Fill the water pans. Evenly distribute the meat on 4 racks, placing it fat side up. When the coals are ready, add a good handful of drained wood chunks to each smoker, then quickly add the water pans and racks of meat to the smokers and cover them well. Resist the temptation to peek, because each time you do you will lose precious heat and moisture. You will probably need to replace coals every 2 to 3 hours; wood chunks will last a little longer. When you replace wood chunks, be sure to check the water level in the water pans; they will probably need to be refilled every 4 or 5 hours. The water level should not drop below half full. Replace with hot tap water, pouring it through the grates without moving the meat to minimize delays.

Meanwhile, add all of the sauce ingredients to a 3-quart saucepan, bring to a boil, and immediately reduce the heat. Simmer slowly for 1½ to 2 hours. Set aside until you're ready to serve.

The meat will take about 12 to 16 hours to cook, until a meat thermometer reads 160°, depending on your heat source and the thickness of the cuts of meat.

The ribs will probably be done in 4 or 5 hours, before the larger cuts. Check to see if the meat pulls easily away from the bones. Remove the ribs from the smoker, then brush them well with the sauce. They are the cook's bonus. Baste the rest of the pork with reheated sauce only when it is ready to be turned, just before its last leg of cooking, about 2 hours before it's done, when it has reduced in size by about a fourth.

When the meat is done, transfer it from the smokers to a large baking pan. As soon as it is cool enough to handle, pull the meat from the bones, then chop it using 2 cleavers or large knives, adding sauce as you chop. Debbie uses a ketchup bottle with holes punched in the lid to

distribute the sauce through the meat. Serve warm, piled high on your plate or on hamburger buns, with potato salad and coleslaw.
Serves 40 to 50

NOTE:
This recipe can be done in a kettle-style grill, such as a large Weber, but because there is no water pan the meat will cook in about 8 hours. Debbie cooks 15 to 20 pounds of meat at a time on hers but warns that you must leave only one of the vents open—just enough to feed some air to the fire, so as to keep it as low as possible. She replenishes charcoal and chunks at least once, after about 4 hours.

TO DRINK:
Lots of cold beer or lemonade

Marinated and Grilled Thick Pork Chops with Summer Squash

Most southerners grew up eating greasy thin panfried pork chops. Today's thick cuts of lean pork lend themselves well to the grill. The marinade is really just a seasoned oil to keep them tender and tasty and to facilitate grilling; the chops need only about a half hour in it. The following recipe is for two but can be multiplied. The Asian seasonings have been found in the southerner's pantry for centuries.

> 2 tablespoons soy sauce or tamari
> 2 tablespoons dry sherry
> 2 tablespoons peanut oil
> 1/2 teaspoon hot red pepper flakes
> 2 to 3 garlic cloves to taste, minced
> a 2-inch piece of fresh ginger, peeled and finely grated,
>   about 2 teaspoons

2 1- to 1¼-inch-thick bone-in pork chops, 8 to 10 ounces each

**3 or 4 small young summer squash such as crookneck
or zucchini**

About 45 minutes before dinner, mix the marinade ingredients in a large bowl and add the chops, turning them several times to make sure they are well coated. Set aside at room temperature for 30 minutes. After 15 minutes, build a charcoal fire or preheat a gas grill to medium-high. Rinse the squash, then cut off the ends and slice them in half lengthwise. Set aside.

When the grill is hot, place the chops on the grill and add the squash to the bowl, tossing it around in the marinade. Cook the chops for 7 minutes on the first side, then turn them. Add the squash to the grill with the chops and spoon the marinade that remains in the bowl onto the chops. Grill the squash for 3 minutes on the first side, then turn it over. After another 3 minutes, remove both the squash and chops to plates and serve immediately with coleslaw.

WINE:
A southern Rhône, preferably Gigondas

Roast Pork with Tequila Glaze

In the South we often baste a pork roast with a honey and mustard glaze spiked with bourbon. In this margarita-inspired version, the roast is marinated in lime juice Cuban style, and the glaze is flavored with tequila.

8 to 10 garlic cloves, peeled

a 3½- to 4-pound pork roast from the loin, bone in

1 cup fresh lime juice, from about 4 to 5 limes

¼ cup tequila

½ cup sugar

1 teaspoon salt

The day before you serve the dish, slice the garlic cloves in half lengthwise so they are very pointed, then slip them into slits made all over the pork roast. Place the roast in a nonreactive container and cover with the lime juice. Rotate the meat several times while it marinates.

About 3 hours before dinner, preheat the oven to 325°. Remove the pork from the marinade, saving the lime juice. Place the meat fat side up in a roasting pan with a rack and place in the center of the oven. After 1½ hours, combine the reserved lime juice, the tequila, the sugar, and the salt in a small saucepan and simmer for 30 minutes. Brush a third of the glaze on the meat, continue cooking it for 5 or 10 minutes, brush on another third of the glaze, cook for another 5 minutes, and brush on the remaining glaze. Cook for a total of 2½ hours or until the meat has reached about 165°. Set the meat aside to rest for 20 minutes before carving. Serve with Black Beans and Rice (Chapter 6) and Mango Relish (Chapter 7).
Serves 6

NOTE:
The pork roast is delicious in a burrito—carved from the bone, diced, and added to flour tortillas with sour cream and hot pepper sauce—also served with the black beans and rice and mango relish.

TO DRINK:
Have margaritas, then serve sangria with the pork.

Summerfield Lamb Shanks with Celeriac and Thyme

This is another recipe from Summerfield Farm, whose excellent lamb and veal I highly recommend (see Ingredients and Sources, Meats).

1 tablespoon peanut oil

2 lamb shanks

½ onion, thinly sliced

¼ pound mushrooms, quartered

1 pound celeriac, trimmed well and cut into ½-inch dice

1¼ cups water

1 tablespoon chopped fresh thyme leaves

½ cup dried tomatoes

1 cup dry white wine

1 cup lamb, veal, or chicken stock

salt and freshly ground black pepper to taste

Preheat the oven to 350°. Place a heavy ovenproof skillet over high heat, adding the oil when the pan is hot. Add the shanks and brown well on all sides. Remove the shanks from the pan and reserve. Reduce the heat and add the onion, mushrooms, and celeriac. Add ¼ cup water and scrape the pan to loosen the drippings. Add the thyme and cook over medium heat for 8 to 10 minutes or until the vegetables begin to soften around the edges.

Add the tomatoes, stir to combine, then place the shanks on top of the vegetables. Add the wine and stock plus the additional cup of water and bring to a simmer. Cover tightly with foil and place the skillet in the oven. Braise until tender, stirring occasionally, about 45 minutes.

Taste the vegetable mixture for seasonings and correct with salt and pepper. Serve immediately.

Serves 2

WINE:
Caillou Blanc from Château Talbot

Onions Stuffed with
Lamb and Rice

This is a real lamb lover's dish. Kentuckian Bill Hughes, quite simply the best meat cook I know, sent me the recipe. If you don't like the muttony taste of the lamb fat, use a little oil in the tomato sauce instead. In Kentucky mutton is the preferred meat for barbecue.

3 large yellow onions, unpeeled

salt to taste

2½ pounds coarsely ground lamb

½ cup finely chopped carrot

½ teaspoon ground cinnamon

1 tablespoon chopped fresh rosemary leaves or 1½
   teaspoons dried, crushed

¾ cup long-grain white rice

2¼ cups water or chicken or lamb stock

freshly ground black pepper to taste

½ cup finely grated carrot, about ½ large

8 whole garlic cloves, peeled

2 teaspoons grated lemon zest

2 cups peeled and crushed tomatoes, about 2 large

1 cup fresh bread crumbs

½ cup chopped parsley

Boil the onions in salted water for 20 minutes. Drain and set aside to cool while you prepare the stuffing and sauce.

Brown the lamb with the chopped carrot, cinnamon, and rosemary in a sauté pan over medium heat until evenly cooked, about 10 minutes. Pour off the excess fat and liquid into another sauté pan.

Add the rice and 1½ cups of the water or stock to the lamb. Season with salt and pepper, then simmer, covered, for 15 minutes. Add the grated carrot and garlic to the lamb fat (or a small amount of oil if you do not want the strong lamb flavor) and sauté until the carrots have begun to melt and the garlic is well glazed. Add the lemon zest, tomatoes, and remaining ¾ cup water, season with salt and lots of black pepper, and cook over medium heat until the sauce has thickened considerably, about 12 minutes.

Preheat the oven to 375°. Slice both the root and stem ends from the onions and peel them. Make a cut from end to end to the center of each onion. Carefully peel away the layers of onion. With a large serving spoon, fill each onion layer with the lamb mixture, roll it back up into approximately its original shape, and stand on end in an 8- by 11½-inch baking dish. Continue making rolls until the dish is closely filled. Pour the tomato sauce over the onion rolls and cover with the bread crumbs.

Bake the rolls for 1 hour. Run the dish under the broiler to brown the crumbs if necessary, sprinkle with the parsley, and serve. The buttery flavor of Green Beans with Pecans (Chapter 6) nicely complements this dish. Serve with a crusty white bread.

Serves 8

WINE:
A full-flavored and zesty Spanish red

Grilled Lamb Chops with Mint Pesto

I lived in Genoa, the Italian home of pesto, before coming home to the South. Real pesto is, of course, pounded in a mortar with pecorino, pine nuts, Genoese basil, and Ligurian olive oil. But mint, a perennial southern favorite, is the traditional accompaniment to lamb in England, whence came so many of the South's early settlers. This cross-cultural recipe is more closely aligned to an English mint sauce than to the pallid mint jelly we have come to serve with lamb. The pesto draws on ideas from all three cuisines—Italian, American, and English—and is at home in the New South. It's perfect with the lamb. The recipe will make about ½ cup of pesto, enough to coat about 12 chops, or 4 servings. Tightly covered, the pesto can be refrigerated for several weeks.

PER PERSON:

3 lamb chops, about 1 inch thick

FOR THE PESTO:

½ cup tightly packed fresh mint leaves

2 garlic cloves

2 tablespoons freshly grated Parmesan cheese

½ cup extra-virgin olive oil

salt and freshly ground black pepper to taste

Build a charcoal fire or preheat a gas grill to medium–high. While you wait for the fire, let the lamb come to room temperature. Add the mint, garlic, and cheese to a blender or food processor and blend together well. Scrape down the sides and add the oil slowly while blending, until the pesto is uniformly smooth. Season with salt and pepper. Set aside while you grill.

Place the chops on the grill for 5 minutes on the first side. Turn them over and spread a heaped teaspoon of pesto on each chop. Grill the second side for about 5 minutes as well. Serve immediately with new potatoes and green beans.

WINE:
A Rutherford Bench Cabernet Sauvignon or a St-Estèphe

Grilled Rabbit

One of the best chefs in the South is Jimmy Noble in North Carolina, whose insistence on the finest ingredients in his restaurants may well make him the closest we have to an East Coast Alice Waters. Most of the foods he serves are cooked either over wood or in wood-burning ovens, and many of those foods are raised by Jimmy himself. He buys free-range chickens for the restaurant, but he raises hens for eggs and grows all of his herbs, lettuces, beets, turnip and other greens, and many other vegetables. The rabbits you eat in his fine establishments were also grown by Jimmy, and he has a burgeoning flock of sheep.

One of the most memorable restaurant meals I've ever had was at Noble's Grille in Winston-Salem. A fresh young rabbit, marinated in olive oil and fresh herbs, was perfectly grilled over an oak and hickory fire alongside fresh leeks and tomatoes. Freshly dug new potatoes were roasted among the embers in his brick oven, and both rabbit and vegetables were napped with a rabbit stock reduction just before being served on bright Italian majolica. I chose one of several Rhône Valley wines he was offering by the glass that evening to accompany the dinner and can honestly say I've never had a better meal.

Rabbits are becoming easier to find in America's supermarkets. If your grocer does not carry them, encourage him to. They are delicious lean white meat, easy to prepare, and take well to all sorts of preparations. They can be grilled or fried like chicken or braised slowly as in the classic German hasenpfeffer, still a favored preparation in southern towns where Germans settled and rabbit hunting is common.

Jimmy bones the rabbits at his restaurants to make for easier white-tablecloth dining. Boning rabbits is a snap, but I never bother. I like to serve this meal outdoors at the picnic table on one of the first warm nights of spring. If you've got a kettle-type grill, you can roast potatoes—coated with extra-virgin olive oil or duck fat, salt, pepper, and thyme—in a pan off to one side of the grill, not over the coals; just be sure to keep them basted.

Jimmy warns, "Be sure not to put any lemon juice or vinegar in your marinade; it breaks down the meat."

If you buy rabbits with the livers included, sauté them in a little butter and onion or treat them any way you would a chicken liver.

2 young rabbits, cleaned, about 2½ to 3 pounds each

1 celery rib

1 carrot

1 small onion, split, or ¼ large onion

1 handful of fresh herbs of your choice

1 quart water

salt and freshly ground black pepper to taste

⅓ cup olive oil

2 garlic cloves, minced

¼ cup chopped fresh herbs such as basil, parsley,
  and thyme

3 shallots, finely chopped

4 tablespoons butter, ½ stick

2 cups dry white wine

Wash the rabbits well and pat dry. Using poultry shears, trim away the belly flaps and place in a saucepan. Cut the hind legs away from the body at the hip joints and place in a large nonreactive baking dish such as glass or stainless steel. Cut the front legs away from the body at the shoulders and add them to the baking dish.

With the backside up, make a shallow slit with a sharp knife into the skin down the length of the backbone. Slip the knife under the outer layer of skin and remove it from the saddle of meat that encases the backbone. Turn the rabbits over and slip the knife down under the last set of ribs. Break the backbone at this point and cut through with the knife.

The saddles should be about 6 inches long. Cut them into 3 equal pieces, cutting off the end where there is no meat. Add the saddle pieces to the baking dish and all the trimmings to the saucepan. To the trimmings add the celery, carrot, onion, and handful of herbs, cover with the water, and simmer for about 1 hour, or until reduced by half, to make 2 cups stock. Strain out the solids and discard; reserve the stock.

Sprinkle the rabbit pieces with salt and pepper. To the oil, add the garlic and chopped herbs, mix well, and pour over the rabbit. Toss the pieces with your hands to make sure they are all well coated with the oil. Cover with plastic wrap and refrigerate until about 45 minutes before serving time.

About an hour before you plan to eat, sauté the shallots in the butter in a sauté pan over medium-high heat for about 5 minutes, then add the white wine. Simmer until the wine has completely evaporated, then add the reserved stock and continue to cook, perhaps turning it down a bit, to thicken while you're grilling: this final reduction will produce the sauce for the rabbit, and it should still be of pouring consistency.

Meanwhile, remove the rabbit from the refrigerator and prepare a charcoal fire or preheat a gas grill to medium. When the grill is ready, place the rabbit pieces on the grill and cook, covered, as you would chicken. The tiny front legs take just a few minutes per side; the saddles will take a little longer; the powerful hind legs a few minutes more or about 10 to 15 minutes per side. The meat should be opaque throughout but not dry. Baste frequently with the oil.

As soon as the rabbit comes off the grill, put the pieces on plates and nap with the sauce. Serve with Panfried Potatoes (Chapter 6) or with grilled leeks (Chapter 4, Grilled Poussins or Cornish Hens and Leeks) and tomatoes (Chapter 5, Frittata of Grilled Vegetables).
Serves 4 to 6

WINE:
A medium-bodied fruity wine such as Vacqueyras from the Rhône Valley or Château de la Chaize Cru Beaujolais. Do not *serve a heavy, tannic red.*

Rabbit Compote

Similar to meat pastes or pâtés, this light and unusual shredded meat spread has gone through several cooks' hands before evolving into this recipe. Paula Wolfert offered chef Lucien Vanel's version in her classic book *The Cooking of South-West France*; at a culinary conference held in New Orleans, chef Susan Spicer demonstrated her variation of that recipe, cooking the rabbit in broth instead of the usual fat. This is my version of Susan's version of Paula's version of Vanel's version of the old French dish. Paula advises starting several days in advance so that the compote has time to mellow.

FOR THE RABBIT AND STOCK:

> 1 skinned rabbit, 2½ to 3 pounds
>
> 2 carrots
>
> 1 celery rib
>
> 1 large yellow onion, halved
>
> 2 bay leaves
>
> a good handful of fresh herbs, including parsley, several
> thyme sprigs, and sage leaves
>
> 16 black peppercorns
>
> 6 cups water
>
> 1½ cups dry white wine
>
> ½ cup olive oil
>
> 1 garlic clove, halved

FOR THE COMPOTE:

> 1 cup whipping cream
>
> 2 teaspoons Dijon mustard
>
> 2 teaspoons chopped shallot
>
> 2 teaspoons chopped fresh herbs of your choice
>
> salt and freshly ground black pepper to taste

Rinse the rabbit well, cut off the 4 legs, and set aside. If any organs are included, set them aside for use in another recipe. Cut the loins from the backbone and set them aside with the legs. Place the remaining bones and carcass in a stockpot and add one of the carrots, the celery, half of the onion, a bay leaf, some of the herbs, and half of the peppercorns. Cover with the water and simmer for about 45 minutes to an hour or until the liquid has reduced by a third, to 1 quart. Strain, cool, and reserve the stock.

Meanwhile, mix the wine and oil together. Peel the remaining carrot and onion half and thinly slice both. Put the reserved rabbit legs and loin pieces in a shallow casserole dish and add the wine and oil mixture. Add the sliced carrot and onion, the garlic, and the remaining herbs and spices. Toss to make sure everything is well coated, cover well, and refrigerate overnight, turning the pieces occasionally.

The following day, strain the rabbit and vegetables from the marinade, saving all. Set the casserole dish aside to use at the stove. Skim the oil from the marinade and place in a heavy sauté pan over medium-high heat. Remove the rabbit pieces and brown in the hot oil, placing them in the casserole dish as they are browned.

Add the marinade vegetables and sauté until lightly caramelized, about 10 minutes. Add the reserved marinade and increase the heat to high to deglaze the pan. Add the reserved quart of stock and the browned rabbit pieces and bring to a boil. Immediately reduce to a simmer and cook for 2 hours, skimming occasionally. When done, the meat should be very tender and pull easily from the bone. Remove the rabbit from the pot and set aside to cool in the marinade casserole.

Strain the liquid and discard the vegetables. Skim the oil from the surface, return the liquid to the pot, and cook over high heat to reduce to about 1 cup.

Meanwhile, remove the bones from the rabbit with your fingers, discard the bones, and shred the meat uniformly by mashing it between your thumbs and fingertips. Remove any cartilage or tough silver skin and be careful to remove all bits of bone—there will be many small pieces.

Add the cream to the reduced liquid and continue to cook to reduce by half, until very thick. Whisk in the mustard and remove from the heat. Add the reduced cream mixture, the shallot, and the herbs to the shredded meat and mix well. Season with salt and pepper. Remove the compote mixture from the casserole dish and pack into a lightly oiled small stainless-steel bowl. Refrigerate for at least 24 hours. Tightly covered, the compote will keep for a week.

Remove the compote from the refrigerator about an hour before you plan to serve it. Turn it out on a serving platter and serve with toasted bread or crackers. Paula suggests serving the rabbit with prunes soaked in hot tea. Her version of the compote contains the sour greens of sorrel. I use paper-thin slices of lemons (seeds removed) as a garnish.

Makes 2 cups, serving 6 to 8

Wine:
Pouilly-Fuissé

CHAPTER
4

Poultry

Southerners hold no claim to chicken; it has been domesticated for thousands of years. We do raise more and eat more than any other Americans; possibly no other region of the country knows more chicken dishes than the South. Ducks, too, are old favorites: archaeological digs in Charleston, South Carolina, reveal them to have been the favored meat in years gone by. The wild turkey that lives in that state is said to be closer to the original than any other living in the wild.

I'm willing to bet that these birds—whether poached or stewed or fried or grilled—find their way to the table for at least one meal a day for most southerners.

Fried Chicken

Fried chicken is arguably *the* quintessential southern dish. Recipes, which are little more than technique, vary as you cross county lines and plot family trees. Barbecue may well be the only other southern specialty with more fierce pride behind it. Show me a barbecue recipe, and I can tell you where it's from; tell me how you like your fried chicken, and it's more than likely how your mother or grandmother did it. In researching this book, I found only coleslaw and brownie recipes with as much variety—and they are not particularly southern.

There are recipes calling for soaking the chicken in milk. Some lay importance on freshness and give you instructions for killing the bird. Some call for coating the bird in batters; others in heavy spices. Many cooks tell you to cover the chicken while it fries, which makes for a very moist—albeit greasy—bird, but I think that that technique—favored among many southern cookbook writers—emerged in this century among homemakers (or home economists) in an effort to keep the kitchen clean. The third edition of *The Virginia House-Wife* (1828) included a recipe. *The Carolina Housewife,* published in Charleston in 1847, included several.

In his book on southern food, Bill Neal insists on cutting the bird (fresh, never frozen) into 9 pieces, with a wishbone (or "pulley-bone," as we called it at my house). He gives explicit instructions for butchering the bird, which he says can be from 3 to 3½ pounds. I was always told that fryers should never be over 3 pounds. Mrs. Dull, whose *Southern Cooking* has informed southern cooks for over sixty years, insists on birds 2 pounds or under. Bill soaks his 9 chicken pieces in buttermilk for 2 hours. Both he and Mrs. Dull cover the frying pan.

John Egerton's definitive *Southern Food* says that all these refinements and special touches are just minor variations on Mrs. Randolph's theme in *The Virginia House-Wife.* He soaks his birds in cold water and adds a little bacon grease to the shortening. But he doesn't cover the pan. Panfried recipes are mostly similar, covered and not. John says that he "gladly leave[s] the deep-frying to the fast-food chains." Not me.

If ever the craft of cooking has risen to artfulness in the South, it's in our frying. Perhaps the reason that so few people can agree on fried chicken recipes is that, in truth, very few people fry it at home these days. And why should we, with Popeye's and Church's in every southern town? My friend

Jack Early, from Bamberg, South Carolina, says that anyone can artfully fry—all you need is clean, hot grease and fresh food. He's right. The deeper the fat, the better. You want the pieces of food being fried not to touch—to sear on all sides immediately upon entering the hot grease. Heat, not the grease itself, then penetrates the food and cooks it at a high temperature. The foods being cooked will not be greasy. Deep frying is a dry cooking technique, as long as the grease is clean and hot enough and the food is not crowded.

Deep-fried chicken is to me the very best. Harriet Ross Colquitt, writing in *The Savannah Cook Book* in 1933, agreed. Her recipe is simple perfection: "Cut up the chicken, sprinkle liberally with salt and pepper, dredge with flour, and fry in deep, and very hot, fat." I might add that clean, fresh lard is the best fat to use, that the temperature should be 365° to 375°, and that the chicken, which should cook in 20 to 25 minutes, should be drained on racks before being served. But other than that, I have no improvements.

I do admit, though, that I do most of my frying outdoors and that open-kettle frying indoors without good ventilation can wreck your kitchen. I have therefore included here another recipe for panfrying chicken, and covered, too. It's followed by the classic gravy that is served over the biscuits and mashed potatoes or rice that accompany the meal. This version is served hot. If you're going on a picnic, however, I do recommend deep-fried chicken, which is so much crisper (and which you can buy at the fast-food joints).

Another popular method of deep-frying poultry in the South involves frying the whole bird, such as a turkey or a whole chicken. When *Vogue* magazine featured my deep-frying an entire bird, I got hundreds of calls from curious cooks. It makes for a very crisp skin and moist meat. A recipe for deep-frying a turkey breast follows those for chicken and gravy.

Panfried Chicken

1 fryer, 2½ to 3 pounds, cut into 8 to 10 pieces, with skin
2½ cups lard or shortening, about 1 pound, or
    mild-flavored oil such as peanut
1 teaspoon salt
1 teaspoon freshly ground black pepper
pinch of paprika or cayenne, optional
1 cup unbleached all-purpose flour

Wash the chicken well in cold water, drain, and pat dry. Put the shortening in a heavy skillet or sauté pan over medium-high heat. Place the salt, pepper, and, if desired, paprika or cayenne in a paper bag with the flour. Shake to mix.

Add the chicken pieces to the bag one at a time, shaking well to coat. Reserve the flour for making gravy. When the shortening has reached 365°, place the coated chicken in the pan, skin side down, one at a time. Start with the dark pieces, which take a little longer. Cook in batches if necessary: you do not want to crowd the chicken, and the grease should come up around the edges of each piece. Cover the pan, reduce the heat a little, and fry for about 5 to 7 minutes, until the underside is brown. Turn the chicken, cover the pan again, and fry for another 5 to 7 minutes. Remove the cover and continue cooking for about 15 minutes more, until the chicken is perfectly crisp and cooked through. Drain on a wire rack, not on papers (where it would sit in and reabsorb excess grease). Keep warm while you make the gravy.

ONION GRAVY

Country gravies like this one can be made with cream, milk, half-and-half, water, or chicken stock—or any combination. If you cut up your own fryer, make a quick stovetop stock with the neck and back of the chicken as you're frying and use that in the gravy. It's delicious.

2 to 3 tablespoons grease from frying

2 tablespoons seasoned flour from frying

2 cups milk or chicken stock or a combination

1 to 2 tablespoons grated onion to taste

salt and freshly ground pepper to taste

Pour the melted shortening from frying out of the pan into a container, leaving 2 or 3 tablespoons of the grease and all of the little browned bits of flour in the pan. Over medium heat, add the flour to the grease, whisking it in and stirring constantly until it begins to brown. Slowly add the liquid and onion and continue cooking, stirring often, until the desired consistency is reached. Correct the seasoning and serve from a gravy boat, but *not* on the chicken.

WINE:
Jean Cordier Vin de Table Blanc cuts through both grease and spice to show pleasant fruit—or try any Chenin Blanc.

Deep-Fried Turkey Breast

One of the new traditions in the South is deep-frying an entire turkey. You need a huge (10-gallon) pot and lots (5 gallons) of oil. And it must be done only outdoors. This recipe, for just the breast, is more feasible, but you still mustn't try it indoors. Once you've eaten fried turkey, though, you'll never go back to baked.

The hardest I ever worked at cooking was for a dinner for four of club sandwiches and fries. I baked the bread, fried the turkey breast, and made all the condiments from scratch. It was also one of the best meals I've ever eaten.

1 fresh bone-in turkey breast, about 5 pounds

2 gallons vegetable oil

ground cayenne pepper to taste

Bring the turkey breast to room temperature, allowing it to drain well of any juices. In a 5-gallon stockpot (preferably with a mesh insert), heat the oil outdoors over a gas burner until it is very hot, about 365°. If you don't have a thermometer, you can test the oil's temperature with a fresh piece of bread, which will take about 1 minute to brown completely when the oil is hot enough for frying.

Pat the breast dry. Sprinkle it all over with cayenne, then *slowly* and carefully lower the breast into the oil. Fry the breast for 4 to 6 minutes per pound or until it is evenly golden brown all over and it floats freely in the oil. A meat thermometer inserted carefully into the thickest part of the breast should register 180° when the breast is fully cooked.

Carefully remove the breast from the pot with long forks or tongs and allow all excess oil to drain away. Carve immediately and serve.
Serves 6 to 8

WINE:
White from the southern Rhône

Chicken Pie

Chicken pie is another illustration of the regional differences within the South. There are pies with no crusts, pies with bottom crusts only, and pies with only a top crust. Some are merely chicken enriched with cream or sour cream; others are filled with peas and mushrooms. In this south Georgia version, celery is the predominant flavor, and the pie is covered with a simple biscuit dough—a variation on chicken and dumplings. This is one of my favorite comfort foods.

FOR THE STOCK AND FILLING:

1 3½- to 4-pound chicken

3 quarts water

4 large celery ribs, trimmed

1 large onion, quartered

2 carrots, broken into pieces

2 bay leaves

a few fresh thyme sprigs and other fresh herbs of your choice

4 eggs

FOR THE BISCUIT CRUST:

2 cups sifted soft southern flour (see Ingredients and Sources), plus a little for dusting

2 teaspoons baking powder

1 teaspoon salt

5 tablespoons butter, lard, or vegetable shortening

½ cup milk

FOR THE FILLING AND FINAL ASSEMBLY:

4 tablespoons butter, ½ stick

3 tablespoons unbleached all-purpose flour

½ cup milk

salt and freshly ground pepper to taste

1¼ cups finely chopped onion, about 1 medium-large

2 tablespoons melted butter or cream

Rinse the chicken well, then put it in a stockpot and cover with the water. Add the celery, onion, carrots, and herbs to the pot, bring almost to a boil, and simmer until the meat is evenly cooked, about 1 hour. While the chicken is poaching, hard-cook the eggs, cool them, peel them, chop them, and set them aside.

Remove the chicken and the trimmed celery ribs from the pot and strain the rest of the solids out of the stock and discard. Refrigerate the strained stock. When it is cool enough to handle, remove the skin from the chicken and discard, then pull the chicken meat from the bones and chop into uniform pieces, discarding any fat. You should have 4 cups of meat. Chop the cooked celery into small pieces. You should have about a cup of celery. Set the celery and chicken aside.

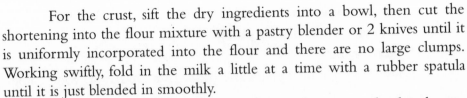

For the crust, sift the dry ingredients into a bowl, then cut the shortening into the flour mixture with a pastry blender or 2 knives until it is uniformly incorporated into the flour and there are no large clumps. Working swiftly, fold in the milk a little at a time with a rubber spatula until it is just blended in smoothly.

Dust a counter lightly with some flour and scoop up the dough onto the counter with the spatula. *Lightly* work the dough, working only with the fingertips, until it is evenly blended. Roll it out about ¼ inch thick into the shape and size of the 2-quart casserole dish in which you will bake the pie (mine is rectangular, about 11 by 8 inches). Cover with a kitchen towel while you prepare the filling.

Preheat the oven to 425°. In a saucepan over medium-high heat, melt the 4 tablespoons butter, then add the flour, stirring constantly until you have a smooth paste. Gradually add 2 cups of the reserved stock and the milk and continue cooking until the mixture is the consistency of thick cream, about 5 to 10 minutes. Season with salt and pepper. Add the onion, reserved chicken, and reserved celery and toss well together. Remove from the heat and turn into a 2-quart baking dish.

Add the eggs, then top with the biscuit dough. I cut biscuits out with a 2-inch metal biscuit cutter dipped in flour, then cover the top of the pie with the biscuits and the scraps. Brush with melted butter or cream, then bake for about 15 minutes. If the biscuits are not browned, you can run them under the broiler for a moment. Serve hot.

Serves 6 to 8 as supper or 8 to 10 as part of a larger meal

Wine:
Oaky and rich Chardonnay from Napa or Monterey

Sweetbreads and Chicken with Madeira

Frank Stitt's successful restaurants in Birmingham, Alabama, are the epitome of fine new southern cooking. The southern-born and -bred young chef blends local ingredients with techniques from Tuscany and the South of France, making his takes on southern cooking at once traditional and modern, steeped in southern heritage and full of flavor. After a trip to Birmingham to sample Frank's cooking, I called him to ask about this dish of sweetbreads and chicken that was on the oft-changing lunch menu.

"People don't usually think of sweetbreads for lunch, but I really like them and think it makes a nice springtime dish served with fresh asparagus and rice pilaf. The cooking is traditional for the sweetbreads. Just deglaze the pan with the best Madeira you can get your hands on and whisk in a little butter to finish off the sauce," he said. Madeira has been popular in the South since colonial days, when ships bound for America often stopped on the Portuguese island to take on water and supplies.

> ³/₄ **pound veal sweetbreads**
>
> ¹/₄ **cup unbleached all-purpose flour**
>
> ¹/₂ **teaspoon salt**
>
> 1 **small breast of chicken, split, boned, and cut into**
>   **2-inch medallions**
>
> 4 **tablespoons unsalted butter,** ¹/₂ **stick**
>
> ¹/₄ **cup Madeira**
>
> ¹/₄ **cup chicken stock**

Four hours before you plan to eat, soak the sweetbreads in several changes of cold water until clean. Place the sweetbreads in a saucepan and cover with cold water. Simmer for 5 to 6 minutes, then cool them in cold water. Remove the membrane and connective tissues, wrap in a dry towel on a sheet pan, and cover with a 2- or 3-pound weight for 3 hours. I like to use a fresh small (less than 4 pounds) fryer for this dish and make cracklings from the skin and a stock from the rest of the body while the sweetbreads are being pressed.

Heat the oven to its lowest setting, then place a plate inside to warm. Slice the sweetbreads into uniform medallions. Mix the flour with the salt. Coat the sweetbread and chicken pieces with the flour. Melt 3 tablespoons of the butter in a sauté pan and sauté the sweetbreads over medium heat until crisp, about 5 minutes per side. Transfer to the warmed plate in the oven. Sauté the chicken pieces until crisp as well, add them to the warmed plate, and finish the sauce.

Pour in the Madeira and stock, raise the heat, and deglaze the pan, shaking it and scraping up any little brown pieces that have stuck to the bottom. Cook until the liquid is reduced by half. Cut the remaining tablespoon of butter into pieces and whisk in the pieces a few at a time. Add the sweetbreads and chicken to glaze them with the sauce and serve immediately. *Serves 2 to 4*

WINE:
Madeira at least 5 years old

Chicken Liver Pizza

In Italy there is a dish called *crostata di fegatini*—a chicken liver tart made with pancetta, vin santo, and grated Parmesan. The following recipe is inspired by the *crostata* and is typical of the *pizze bianche*—white pizzas—being offered by young chefs in the South with their increasingly popular wood-fired ovens. I've replaced the pancetta with country ham and the vin santo, an artisanal dessert wine, with sherry, both traditional southern ingredients. Chicken livers have long been favored in the South.

Even without a wood-fired oven, you can easily obtain a crisp crust by using a pizza stone (readily available in kitchenware shops) or quarry tiles preheated in your oven. Transferring the pizza to the stone may prove difficult, however, without a peel, the big paddle you slide underneath risen pizzas and bread loaves to quickly flick them into the oven. If your kitchen-ware shop doesn't have a peel, try the local restaurant supply house.

FOR THE DOUGH:

> ½ ounce fresh compressed cake yeast or 1 teaspoon preservative-free active dry yeast plus ¼ teaspoon sugar or honey
> 1¼ cups warm water, 110° to 120°
> 1 pound unbleached all-purpose flour, about 3¼ cups, plus flour for dusting
> 1½ teaspoons salt
> 2 teaspoons fruity olive oil, plus a little more if you're using a sheet pan

FOR THE TOPPING AND ASSEMBLY:

> 10 ounces trimmed chicken livers, about 1¼ cups
> 3 tablespoons dry sherry
> 2 tablespoons extra-virgin olive oil
> 1 small sweet onion, cut into rings
> ¼ pound country ham, julienned, about 1 cup
> salt and freshly ground pepper to taste
> 2 ounces Parmesan cheese, freshly grated, about ½ cup
> 1 tablespoon fresh marjoram or oregano leaves
> 2 ounces Parmesan cheese, freshly shaved, about 12 2-inch squares
> cornmeal for dusting stones and tiles

In a medium mixing bowl, dissolve the yeast (and sweetener if you're using dry yeast) in ¼ cup of the water. Set aside for about 10 minutes in a warm place until the mixture is bubbly and creamy. Add a cup of the flour and mix until smooth.

Mix the rest of the flour and the salt together in a large warm mixing bowl, making a well in the center. Pour in the yeast mixture and the oil and mix well, gradually adding the remaining water and mixing the dough until it forms a ball and no longer sticks to your hands or the bowl. Knead the dough until it is satiny and evenly elastic, about 10 minutes.

Sprinkle the inside of a large bowl with flour, form the dough into a ball, and place in the bowl. With a razor blade, cut an X into the top of the dough, sprinkle it with a little more flour, and put the entire bowl in a plastic bag, loosely sealed. Set aside in a warm, draft-free place to rise until doubled in volume—1 to 3 hours.

When the dough has doubled, punch it down and knead it for a few minutes on a floured surface. If you're using a pizza stone or quarry tiles, place them in the oven now as you preheat it to 500°. If you're using a baking sheet, lightly grease a half sheet pan (12 by 17 inches) or two 12-inch pizza pans and set aside.

If you're cooking 2 pizzas, divide the dough in half, then bake them one at a time so that the crust is crisp and hot when served. Pizzas cooked in baking pans can be rolled out to roughly the shape of the pans and pressed into place. Do not make a very large edge, or it will be tough.

Pizzas baked on stones or tiles should be rolled out on a floured board or on a counter with room to maneuver a peel under the dough. Use a rolling pin to roll the dough into two 12-inch circles, then press and pull them into shape. Do *not* throw it in the air and toss it around, or you'll end up with a tough, overworked dough. Let the dough rest for 10 minutes or so while you make the topping.

Make sure there are no off-color pieces of the gall bladder attached to the livers and that they are trimmed of all fat. Place them in a bowl and cover with the sherry.

Place the oil in a sauté pan over medium heat and add the onion and ham. Cook until the onion is just barely becoming transparent, about 5 minutes. Carefully add the livers and sherry and cook without stirring, but occasionally shake the pan lightly until the livers are just beginning to color, about 2 minutes. Turn off the heat and allow the livers to cool. Season with salt and pepper.

When the livers have cooled somewhat, sprinkle the grated Parmesan on the prepared dough, followed by the marjoram, the livers, and the shaved Parmesan. If you're making 2 pizzas, divide the ingredients evenly between them, assembling one pizza, cooking it, and then assembling the

other. Dust preheated stones and tiles with cornmeal and quickly slide the pizzas onto them via the peel. Simply place pizzas in pans in the oven. Those on tiles will take about 15 minutes to brown; in pans, about 20 minutes. Serve immediately with a green salad. Allow the oven and stone or tiles to reheat before cooking a second round.
Serves 2 to 4

WINE:
Bourgogne Blanc

Chicken Liver Pâté

This easy country-style terrine can be made with ground lean pork or veal. It's a hit at a party, cut into little slices and served with crackers and mustard.

> **1 pound chicken livers**
> **4 shallots, minced**
> **1/2 cup butter, 1 stick**
> **1 cup fresh French bread crumbs**
> **grated zest of 1 orange**
> **1/2 cup brandy**
> **2 teaspoons salt**
> **1/2 teaspoon freshly ground black pepper**
> **1 teaspoon mixed dried herbs such as herbes de Provence**
>   **or Italian seasoning**
> **1/2 teaspoon quatre-épices (see note)**
> **1 pound ground lean pork or veal**
> **4 eggs**
> **1/2 cup whipping cream**
> **fresh pork fat, cut into thin slices**

Clean the livers of any sinew or spots and set aside. In a sauté pan over medium heat, sauté the shallots in the butter until transparent, about 5 minutes. Add the livers and sauté for another 5 minutes. Put the bread crumbs in a large mixing bowl and add the liver and shallot mixture. Add the orange zest and brandy, toss well, cover, and refrigerate for 6 hours or overnight.

In a separate bowl, add the seasonings to the ground meat. Remove the liver mixture from the refrigerator and puree in a food processor. Beat the eggs lightly into the cream, add to the food processor, and blend again until smooth. Add the puree to the ground meat and mix well together, then process in batches in the food processor until it is all well blended.

Preheat the oven to 350°. Line a standard loaf pan or a 1½-quart terrine with the pork fat and fill with the forcemeat. Cover with foil and place in a pan holding enough hot water to come halfway up the sides of the loaf pan. Bake for 1½ hours, remove from the oven, place a heavy object such as a brick or can of food on the pâté, and cool. Refrigerate with the weight overnight, then serve on crackers or toast points or alongside a salad with French bread and mustard.

NOTE:
Quatre-épices is a traditional spice mix for pâtés and terrines. Use ¼ teaspoon of freshly ground white pepper plus pinches of nutmeg, cloves, cinnamon, and ginger, preferably all freshly ground.

WINE:
Sangre de Toro

Thai Chicken Salad

Terrell Vermont is a southern food writer based in Atlanta who has traveled extensively in Thailand, learning from the native cooks in the countryside outside of Bangkok. When she sent me this recipe, she noted: "In northeastern Thailand, where I learned to cook this dish, the chicken was simmered in a huge pot over an open fire by a tiny, sparkling woman amused to have such a long, lanky foreigner watching her every move. The roasted rice adds a nice, nutty taste. The flavors will knock you out, and the entire dish can be readied a day ahead, needing only to be tossed together at the end."

This makes a delicious summer lunch, and, as Terrell points out, it is perfectly delicious without the chicken!

4 chicken breast halves with skin and bone

1 quart chicken stock or water

½ cup chopped red onion, about ½ medium

⅓ cup long-grain white rice

4 carrots, peeled and very thinly sliced

¼ cup fish sauce (see note)

⅓ cup fresh lime juice plus limes for garnish

1½ teaspoons sugar

½ cup fresh mint leaves

¼ cup cilantro leaves plus more for garnish

1 to 3 teaspoons ground dried red pepper to taste,
  preferably from Asia

fresh lettuce leaves

Put the chicken breasts in the stock or water in a saucepan, bring to a boil, reduce the heat immediately, and cover. Poach at a simmer for about 20 minutes. Drain the chicken and allow it to cool. Remove the skin and bones and discard. Pull the flesh into thin bite-size pieces.

Put the onion into a strainer and pour boiling water over it, then rinse with cold water and drain. Refrigerate both the chicken and the onion until just before assembling the salad.

Roast the rice in a dry skillet over medium heat for a few minutes, shaking every now and then to prevent it from burning. It should turn the color of café au lait. Remove from the heat and cool, then place in a mortar and pestle and grind until it is all broken up.

Place the carrot slices in a large bowl and dress with the fish sauce, lime juice, and sugar. Refrigerate. When you're ready to serve the salad, add the chicken and onion to the vegetables, toss thoroughly, and add the herbs and red pepper. Toss again. Add the crushed rice, toss again, and taste to see if you need any more fish sauce, lime juice, or pepper.

Serve on a bed of leafy lettuce with a few lime wedges and cilantro sprigs as garnish.

Serves 4 as a main course

NOTE:
The brand of fish sauce we use is Tiparos. The sauces vary widely, so you may want to adjust this measurement to taste.

WINE:
Young, crisp wine with low alcohol content, such as a German Riesling

Grilled Poussins or Cornish Hens and Leeks

Poussins are very young chickens ($3^{1}/_{2}$ weeks old) that are becoming widely available in the United States. Palmetto Pigeon Plant (see Ingredients and Sources, Meats) in Sumter, South Carolina, processes thousands of them. Once known as *squab chicken,* they are tastier and more tender than Cornish game hens (which are neither wild nor Cornish). Poussins weigh from $^{3}/_{4}$ to $1^{1}/_{4}$ pounds, dressed. Cornish hens (not necessarily females) are six weeks old; they can weigh as much as 2 pounds.

If you can't find fresh poussins, buy large Cornish hens and split them in half. I trim the wing tips and backbones and make a quick stovetop stock with the other giblets (except the liver, which I fry as the cook's bonus) to flavor the rice and cracked wheat pilaf that I serve with the dish.

**4 poussins, about 1 pound each, or 2 Cornish hens, about
  2 pounds each
salt and freshly ground black pepper to taste
2 garlic cloves, minced
¼ cup extra-virgin olive oil
2 or 3 fresh thyme sprigs
4 leeks**

Cut the backbones and the wing tips from the birds with poultry shears. Use them to make a quick broth with the giblets.

Lay the birds flesh side down in a large nonreactive roasting pan. Season them with salt and pepper, then turn them over and season the flesh side. Mix the garlic with the oil, then pour the oil over the birds. Strip the thyme leaves from the stems—you should have a couple of teaspoons—and sprinkle them over the birds. Marinate at room temperature for 30 minutes.

Meanwhile, build a charcoal fire or preheat a gas grill to medium-high. Clean the leeks by splitting them lengthwise down to, but not into, the root base and washing them well under running water. Leave the root end intact. Cut off most of the upper green leaves.

When the fire is ready, remove the birds from the marinade and place them flesh side down on the grill. Cover and cook for 5 minutes, then turn the birds over, and add the leeks to the grill. Drizzle the birds and leeks with any leftover marinade, cover the grill, and cook for another 5 minutes. Turn the leeks, then cook for another 5 minutes. Transfer the birds to plates and the leeks to a cutting board.

Slice the base off the leeks, remove the charred outer leaves, and slice the leeks, if desired, into bite-size pieces. Serve the birds and leeks with a pilaf of rice and cracked wheat cooked in broth and the green vegetable of your choice. I am partial to blanched kale stir-fried with hot chili sesame oil, finished with lemon juice, and tossed with the rice.

Serves 4

Wine:
A big white Burgundy or an estate-bottled Pouilly-Fuissé

Grilled Quail with Raspberry Vinaigrette

Many former cotton plantations in the South remain large tracts of land maintained as quail preserves. The plantations require serious management: favorite food and cover crops are planted for the birds, feral cats must be controlled, and forest floors are burned to control undergrowth. Hunters pay a premium for hunting rights on these quail havens. The southern quail (*Colinus virginianus*), called "bobwhite" for the sound of its call, eats harmful insects and weed seeds, and is therefore a boon to southern farmers. Corn is often a bumper crop on these quail plantations.

The white flesh of the bobwhite is renowned for its delicious flavor, but what most southerners now know as quail is actually the European or pharaoh quail (*Coturnix coturnix*), widely raised for the table. A migrating species, the pharaoh quail have both white and dark meat, like chicken. They lay an average of 15 eggs per clutch (of which 12 survive), so they are favorites of breeders. Manchester Farms in Dalzell, South Carolina, has been raising them for the food market since 1971 (see Ingredients and Sources, Meats).

Very popular with restaurants is a boned bird, suitable for stuffing and eating with knife and fork. But most southerners either fry or grill quail, then eat the delicious little birds with their hands. Chef Frank Stitt suggests serving the grilled quail over mixed salad greens with his raspberry vinaigrette (recipe follows). I serve 1 quail as an appetizer or 1½ or 2 as dinner.

> **6 quail**
>
> **5 tablespoons raspberry vinegar**
>
> **1 cup plus 3 tablespoons mild olive oil or part olive oil and part vegetable oil**
>
> **2 to 3 tablespoons of chopped fresh herbs such as thyme and parsley**
>
> **salt and freshly ground black pepper to taste**
>
> **½ pint raspberries**
>
> **1 small shallot, finely chopped**
>
> **1 tablespoon Dijon mustard**

1 tablespoon honey

1 tablespoon chopped parsley

1 egg yolk

juice of 1 lemon

5 to 6 ounces mixed lettuces: some bitter, such as radicchio, endive, and/or watercress; some red leaf or red oak leaf; and some Boston or green leaf

½ cup walnut pieces, optional

1 cup cooked lentils (optional; see note)

About 30 minutes before dining, use kitchen shears to cut the birds up the backbone so that they will lie flat. Splash the quail with a tablespoon of the raspberry vinegar, 3 tablespoons olive oil, and some chopped herbs. Build a charcoal fire or preheat a gas grill to medium-high.

When the fire is hot, remove the quail from the marinade and season with salt and pepper. Place the birds with their legs up on the hot grill (or legs down under a very hot broiler), cover the grill, and cook for 5 minutes. Turn the birds and baste with the leftover marinade. Cover the grill again and cook until just done, about another 5 minutes.

Meanwhile, make the vinaigrette. Remove the ripest raspberries (about 6 to 10) and crush them in a small bowl. Set the remaining raspberries aside. Add shallot, remaining vinegar, mustard, honey, parsley, and salt and pepper to taste. Whisk together, then add the egg yolk, whisking continually. Slowly whisk in the remaining olive oil, then season to taste with lemon juice.

Transfer the cooked birds to large individual serving plates covered with mixed salad greens, drizzle with the vinaigrette, and garnish with the reserved raspberries. Frank adds some walnut halves and cooked lentils to the salad as well.

NOTE:
To cook lentils, simmer in water to cover with finely chopped carrots, celery, onion, and a bouquet garni until just tender, about 45 minutes.

WINE:
Fleurie (Cru Beaujolais)

Duck Breasts with Cabbage and Apples

This is an easy winter's meal that takes little time and effort. It uses only the breasts of ducks, which cook very quickly. If your market sells only whole ducks, first remove the breasts. Remove the legs, season them well, cover with melted duck fat (see the recipe for Duck and Oyster Jambalaya) and/or lard, and cook in a slow cooker overnight for the French classic, confit. The confit will last a long, long time in the refrigerator as long as the meat is totally covered by a layer of fat. Use the rest of the carcass to make a quick stock to use in this dish (just add some aromatic herbs and vegetables to the carcass, cover with 2 or 3 cups of water, and cook at a low boil until the liquid is reduced by half).

> **2 whole duck breasts, boned and split, with skin**
> **salt, freshly ground black pepper, and cayenne pepper**
> **to taste**
> **1 large onion, chopped**
> **1 small, compact cabbage, about 2 pounds, trimmed of**
> **outer leaves and quartered**
> **1 cup chicken or duck stock**
> **2 tart cooking apples, cored and cut into eighths**

Score the skin of the breasts in a crosshatch pattern, cutting down to but not into the flesh of the duck. The gashes should be about ³/₄ inch apart. Sprinkle both sides of the breasts with salt, pepper, and cayenne.

Place a large heavy sauté pan or cast-iron skillet over medium-high heat and wait for it to get hot. Place the breasts skin side down in the hot pan and cook until the skin is very crisp and brown and most of the fat has rendered out into the pan, about 5 minutes. If the skin is browning too quickly, turn down the heat. Turn the breasts over once to sear briefly on the other side and set aside on a platter.

Add the onion to the pan and sauté until transparent, 5 to 10 minutes. Add the cabbage wedges to the pan and spoon fat up over them so that they are all coated. Add the stock, increase the heat, and bring to a boil. Immediately reduce to a simmer, cover, and cook for 5 to 7 minutes. The cabbage wedges should still be firm; if they are not cooking evenly, *carefully* turn them over with a large set of tongs.

Intersperse the apples among the cabbage wedges and add the duck breasts and any juices that may have drained onto the platter. Don't put the breasts down in the stock; they should rest on top of the cabbage wedges. Cover the pan again and simmer for another 5 minutes.

Serve each plate with a duck breast and a wedge of cabbage, then spoon the apples and some pan juices over the cabbage. You can reduce those juices to a thicker consistency if you like. Serve with a condiment such as the Green Tomato Chutney in Chapter 6 and boiled potatoes dressed with a little butter and parsley.
Serves 4

WINE:
Grignolino

Duck Sausage

Duck is my favorite meat, and it lends itself well to many preparations, including this savory sausage. The sausage is delicious as is, but it's a welcome addition to many soups and gumbos, pasta dishes, and pots of greens. You can poach the sausages and freeze them for use later, or you can brine them and then smoke them—but I often just grill them over a low fire. I particularly like to sauté them with leeks and pears or to add them to a simple pasta dish. You'll need a meat grinder and a sausage stuffer to make the sausages.

> 1 duck, about 5 pounds
> 2 teaspoons salt
> 2 teaspoons freshly ground black pepper
> 4 garlic cloves, peeled
> ½ teaspoon quatre-épices (see note in Chicken
>   Liver Pâté recipe)

**2 teaspoons mixed dried herbs such as herbes de Provence
or Italian seasoning**

1 small onion, chopped

¼ teaspoon cayenne pepper

½ cup dry sherry

4 feet prepared hog casings (see note)

Bone the duck. Remove most of the fat and the skin, but leave the skin on the breast halves. Render the extra fat as described in the next recipe for use in another recipe. Make a stock from the carcass (see the preceding recipe).

Chop the meat into small pieces, being careful to remove any tendons or sinew, and place in a nonreactive container. Add the seasonings and onion and mix in well, then add the sherry, cover the container, and refrigerate for several hours or overnight.

Run the ingredients through the coarse disk of a meat grinder, then attach the sausage stuffer to the meat grinder and pull the length of casings up onto the sausage horn. Tie off the free end of the casings. At this point you can taste the sausage by frying a little bit in a pan or by poaching it for a few minutes. Adjust the seasoning to your own taste. Run the ground duck mixture through the grinder again and into the prepared casings. Make sure there are no air pockets in the sausage, pricking it with a pin in several places. Tie off the open end, then lower the sausage into a large sauté pan or skillet of simmering water or stock (I use the stock made from the carcass) and poach for about 5 to 10 minutes or until the sausage is firm. Prick the sausage again if necessary where pockets of grease or air appear.

Remove the sausage from the poaching liquid. It is now ready to be finished off in a skillet or on the grill, added to a stew or a sauce, or frozen for later use.

Makes about 1½ pounds

NOTE:

Casings are available from most butchers. They are often frozen and/or packed in salt. To prepare them, run water from a faucet through them several times until they are free of all salt crystals.

WINE:

For grilled sausages, a Provençal rouge; for sausage sautéed with leeks and pears, a Provençal rosé

Duck and Oyster Jambalaya

Rice is a staple in many corners of the South, and pilaus (pronounced perLOE in South Carolina) such as this one are common daily and festive fare. The great town houses of Charleston were built by wealthy rice planters and merchants, and the crop remained the backbone of the coastal Carolina and Georgia economy until the Civil War. Rice was soon thereafter introduced into Louisiana, Texas, and Arkansas.

By the turn of the century, when *The Picayune Creole Cook Book* was published in New Orleans, it boasted:

The consumption of rice has increased enormously of late, and it will continue to become more and more a popular article of food when the people of the great North and West learn how to cook it as well as the Creoles of Louisiana.

An entire chapter was devoted to Louisiana rice cookery in the still-popular volume, including several for jambalaya—pilau by another name.

Pilaus are also at home in northern Florida, where Minorcans settled. Jeanne Voltz and Caroline Stuart wrote in *The Florida Cookbook,* "The Minorcan-style pilau is Spanish in character, showing the influence of the Moors who occupied southern Spain for centuries." Around St. Augustine a pilau is likely to contain their local incendiary datil pepper, brought to the area by the Minorcan settlers in the late eighteenth century.

FOR THE STOCK AND DUCK:
- **1 duck, 4 to 5 pounds**
- **2 quarts water**
- **1 large onion, unpeeled and quartered**
- **1 large or 2 small carrots**
- **1 celery rib**
- **1 bay leaf**
- **a handful of fresh herbs of your choice**

FOR THE JAMBALAYA:

- 1 large onion, chopped
- 1 large green bell pepper, chopped
- 1 jalapeño chili, seeded and chopped
- 2 celery ribs, chopped
- 2 garlic cloves, minced
- 1 pound vine-ripened tomatoes, about 2 cups peeled and chopped, with their juice
- 1 tablespoon tomato paste
- ¼ cup chopped parsley
- 1 quart standard oysters with their liquor (selects are too big)
- 3 cups long-grain white rice
- 1 center slice of country ham, about ½ pound if bone in, trimmed of fat and bone and diced
- 1 teaspoon salt or to taste
- freshly ground black pepper to taste

Remove all of the skin and fat from the duck and set aside. Cut the duck into pieces and place them in a stockpot with the water, onion, carrot, celery, and herbs. Simmer for 1 hour, drain, remove the duck pieces, and discard the aromatic herbs and vegetables. Put the stock in the refrigerator to cool off.

Meanwhile, chop the duck skin and fat and puree it in a food processor in batches. Put a shallow layer of water—a couple of tablespoons is fine—in the bottom of a heavy pot over low heat and add the puree. Wait until most of the water has evaporated and the melted fat is clear, then strain into a container and keep covered and refrigerated. It will last for several months if you remove all traces of liquid. I place it in a flexible plastic container overnight, then remove the congealed fat the next morning. Add the congealed stock at the bottom of the container to leftover stock from the jambalaya before freezing it for use later.

As soon as it is cool enough to handle, pick the duck meat from the

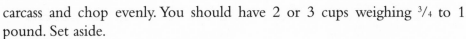

carcass and chop evenly. You should have 2 or 3 cups weighing ³/₄ to 1 pound. Set aside.

In a large pot or Dutch oven with a tight-fitting lid, heat 3 tablespoons of the rendered duck fat over medium-high heat. Add the onion, pepper, chili, celery, and garlic and sauté, stirring occasionally, until the vegetables are limp, about 10 minutes.

Add the tomatoes and their juice, the tomato paste, and the parsley and cook until most of the liquid is gone, about 10 minutes. Meanwhile, remove the duck stock and oysters from the refrigerator. Drain the oysters, saving their liquor; taste it for saltiness.

Pour the oyster liquor into a measuring cup and return the oysters to the refrigerator. Skim any fat from the surface of the duck stock and add it to the oyster liquor to total 5 cups.

Add the rice, ham, reserved duck, and oyster-duck stock to the pot and stir once to mix all the ingredients. Add the teaspoon of salt, more or less, according to the saltiness of the oyster liquor and country ham. Season with pepper. Simmer the jambalaya, tightly covered, for 20 minutes.

Meanwhile, prepare corn bread (Chapter 8), a perfect accompaniment to the jambalaya.

Turn off the heat and fluff the rice with a big spoon as you fold in the oysters. Do not stir. Wait another 10 minutes or so for the oysters to plump and serve with corn bread and a green salad.

Serves 10 to 12

WINE:
A fruity white wine with body, flavor, and just a touch of sweetness, such as Reichsgraf von Kesselstatt Riesling

Duck Etouffée with Corn Cakes

This is marvelous new Creole cooking inspired by a recipe from chef Tom Cowman of New Orleans's Upperline restaurant. In their lovely uptown setting Tom and owner JoAnn Clevenger offer both traditional and upscale Creole dishes amid constantly changing artwork and flowers. They even have their own Duck Festival, during which they offer my favorite bird prepared a dozen ways, with Duckhorn Vineyards Merlot and Sauvignon Blanc as the featured wines.

This recipe takes all day, but it's mostly unattended cooking. Tom roasts his ducks, but I usually simmer mine gently for several hours the day before I plan to serve. The duck falls from the bone and yields a rich stock. I also make my roux with duck fat, because it's delicious.

FOR THE DUCK AND STOCK:

> 1 4- to 5-pound duck
>
> 3 quarts water
>
> 1 large onion, unpeeled and quartered
>
> 1 large or 2 small carrots, broken into pieces
>
> 2 celery ribs, broken into pieces
>
> a handful of fresh herbs such as parsley, thyme, savory,
>   and oregano
>
> 1 bay leaf
>
> several whole black peppercorns
>
> 1 whole clove

FOR THE ROUX:

> ½ cup rendered duck fat or butter, 1 stick
>
> ⅓ cup unbleached all-purpose flour

FOR THE ETOUFFÉE:

> ¾ cup finely chopped onion, about 1 small
>
> ⅓ cup finely chopped celery
>
> ⅓ cup finely chopped carrot
>
> ¾ cup finely chopped green bell pepper, about ½ large

1 garlic clove, minced

½ teaspoon salt

freshly ground black pepper to taste

1 teaspoon hot red pepper flakes

½ teaspoon mixed dried herbs such as herbes de Provence
or Italian seasoning

Rinse the duck well and remove most of the skin and any excess fat, setting it aside to use for the roux. Place the duck, including the neck and giblets except the liver (which I fry in a little butter or duck fat as the cook's bonus), and the water along with the rest of the ingredients in a stockpot and cook at a low simmer for 2 or 3 hours or until the liquid has reduced by a third, skimming the pot occasionally.

Strain out the solids, cool, and refrigerate the stock. Remove and discard any fat that congeals on the surface of the stock. Reserve 2 quarts stock for the étouffée; freeze any extra for another use. Pick the meat from the duck carcass and discard the bones and the stockpot vegetables. You should have a good pound of meat.

Meanwhile, as the stock is cooking, render the duck fat as described in the preceding recipe. Then make the roux: Preheat the oven to 350°. Melt the fat over low heat and whisk in the flour so that it is uniformly incorporated. Spread the mixture on a baking sheet and bake, stirring every 10 or 15 minutes, until it is dark brown, about an hour.

About 3 hours before you plan to eat, warm the roux over medium heat in a large heavy stockpot or Dutch oven. Add the onion, celery, carrot, and bell pepper. Cook the vegetables in the roux, stirring often, until they begin to wilt and the onion is becoming transparent, about 10 minutes.

Add the garlic, salt, peppers, herbs, and reserved stock and bring to a low boil. Cook at a low boil for about 2 hours, skimming any scum from the surface and stirring the pot from time to time. It should reduce by two-thirds.

Reduce the heat and stir in the reserved duck meat. Meanwhile, make Corn Cakes (Chapter 8), omitting the jalapeño. Serve 1 corn cake per person as an appetizer or 2 for dinner.

Serves 12 as an appetizer or 6 as an entrée

WINE:
Barbera d'Asti

CHAPTER
5

Eggs and
Cheese

This chapter is an assortment of savory dishes that are more dairy than grain or vegetable. Deviled eggs and pimiento cheese, southerners' favorite sandwich spread (and dip for raw vegetables), are grouped with omelets and baked cheese dishes that are delightful lunch and supper fare. Recipes for sweet custards and cheesecakes are found in Chapter 9. Some of these recipes make good side dishes: try the Sweet Potato Flan instead of mashed potatoes or the Sweet Onion Tart instead of macaroni and cheese.

Sweet Onion Tart

Onions that are as sweet as apples are grown throughout the South. Georgia's Vidalia, Texas's 1015, and South Carolina's Wadmalaw Sweets are now widely available (see Ingredients and Sources, Sweet Onions). They appear on the market as large bulbous spring onions in April, then the mature onion is sold during the months of May and June—or while supplies last. There are several cookbooks devoted solely to sweet onions, and recipes that feature them range from salads to desserts.

This simple tart is one of my favorite ways to eat them. It can be served as a first course, as a side dish, or with a salad as lunch.

Don't feel you have to use a southern onion for this dish; sweet ones are being grown in Washington state (Walla Walla Sweets) and in Hawaii (Mauis). Check your local market first; there may well be a sweet onion being grown in your own backyard.

FOR THE CRUST:

2 cups unbleached all-purpose flour, plus flour for dusting

¾ teaspoon salt

10 tablespoons chilled butter

¼ to ¾ cup ice water as needed

FOR THE FILLING AND ASSEMBLY:

3 tablespoons bacon grease or butter

2 pounds sweet onions, sliced, about 4 cups

1 garlic clove, minced

salt and freshly ground black pepper to taste, optional

1 cup sour cream

3 eggs, beaten

To make the crust, put the flour and salt in a large bowl and mix together. Cut the butter into pieces and add to the flour. Cut it into the flour with a pastry blender or 2 knives until distributed evenly. Use a fork to mix in the water, adding it gradually by dribbling it in. As soon as you feel that the dough will hold together, stop adding water and press the dough into a ball with your hands.

Place a piece of wax paper on the counter and dust lightly with flour. Place the ball of dough on the paper, dust with flour, and put another piece of wax paper on top. Roll it out into a 6-inch circle. Wrap the dough well and refrigerate for at least 30 minutes—preferably an hour or two.

Preheat the oven to 350°. Remove the dough from the refrigerator, unwrap it, and place it on a lightly floured counter. Give it a few whacks with your rolling pin, then roll it out to a 14-inch circle. Roll it up off the counter onto the pin and over an 11-inch tart pan. Unroll it into the pan and press into place. Trim and discard any extra dough.

Bake the crust "blind"—line it with wax paper, then fill with beans, rice, coins, or pie weights—for 15 minutes. Remove from the oven, remove the weights, and set aside.

Heat the bacon grease or butter in a skillet over low heat and add the onions and garlic. Cook until completely wilted and just beginning to turn golden, 20 to 30 minutes, stirring occasionally. Do not let them brown. Turn them out into the partially baked tart shell and spread them around evenly. Sprinkle with salt and pepper if desired.

Drain the sour cream of any watery liquid and turn it out into a bowl. Beat it smooth, then stir in the beaten eggs until mixed evenly. Spoon the mixture evenly over the onions in the tart shell.

Bake on the middle rack of the preheated oven for about 45 minutes or until the top just hints of gold and a knife poked into the tart comes out clean.

Serves 8

WINE:
Chenin Blanc

Rustic Omelet of Potherbs and Potatoes

When I lived in Italy, I was struck by the similarities among many traditional Italian foods and the foods of the American South. Polenta was no more than cornmeal mush. The profusion of ice creams and other desserts laid bare a sweet tooth as bad as ours. The eggplants and tomatoes in their markets looked like those in many backyard gardens back home. The cooking up in the hills behind Genoa, with its well-seasoned cast-iron skillets, wood-burning stoves, and use of wild greens, was not unlike that of the southern reaches of Appalachia.

　　We would go to the home of Celeste Martini, the mother of my friend Gianni, in the Ligurian Apennines, where we would base ourselves for early-morning and late-afternoon mushroom hunts. Celeste would cook an omelet filled with wild greens in her potbellied stove fueled by fruit-tree cuttings. In Genoa, Gianni would cook his frittata on top of the stove, inverting the omelet onto a plate after the eggs had set and sliding it back into the skillet to complete the cooking. This country omelet is closer to Spain's filled with potatoes than to its loftier French cousin. And with its mixed potherbs, the frittata, as it's called in Italy, rightfully belongs in any southern cook's repertory.

　　To approximate the taste of wild Ligurian or Appalachian potherbs, I combine a good handful of herbs with about a pound of leafy green vegetables, always including some bitter greens. I might include a few leaves each of mitsuba (Japanese parsley) from my herb garden, along with chicory, French sorrel, sage, basil, lovage, chervil, hyssop, and a little tansy. Borage is invariably included in Liguria, as is wild marjoram. To these I add about a pound of whatever mixed greens are available from the greengrocer (and there's usually a preponderance)—a handful each of Swiss chard, spinach, watercress, parsley, arugula, kale, and mustard and beet greens. When serving three or four, I remove the outer leaves from three heads of Belgian endive and add them to the mix, reserving the rest as a bed for a salad. Washed, picked clean, and drained, the herbs and greens should weigh about a pound, still wet. They will fill an average colander.

I bake these Italian-inspired omelets in well-seasoned cast-iron pans, then place the skillets in closed cardboard boxes to keep them warm to take on fall picnics. Serve with the Salad of Roasted Peppers, Onion, and Endive in Chapter 7.

FOR THE POTHERBS:

a handful of fresh herbs such as basil, chervil, parsley, lovage, and marjoram

1 pound fresh mixed greens, including some bitter ones

FOR THE OMELET:

2 tablespoons olive oil

8 to 10 eggs

salt and freshly ground black pepper to taste

¾ pound potatoes, 2 to 3 medium, cooked, peeled, and diced

Fill the sink with cold water and add the herbs and greens. Shake them around in the water until they are free of all dirt and sand. It may take several changes of water.

Stem the greens, discarding any blemished or yellow leaves, and place them in a colander to drain. It should be full of greens (about 12 loosely packed cups).

With kitchen shears in one hand, grab handfuls of the washed greens. Above a large kettle over low heat, cut the greens into small pieces, allowing them to fall into the empty pot. Cook the greens with only the water that clings to them, uncovered, stirring frequently, for about 15 minutes or until they are completely wilted but still bright green.

Remove the greens from the pot and drain, squeezing all of the juice from them by twisting them in a clean towel. Reserve the juice to use in vegetable soups. Set the prepared potherbs aside.

Heat a gas oven to 500°; set an electric oven to broil (see note following the next recipe).

In a well-seasoned 10-inch cast-iron skillet, heat the oil over medium heat. Swirl it to coat the bottom and sides of the pan.

In a large bowl, beat the eggs until foamy. Season with salt and pepper, then add the potatoes and potherbs. Pour the mixture into the skillet and lower the heat. Sprinkle the top of the omelet with salt and pepper.

Cook over low heat until the omelet is well set, about 10 to 12 minutes, shaking the pan occasionally and running a knife between the edge of the omelet and the pan, letting any of the egg mixture trickle down the sides so that it is cooked evenly.

When well set, remove the pan from the burner and put the omelet under the broiler, about 4 inches from the heat. Cook until it is puffy and golden, about 2 to 3 minutes. Remove from the oven and let the omelet cool in the pan for a few minutes before serving it warm or at room temperature from the skillet.

Serves 4 to 6

WINE:
A white wine from Bordeaux or Gascony

Frittata of Grilled Vegetables

This hearty Italian-style omelet is perfect picnic fare. If you don't feel like getting out the grill, you can broil the vegetables in the oven.

    1 medium eggplant
    salt
    1 medium vine-ripened tomato
    1 fennel bulb
    ¼ cup olive oil
    8 to 10 eggs
    freshly ground black pepper to taste
    1 tablespoon chopped fresh basil

Slice the eggplant lengthwise into several thick slices. Place them in a colander and sprinkle liberally with salt. Turn the slices over and sprinkle the other side. Leave to drain.

Build a charcoal fire or preheat a gas grill to medium-high. Cut the tomato in half crosswise and place cut sides down on a platter. Core the fennel bulb and place it with the tomato. When the eggplant has drained some of its moisture and the fire is hot, wipe the salt from the eggplant slices with a paper or cloth towel and add them to the platter.

Lightly brush the eggplant slices, the tomato skins, and the fennel with some of the olive oil, then place them on the grill, oiled sides down. Cover the grill and cook until the eggplant is scored with grill marks and the tomato skin shrinks from the flesh. Lightly brush the top sides of the vegetables with oil and turn them. Cook for a few minutes on the second side, then remove to the platter.

Peel the eggplant slices and dice them. Core, peel, seed, and dice the tomato halves. Chop the fennel bulb. Pat any excess moisture or oil off the vegetables.

Heat a gas oven to 500°; set an electric oven to broil (see note).

In a well-seasoned 10-inch cast-iron skillet, heat the remaining oil over medium heat. Swirl it to coat the bottom and sides of the pan.

In a large bowl, beat the eggs until foamy. Season with salt and pepper (remembering that the eggplant may be salty), then add the grilled vegetables. Pour the mixture into the skillet and lower the heat. Sprinkle the top of the omelet with salt, pepper, and the chopped basil.

Cook over low heat until the frittata is well set, about 10 to 12 minutes, shaking the pan occasionally and running a knife between the edge of the omelet and the pan, letting any of the egg mixture trickle down the sides so that it is cooked evenly.

When well set, remove the pan from the burner and put the omelet under the broiler, about 4 inches from the heat. Cook until it is puffy and golden, about 2 to 3 minutes. Remove from the oven and let the omelet cool in the pan for a few minutes before serving it warm or at room temperature from the skillet.

Serves 4 to 6

NOTE:
These omelets can be baked entirely in the oven at 350° for about 45 minutes.

WINE:
Rully Blanc from the Côte Chalonnaise

Pimiento Cheese

A spread of sharp Cheddar spiked with roasted pimientos is often found on southern picnics and sideboards, but the cheese is usually grated beyond recognition and canned pimientos swim in as much mayonnaise as Cheddar. In South Carolina we usually call this "palmetto cheese" after our state tree. This version was inspired by a recipe from Alice Marks, one of Charleston's great cooks. It's chock-full of roasted peppers and olives and is delicious in sandwiches, on crackers, or with crudités.

FOR THE MAYONNAISE:

> 1 egg
>
> 1 teaspoon prepared mustard
>
> cayenne pepper to taste
>
> ¼ teaspoon salt
>
> 1 cup mild-flavored oil such as peanut
>
> 1 tablespoon fresh lemon juice

FOR THE SPREAD:

> ¾ pound sharp Cheddar, coarsely grated, about 4 cups
>   loosely packed
>
> 1 cup roasted, peeled, seeded, and chopped pimientos or
>   red ripe bell peppers (see Salad of Roasted Peppers,
>   Onion, and Endive in Chapter 7)
>
> ½ small onion, grated
>
> ½ cup large pimiento-stuffed olives, about 1 dozen sliced
>   into thirds
>
> cayenne pepper or Tabasco or other hot pepper sauce to
>   taste, optional

For the mayonnaise, put the egg, mustard, cayenne, and salt in a blender at high speed for about 20 seconds. Add the oil very slowly, in droplets at first, and blend until all of the oil has been bound with the egg mixture and the mayonnaise is thick and creamy. Add the lemon juice and blend to incorporate.

You'll need ¹/₂ cup for this recipe; store the rest tightly capped in the refrigerator for no more than a week.

Mix all of the spread ingredients together, including the ¹/₂ cup mayonnaise; then, if desired, season with cayenne or hot pepper sauce.
Makes 3 cups, enough for 6 sandwiches

Deviled Eggs

The oyster plate was the wealthy southern bride's prized piece of china in the mid-nineteenth century. Molded to hold half a dozen oysters on the half shell, these plates were often made in France by the finest porcelain artisans, hand-painted, and sometimes gilded.

In contrast, the mass-produced deviled egg plate was a common bridal shower gift in the 1940s, 1950s, and 1960s, when the cocktail party was perhaps at its peak. No southern bride, rich or otherwise, was without the funny piece of china with its 24 egg-shaped indentations to hold the stuffed eggs. Often the plate was relegated to the back of a shelf, but it would always come out for parties. I rarely see them these days except at estate sales, often alongside the now prohibitively expensive and very collectible oyster plates.

I don't use a deviled egg plate, because it doesn't hold enough eggs for a party, and the eggs are much easier to handle when they're cut in half crosswise rather than lengthwise. You'll have to cut a little slice off both ends so they'll stand on their own.

Deviled eggs are traditionally loaded with mayonnaise, but my sister Sue makes hers with butter, and they're so much better. If you're having just a few guests, you may want to cook only a dozen eggs, but if you're having a party, go ahead and make the full recipe, then watch these disappear from the hors d'oeuvre table. This is another recipe that is meant to be used simply as a guideline. Flavor the eggs however you wish.

2 dozen eggs at room temperature

3 tablespoons, more or less, butter at room temperature

1 tablespoon prepared mustard

1 very small onion, grated

salt, freshly ground black pepper, and cayenne pepper
   to taste

1 tablespoon each, more or less, of any 4: finely chopped
   or ground cooked country ham or shrimp, anchovy
   paste, curry powder, chopped fresh herbs, freshly grated
   Parmesan cheese, drained capers, chopped pitted olives,
   or sweet pickle cubes

paprika, optional

Place the eggs in a large pot, cover with cold water, and bring to a boil. Immediately cover the pot and turn off the heat. Let stand for 15 minutes, then drain the eggs and plunge into cold water. Tap each egg all over, then roll lightly on a counter to loosen the shells. Peel the eggs; it's easier if you start at the large end. Dip the peeled eggs in the cold water bath to help remove any clinging pieces of shell.

When all of the eggs are shelled, slice a bit off both the top and bottom ends of each egg so that the filled halves will stand on end, then cut each in half crosswise. Transfer the yolks to a mixing bowl and mash them all together with the butter, mustard, and onion. Season with salt, pepper, and cayenne.

Divide the egg yolk mixture into 4 small bowls and season each batch differently with one of your chosen fillings.

Stuff the egg yolk filling into the standing egg white halves, using a pastry bag or a teaspoon. Dust with paprika if desired. Cover the eggs with plastic wrap so that it does not stick to the eggs and chill before serving.
Makes 48 stuffed egg halves

Oeufs en Gelée

This old Provençal dish used to appear in the South as jellied eggs, but it had all but disappeared until Hubert Sandot, a Creole chef in New Orleans, started putting it on his menus. Southerners have always had an affinity for congealed dishes, both sweet and savory. This is a delightful change from tomato aspic as a first course or atop a bed of greens as lunch.

Jellied eggs are usually flavored with port, but the Madeira is preferable with the tomato and basil. The recipe is utter simplicity, but you must work carefully and methodically. Read the recipe through before you begin.

> **butter or oil**
> **2 tablespoons white or red wine vinegar**
> **salt**
> **4 very fresh eggs**
> **1 cup clear beef broth**
> **2 teaspoons unflavored gelatin**
> **⅓ cup Madeira**
> **4 small basil tops of paired leaves**
> **1 large vine-ripened tomato, peeled, seeded, and cubed**
> **freshly ground black pepper to taste**
> **2 ounces country ham or prosciutto, thinly sliced**

Lightly butter or oil the bottom of a large sauté pan and fill with water (measure it as you pour it in) about 2 inches deep or about two-thirds full. Add the vinegar and a teaspoon of salt for every quart of water. Bring to a boil, then reduce the heat to a simmer.

Break each egg into a shallow bowl and slip it gently into the water. Cook the eggs for 3½ minutes. The whites should be firm. Transfer them with a slotted spoon to a towel.

Bring the beef broth to a boil and set aside. In a small stainless bowl, soften the gelatin in the Madeira and stir until it is dissolved, then pour the hot stock over the mixture, stirring well. Set the bowl over ice and stir occasionally until the mixture begins to thicken, then remove from the ice bath.

Rinse four ¹/₂-cup ramekins or custard cups with water and place them in a baking dish. (Having them in a baking dish makes them easier to handle and controls spillage.) Pour a little bit of the jelly into each and chill on the ice or in the refrigerator for a few minutes, until the jelly sets. Place a basil top upside down in each ramekin, then a layer of tomato cubes in each, seasoning with salt and pepper. Pour a little more of the jelly into each mold.

Trim the poached eggs so they will fit the molds. Put a thin slice of meat in each ramekin, then add a poached egg to each. Put another thin slice of meat on top of each egg, then fill the molds with the jelly. Set in the refrigerator to chill for at least 1 hour. Cover them with plastic wrap after an hour if you aren't going to serve them then.

To serve, run a thin sharp knife around the edge of the jelly, invert the mold over a bed of crisp greens, and give it a little whack with your hand. If it does not slip out, you can dip the mold briefly in hot tap water or wrap the mold in a hot towel to unmold them. I like to serve these as a summer brunch with Orange Biscuits (Chapter 8).
Serves 4

Wine:
Madeira at least 5 years old

Goat Cheese Strata

Strata is the Italian name of a baked cheese dish—like macaroni and cheese with bread instead of pasta—that is often served as part of a large country breakfast in the South. In this version I've used chèvre instead of the usual Cheddar and added some garlic and fresh herbs for an intriguing flavor. It's still a wonderful breakfast item but also works as a side dish. Place big squares of it on a pool of the tomato sauce on page 44 and you've got a great lunch item.

butter

8 slices of home-style white bread, crusts removed

3 eggs

¼ teaspoon salt

2 cups milk

½ pound goat cheese, crumbled

1 garlic clove, minced

2 tablespoons chopped fresh herbs of your choice

The night (or at least 8 hours) before you plan to serve, butter an 8-inch square baking dish and line the bottom with 4 slices of bread. Beat the eggs until light, then mix well with the remaining ingredients. Pour some of the mixture over the bread slices in the pan, then alternate with the remaining bread slices and the cheese mixture. Refrigerate the strata overnight.

The next morning (or half hour before serving), preheat the oven to 450°. Bake the strata for about 25 minutes and serve piping hot.

Serves 4 to 6

WINE:
Sangiovese if served with the tomato sauce or a Fumé Blanc

Garlic Cheese Grits

One of the most popular side dishes throughout the South is this baked casserole of cheese grits spiked with a little garlic. Some cooks whip the egg whites separately, then fold them into the mixture at the last minute to make a real soufflé, but I never bother.

> 4 tablespoons unsalted butter, ¹/₂ stick
>
> ³/₄ cup coarse stone-ground grits
>
> 3 cups water
>
> ¹/₂ teaspoon salt
>
> 1 cup grated Cheddar cheese, about 3 ounces
>
> ¹/₂ cup freshly grated Parmesan cheese, about 2 ounces
>
> ¹/₂ cup milk
>
> 2 eggs, beaten
>
> 1 garlic clove, minced
>
> ¹/₄ teaspoon cayenne pepper

Use a little of the butter to grease a 1¹/₂-quart soufflé pan or casserole dish with tall sides. Preheat the oven to 350°. Put the rest of the butter, the grits, the water, and the salt in a heavy saucepan and bring to a boil over medium-high heat, stirring occasionally so that the grits do not stick to the bottom of the pan. Continue to cook the grits until most of the water is absorbed, stirring often, about 10 minutes.

Add the remaining ingredients and stir until the cheese is melted. Turn out into the greased pan and bake until a knife poked in the center comes out clean, about 50 minutes to 1 hour. Serve immediately.

Serves 4

Sweet Potatoes with Horseradish

This is my favorite dish in this book. Every time I taste it, I am amazed at how new the flavor of sweet potatoes seems to me. The dish pairs well with either roast lamb or chicken and is even delicious at room temperature—I'll take these cold and left over over pizza any day!

I first had this dish prepared by chef Frank Lee in Charleston. He served it with a perfectly roasted rack of lamb with a clear, natural gravy. Frank also makes these sweet potatoes into a soup by pureeing them with stock and a little cream.

Try to find rather small sweet potatoes, all the same size, that are pointed at the ends.

4 small to medium sweet potatoes, about 1½ to 1¾ pounds
3 tablespoons grated horseradish, preferably fresh
1 cup whipping cream

Preheat the oven to 400°. Peel the sweet potatoes and slice them evenly into ¼-inch disks. Toss all the ingredients together in a mixing bowl so that the potatoes are coated evenly, then turn them out into a baking dish such as a 9- by 13-inch casserole. Cover the pan with foil and bake for 30 to 45 minutes or until the sweet potatoes are slightly soft or al dente. Serve immediately.

Though I've never owned a microwave, I have cooked this dish in one at a friend's beachfront condo. Loosely cover the dish with plastic wrap instead of foil and cook on high for 10 minutes, stopping twice at 4-minute intervals to toss the potatoes around so that they cook evenly.

Serves 4 to 6

Sweet Potato Ravioli with Roasted Garlic Crème Fraîche

This recipe is of neither Italian nor southern heritage, but it is not unlike similar pumpkin-filled pasta dishes found throughout Italy, where fresh sage is often the herb of choice. I make my version in the dead of winter, when sweet potatoes are widely available and even outdoor chive plants thrive.

If you're going to make your own pasta, you'll need to begin this recipe an hour or so before you plan to eat: the pasta dough should rest before you roll it out. If you have a source for fresh pasta in sheets, of course you needn't make your own. You will need about ¹/₂ pound of flat pasta sheets. You can also use wonton wrappers, though they do taste a little different. It will take about 24 wonton wrappers (¹/₂ pound). Instructions for filling the wonton wrappers follow those for the homemade pasta. I've made this recipe alone—including rolling out the dough—in my three- by four-foot kitchen. If you've got the time and inclination, go ahead and make your own pasta. It's fun.

If you don't have a source for crème fraîche, you can make a good substitute by using the recipe that follows, but you'll need to make it a day in advance.

FOR THE PASTA AND ROASTED GARLIC:

> 1¹/₂ **cups unbleached all-purpose flour, not a soft southern flour, which doesn't have enough gluten to make pasta**
> **pinch of salt**
> **2 eggs**
> **1 head of garlic**
> **olive oil**

FOR THE FILLING:

> **1 cup boiled or baked (about ¹/₂ pound), peeled, and mashed sweet potatoes**
> **1 egg, beaten**
> ¹/₄ **pound Parmesan cheese, grated, about 1 cup**

¼ **cup finely chopped fresh chives**

¼ **teaspoon salt**

¼ **teaspoon freshly ground white pepper**

TO ASSEMBLE THE DISH:

1 cup crème fraîche (recipe follows)

salt and freshly ground white pepper to taste

Preheat the oven to 400°. Place the flour and salt in a food processor and process briefly to combine. Beat the eggs lightly in a separate small bowl or cup and, with the processor running, add them in a stream. Continue processing until the dough forms a ball.

Remove the dough from the processor and knead until fairly smooth, about 5 or 10 minutes. The dough will be stiff but will start to show some signs of elasticity after you've kneaded it for a while. Wrap well in plastic wrap and refrigerate for about an hour. Meanwhile, place the garlic head in a ramekin or custard cup, drizzle with olive oil, and bake until it gives to the touch, about 45 minutes.

Just before removing the dough from the refrigerator, prepare the filling: Mix all the ingredients together well. Set aside while you prepare the ravioli. Put a large pot of salted water on to boil. Trying to work quickly but carefully—you don't want the dough to dry out or to absorb the filling—remove the dough from the refrigerator and run it through a pasta machine or roll it out by hand until it is as thin as it can be and still hold the filling. You should have about 12 feet of pasta about 4 inches wide. I hang four 3-foot lengths of dough over a broom handle across the backs of two chairs and cover them with damp kitchen towels.

Dust a large surface lightly with flour; dust your hands as well. You will also need to have another surface covered with another kitchen towel dusted lightly with flour. Remove one of the 3-foot-long sheets of dough from where it hangs and cut it in half, placing the 2 sheets on the dusted counter. Place heaped teaspoons (2 to 3 teaspoons) of the filling in the middle of one of the sheets at 3-inch intervals. Cover with the second sheet of pasta and, working from the far side toward you, gently press the top sheet onto the bottom, pressing out any air bubbles before completely sealing in the spoonfuls. Cut all along the outer edges and between the fillings with a ravioli crimper to seal the edges, then place the ravioli on the floured towel, not touching, and cover them while you continue making the rest of the ravioli.

If you're using wonton wrappers, you'll also need a flour-dusted counter and towel. Spread the wonton wrappers out on the surface, put a heaped teaspoon of filling on each wrapper, and moisten the left and bottom edges of each sheet with water, painting an L shape. Fold the wonton over, bringing the far right corner diagonally across the filling to meet the near left corner. Press the edges together, pushing out any air bubbles as you do, then bring the folded corners together to form traditional wonton shapes. Place on a clean kitchen towel dusted with a little flour, not touching, until all of the wontons are filled. Immediately prepare the sauce and cook the pasta.

Cook the ravioli in the pot of salted boiling water for 2 to 5 minutes while you prepare the sauce.

Put the crème fraîche in the top of a double boiler over simmering water. Cut the base off the head of garlic and remove any loose papery covering. Squeeze the roasted garlic into the crème fraîche and whisk it in well. Heat until just warmed through, season with the salt and white pepper, and serve immediately over the ravioli.

Serves 4

WINE:
An Australian Chardonnay

CRÈME FRAÎCHE

The day before you want to use it, mix together 2 parts cream to 1 part sour cream in a nonreactive container. Allow to sit at room temperature for 6 to 8 hours. Place the mixture in a funnel lined with a coffee filter or something similar and set aside to drain for 2 or 3 hours, until thick.

Mix in a teaspoon of lemon juice for each cup of crème fraîche. It will last about a week kept well covered in the refrigerator.

Mashed White and Sweet Potatoes

I don't know anyone who doesn't like mashed potatoes. Whether served alongside baked or grilled meats, poultry, or vegetables, a puree of potatoes is comfort food at its finest. The basic recipe with the country-fried steak in Chapter 3 is plain and simple, but mashed potatoes can be doctored all sorts of ways to complement other meals, too.

I particularly like them mashed with sweet potatoes, but you can add a puree of cooked fennel, parsnips, or turnips as well. Whip some of the roasted garlic crème fraîche from the preceding recipe into mashed potatoes when you're serving roast meats and you'll get rave reviews. The French like to boil their potatoes, then use the potato water to whip into their potato puree; a little olive oil is a delicious touch in place of the usual butter.

Use this potato recipe as a blueprint, not the ultimate say-so. Just be sure not to try to mash the potatoes in a blender or food processor—they'll get gummy. And, according to Time-Life's excellent book on vegetables from its Good Cook series (now, unfortunately, out of print), you mustn't bake your sweet potatoes at temperatures over 375° if you want them to be sweet.

> **3 large white baking potatoes**
> **3 large sweet potatoes**
> **1½ cups whipping cream**
> **salt and freshly ground white pepper to taste**

Preheat the oven to 375°. Scrub the potatoes well and prick the white potatoes in 2 or 3 places with a fork. Place the potatoes in the oven directly on the racks and bake until they give to the touch. Depending on the size of the potatoes, they should take 45 minutes to an hour. The sweet potatoes may be done a few minutes before the white potatoes.

Put the cream in a small saucepan and bring to a boil, then turn off the heat.

Scoop the flesh out of the baked potatoes into a large mixing bowl and mash with a potato masher or by putting it through a food mill. Beat the cream in a little at a time with a heavy wire whisk, seasoning with the salt and white pepper. Serve immediately.

Serves 8

Potato Pie with Caramelized Onions and Shiitake Sauce

This is another wonderful recipe from Michael McNally of Philadelphia's London Grill, and while I may be his only southern connection, this pie reminds me of the many English dishes that early colonists brought to the South.

My friend Ben Cramer grows exotic mushrooms on his farm just outside Charleston. Freshly picked shiitakes are a welcome addition to the southerner's pantry. Ask your grocery or natural foods store to carry them if it doesn't already.

This pie has the shortest, richest crust I've ever tasted, and the entire dish includes a pound of butter! Serve it for lunch or late supper with a big green salad. My vegetarian friends love this one.

FOR THE CRUST:

2 cups unbleached all-purpose flour, plus flour for dusting
pinch of salt
¼ cup freshly grated Parmesan cheese
2 tablespoons minced fresh herbs such as chives, basil, or parsley
1½ cups cold butter, 3 sticks
½ cup ice water

FOR THE FILLING AND ASSEMBLY:

½ cup butter, 1 stick
2 very large Spanish onions, thinly sliced
1½ pounds potatoes, about 2 baking potatoes
salt and freshly ground black pepper to taste
1 egg
2 tablespoons whipping cream

FOR THE SAUCE:

1 pound fresh shiitake mushrooms, sliced
2 garlic cloves, minced

salt and freshly ground black pepper to taste
2 cups veal, chicken, or vegetable stock

To make the crust, put the flour, salt, cheese, and herbs in a large mixing bowl and toss well. Add the butter, cut into pieces, and with a pastry blender or 2 knives cut it in until it is incorporated uniformly into the flour. Dribble in the ice water, stirring the mixture with a fork, until it will all hold together.

Divide the dough in half and wrap each piece in plastic wrap or wax paper and refrigerate.

For the filling, melt 6 tablespoons of the butter in a heavy pan over medium heat and add the onions. Cook until thoroughly softened, stirring occasionally, about 20 minutes. Turn the heat up to high and, stirring constantly, cook until the onions are caramelized all over, well browned but neither dry nor burned.

Transfer the onions to a plate and refrigerate. Add the remaining 2 tablespoons of butter to the pan, swirl it around, and remove from the heat.

Preheat the oven to 350°. Dust a counter and rolling pin well with flour. Remove the dough from the refrigerator and roll one of the pieces several inches bigger than the ring mold, pie plate, or springform pan that you're using (I like to use an 8-inch springform so that the finished product resembles the raised pies of England). Pick up the circle of dough on the rolling pin and place it down in the pan, pressing lightly into place and letting any extra hang over the edge.

Remove the cooked onions from the refrigerator. Peel the potatoes and cut them into ¼-inch slices. Pat the slices dry with a cloth or paper towel. In the bottom of the dough-lined pan, put a layer of potatoes, season with salt and pepper, and add a layer of the onions. Repeat until the pie is filled, then set aside.

Roll out the second piece of dough to a thickness of about ¼ inch. Place the filled pan down on top of the dough just enough to create an impression of the plate, then remove and set aside. With a knife or pizza cutter, cut out a circle of dough that will fit exactly over the top surface of the pie just inside the lower crust. Lift it up and set it over the filled pie. (Note: You will probably have some dough left over, particularly if you used an 8-inch pan. I simply press it into a small tart pan, slip into a freezer bag, and freeze for later use.)

Bring the dough that hangs over the sides of the pan up and over the top and crimp into place, sealing the top. Cut 3 steam holes into the top of the crust and paint it with an egg wash made of the egg and the cream. Bake for 1 hour.

Meanwhile, place the reserved pan with the 2 tablespoons butter over high heat and add the mushrooms, stirring to coat them well. Cook until the mushrooms have given off most of their liquid and are golden brown, about 15 minutes, stirring most of the time to keep them from sticking to the pan or burning.

Add the garlic, stirring constantly, and cook for 30 seconds. Season with salt and pepper, add the stock, and cook until just shy of a beautiful, thick sauce. Remove from the heat until the pie comes out of the oven, then cook further to reduce and thicken the sauce.

Serve the pie hot with the shiitake sauce.

Serves 8

WINE:
Chassagne-Montrachet

Panfried Potatoes

These potatoes are boiled first so they fry quickly and the interiors are airy in contrast with the golden brown exteriors. They take about 30 minutes to prepare, and you'll want to serve them hot, so plan accordingly.

2 pounds potatoes, about 12 medium new potatoes, 6 medium white potatoes, or 2 or 3 Idahos

¼ cup oil—mostly peanut or corn, with a little olive oil for flavor

1 teaspoon salt

freshly ground black pepper to taste

**1 teaspoon mixed dried herbs such as herbes de Provence
or Italian seasoning**

2 or 3 garlic cloves to taste, minced

Leave the potatoes unskinned, but cut small new potatoes in half or larger potatoes into 1½-inch wedges. Cook them in boiling water until they are partially cooked but are still firm and hold their shape, about 10 minutes depending on the type of potato.

Heat the oil in a large heavy skillet over medium-high heat. When it is hot, add the potatoes. They should form one layer that covers the bottom of the pan. Sprinkle half of the salt, some pepper, and half of the herbs, crushed, over the potatoes. Fry without stirring for about 10 minutes or until the potatoes are golden brown on the bottom.

Shake the pan gently to loosen the potatoes, then turn them with tongs or a metal spatula. If they're browned but still sticking to the pan, scrape them off the bottom of the pan with the spatula turned upside down, pushing firmly. Make sure all the potatoes are turned over.

Sprinkle the rest of the salt and herbs over the potatoes and fry until they are well browned all over, turning the wedges if necessary, about another 10 minutes. About 30 seconds before removing the potatoes from the pan, sprinkle them with the garlic and shake the pan to distribute evenly.

Lift the potatoes from the pan with a slotted utensil that will allow the oil to drain off into the pan. Serve immediately.

Serves 4

Onions and Their Kin

Seventeenth-century gardeners in coastal South Carolina were quick to get their garden seeds sown in February, along with the onion and leek sets. By the time Mrs. Hill (1872) wrote her cookbook in Georgia, southerners were using several other members of the lily family in their kitchens. She gave four recipes for shallots and several for onions, including an onion custard not unlike the Vidalia onion tart in this book. "For seasoning, the red onion will answer," she advised, "but only use the white silver-skinned for boiling, stewing, etc." Her leek recipe is perfect: "Skin them; lay in cold water an hour; boil in salted water until they yield to pressure. Put them upon a hot covered dish; pour over melted butter."

Some fifty years earlier in Virginia, Mary Randolph had written a recipe for potatoes mashed with onions, noting that "you will be guided by your wish to have more or less of their flavor." Cajuns and Creoles in Louisiana would obviously want more of that bold flavor, given their Spanish and French heritage, but, as culinary historian Karen Hess has pointed out, Mrs. Randolph's heavy use of garlic in old standbys from England, where so many of her recipes originated and where garlic had been conspicuous in its absence up until then, is indicative of a new palate in the South.

Southern Appalachia has its own wild leek, the ramp, whose harvest in mid-April sparks ramp festivals and cookoffs in at least six West Virginia towns. Ramps are downright stinky but delicious—raw, boiled, sautéed, fried, pickled, in soup, and baked with fish. I've seen tears well up in one grown man's eyes at the mere mention of the possibility of having some ramps; he had grown up in the Tennessee hills and hadn't had any since childhood.

You'll see more than tears at the mention of sweet onions. In what was once a virtual monopoly all but owned by onion growers in and around the tiny town of Vidalia, Georgia, applelike onions from Texas, Mexico, Hawaii, South Carolina, and Washington state have flooded the market.

I love baked onions, roast garlic, grilled leeks, and a garnish of chives on just about anything. Most of my one-pot meals and sauces start with the sautéing of some onions, shallots, or garlic. I can't imagine a southern meal without these lilies of the table, if only the scallions in the salad.

Fried Sweet Onion Rings

You can't go wrong with onion rings, especially if they're made with sweet onions. You can simply dip onion rings into milk and then into flour; they will fry to a golden brown with a crispy coating. Some recipes call for a sticky batter; others call for thin ones. Some have baking powder, and some have egg whites. This one is made with beer—something most southerners have sitting around.

This is a large recipe to serve eight people, but I figure if you're deep-frying, you may as well get your money's worth out of the oil. I use an outdoor burner and a large pot. I still have to work in batches, but I offer baskets of onion rings as they come out of the fryer. My guests enjoy a drink on the patio while I fry the onions.

Start making the batter up at least an hour before you plan to fry because it must rest.

> 2 cups unbleached all-purpose flour
>
> ³/₄ teaspoon salt
>
> a 12-ounce can of beer, flat and at room temperature
>
> ¹/₄ cup peanut oil, plus peanut oil for frying
>
> 4 large, rather flat sweet onions, about ³/₄ pound each
>
> 2 egg whites

In a large mixing bowl, combine the flour and salt. Combine the beer and the oil. Pour the liquid into the dry ingredients, stirring with a wire whisk only until combined. Do not beat the batter. Let it stand for at least an hour.

To prepare the onions for frying, cut ¹/₂-inch slices of peeled onions and carefully separate them into rings. Large flat onions will separate into nice rings almost all the way to the center. Save the centers to use in a salad or another dish.

When you're ready to fry, heat at least 2 inches of oil in a large pot over high heat. While the oil is heating, beat the egg whites until they hold stiff peaks, then fold them into the batter, working lightly.

When the oil has reached 365°, dip the rings into the batter and then drop them into the oil. Do not crowd the pot. Fry until golden brown all over, then remove from the pot, holding each onion ring over the pot for a moment so that any excess oil drains off. Place on a rack, then continue frying. Serve when you have a plateful. They stay hot for a while. Be sure to wait for the oil to return to 365° before adding the next batch and try to maintain that temperature throughout the frying.

Let your diners salt their own onion rings. They'll get soggy if you salt them before serving.

Serves 8

Sweet Onion Confit

Young chefs throughout the country are cooking a global cuisine that draws on techniques and ingredients from around the world. It's especially gratifying to me to see traditional southern condiments—chutneys, relishes, pickles, and preserves—not to mention the desserts, making their way onto the menus of some of the nation's finest restaurants. Southern chefs, of course, are not immune to this cross-cultural trend; their restaurants offer Mediterranean and Asian fare along with grits and greens.

The finest foods, though, are always the freshest. It matters not whether you are frying chicken or making coq au vin: a freshly killed, organically raised bird that was not bred for its breast size or precociousness will always taste better. I always order those menu items that are preceded by the words *fresh local*—whether ramps in the mountains, peaches in the foothills, or soft-shell crabs on the coast. And I try to buy fresh local products as often as possible.

Sweet onions are now grown in several states, not just in southern Georgia, and they are shipped throughout the country. I've seen menus offering Vidalia onion marmalade, Maui onion compote, and Walla Walla onion jam—though none of the preparations is traditional. This sweet onion confit is a delicious condiment that combines a technique from the South of France with our fine local onions. I like to spread it on bread, add it to sauces, and garnish roast meats with it. It is also delicious pureed with roasted peppers or with mayonnaise.

Chef Frank Stitt in Birmingham uses a Vidalia onion confit atop corn bread crostini (Chapter 8) smeared with sautéed rabbit livers; chef Stephan Pyles in Dallas serves his with venison. Both chefs cook the onions fairly quickly, with some vinegar to cut the small amount of fat used. Mine leans more toward tradition and will keep for several weeks. Though widely available, sweet onions do not keep well. This recipe is a perfect way to extend their shelf life.

1 cup rendered duck fat (see Duck and Oyster Jambalaya, Chapter 4)

3 pounds sweet onions such as Vidalia, Wadmalaw, Maui, or Walla Walla Sweet, peeled and sliced stem-to-root into ¼-inch slices

4 bay leaves

1 fresh thyme sprig

1 teaspoon salt

3 whole black peppercorns

2 whole allspice berries

In a large heavy sauté pan or Dutch oven, melt the duck fat over medium heat. Add the onions and seasonings and stir carefully to coat the onions in the fat but not to break up the bay leaves. Make sure there are no pieces of onion skin or any yellowed or soft spots on the onions. If there are, remove them from the pan. Cook, stirring occasionally so they don't stick or brown, until the onions are translucent, about an hour.

Meanwhile, sterilize a quart jar and lid by placing them in a simmering water bath and leaving them there until needed.

When the onions have finished cooking, remove the herbs and spices and discard, then put the confit in the jar. Run a chopstick or tool designed for the purpose around the inside of the jar to release any air bubbles, then seal.

The onions will keep for several weeks. I put the confit out with hearty bread on the hors d'oeuvre table. Always use a clean utensil to remove the confit and be sure to leave a layer of fat on top of the onions as an extra seal.

Makes 1 quart

Vidalia Onion Tarte Tatin

This terrific vegetable dish comes from my Charleston friend Donna Skill. Sweet onions are now available throughout the country in the late spring and early summer—be sure to use a sweet hybrid for this recipe so the onions will caramelize. You'll need to start several hours before you plan to serve. Sweet onions are so much juicier than white or Spanish onions; it takes a long time for the juices to cook out. If you've got the time, you should really cut them the day before you plan to use them in this recipe to let them air-dry. Don't worry if they turn a little dark; they're going to brown in the tart anyway.

> 2½ **pounds sweet onions such as Vidalia, Wadmalaw,**
>   **Texas 1015, Walla Walla Sweet, or Maui**
> ½ **cup butter, 1 stick**
> ½ **cup sugar**
> **1 sheet frozen puff pastry**
> **all-purpose flour for dusting**
> **1 teaspoon chopped fresh thyme leaves**
> ½ **cup chopped scallion, both white and green parts**
> **1 shallot, chopped**

Ahead of time if possible (as much as a day before), slice the onions in half stem-to-root, then slice off the tops. Slice the bottoms, leaving a hint of the tough base above the roots to help hold the onion together. Peel the onions. Place on a cloth or paper towel over some newspaper and allow to air-dry.

In a 10-inch cast-iron skillet, melt the butter, add the sugar, and remove from the heat, stirring to mix well. Add the onions, root ends down and curved edges touching the outside of the pan. Shove the onions into the pan, cramming it full. You should have enough to tightly pack the skillet.

Place the skillet over medium heat and cook until bubbles appear. Turn down the heat a bit and continue to cook until most of the liquid has cooked out of the onions and they begin to collapse, 1½ to 3 hours, depending on how juicy your onions are and how high the heat. You must not stir the onions, because you want them to stay in place, but it is okay to shake the pan a little bit. I turn the skillet around on the burner several times while it is cooking to be sure there are no hot spots. Remove the pan from the heat the moment the remaining sugar in the bottom of the pan caramelizes. Tilt the pan slightly to be sure there is no clear liquid left.

Preheat the oven to 400° and take the puff pastry out of the freezer to thaw. Several manufacturers make a 17¼-ounce package that contains 2 frozen sheets. They take about 20 minutes to thaw. After they have thawed, remove one of the sheets and wrap the other well in its original covering, then a layer of aluminum foil. Refreeze immediately.

Dust a counter and rolling pin well with flour and place the thawed sheet of puff pastry on the counter. Sprinkle the pastry with the thyme leaves and roll it out so that it forms a circle about 12 inches in diameter.

Sprinkle the chopped scallions and shallot all around the sweet onions in the pan, then lift up the puff pastry sheet and place it down on top of the onions. Let it sit for a moment, then press it down over the onions and down the sides between the onions and the sides of the skillet. You may have to use a thin tool such as a hard plastic spatula to wedge the pastry down the sides.

Place the tart in the oven and bake for 30 minutes or until golden brown. Transfer to a rack to cool.

To serve, invert a large plate over the skillet. Invert the skillet and lift it from the tart. Slice carefully with a serrated bread knife and serve.
Serves 8 to 10

WINE:
A fruity white Côtes du Lubéron or Chenin Blanc

Braised Chayote

Chayote (pronounced like coyote) is a gourd native to tropical America. It is well known throughout Central America and the Caribbean, as well as in the southernmost reaches of the South. In Louisiana they call it *mirliton* and, in much of the Caribbean, *christophene.* It grows on a vine that can be trained on fences and trellises, and many tropical gardeners are as proud of their chayotes as they are of their passion fruits.

Each chayote, apple green and crisp, weighs about ³/₄ pound. It is shaped like an avocado or a pear. You can prepare it any way that you would summer squash, but because it's harder, it takes more time to cook, about 20 or 25 minutes. It is most often halved and stuffed, but this recipe from Charleston's Scott Fales is a pleasant change from ordinary squash fixings. "When I serve this," Scott told me from the porch of his popular Pinckney Cafe, "people love it, but they always have to ask what it is."

You'll need about ¹/₂ pound of chayote per person. To prepare them for cooking, you should peel them. The skin of very young chayote is edible, but I usually peel it anyway because it will toughen when cooked. The seed, however, is slightly nutty; include it if you want to.

> **3 tablespoons butter**
>
> **1 cup chopped onion, about 1 medium**
>
> **1 cup diced carrot, about 2 large**
>
> **3 cups peeled and diced chayote, about 3**
>
> **12 grains each freshly ground black pepper and coriander, about ¹/₄ teaspoon each**
>
> **salt to taste**

In a heavy sauté pan with a lid, melt the butter over medium heat, add the onion and carrot, and cook for 5 minutes or so until they soften. Add the chayote, pepper, coriander, and salt. Turn the heat to low, cover the pot, and cook until tender, about 15 minutes.

Serves 4

Okra

It's too bad that some people find the mucilaginous quality of okra unappealing, because its flavor is one of the best in the vegetable kingdom. It can be cooked so that it's not at all slimy, but okra haters are often violently opposed to even trying it. Native to Africa, okra came to America with the slave trade and has stayed firmly entrenched in the cuisines of the African diaspora. Creole cooking relies heavily on it, whether in Brazil, the Caribbean, or New Orleans. Most southerners join the ranks of Middle Easterners, Southeast Asians, and Indians, who feature it often in their menus.

Okra will grow in more northern climes, but it is little understood in America outside the South. One cookbook author whose work I regard highly features several okra recipes in one of her books, but a photograph shows old, blackened okra. I can only imagine that she's never had the real thing. There is no vegetable that I spend more time choosing before I buy it than okra: finger length, bright green, no blemishes (not even a hint of darkness on the tip), and no hard spines; it must give to the touch and have a fresh smell that hints of the salt marsh. It should be cooked the day it is picked and should not be refrigerated. If you can't find freshly picked okra, use frozen.

The older nonhybrid okra varieties are the best (see Ingredients and Sources, Garden Vegetables); ask the farmers at your farmers' market to grow them for you if you can't find or grow them yourself. If you live in the Cotton Belt (cotton, like okra, is a member of the Hibiscus family), grow the Clemson Spineless; it will be a prolific producer in less than two months. Okra plants are easy to grow, and they produce large, typically showy hibiscus flowers. If you grow your own, you'll never have to shop so diligently for okra; almost every morning you'll be able to pick perfect, small pods.

To prepare okra for the table, simply cut the stem end down to but not into the pod. If you cut into the pod, the mucilaginous liquid will escape and the dish will be slimy. That's fine for thickening gumbo, or if the okra is to be cut up, dusted with flour or corn flour, and fried. But if you want the okra as a side dish, be fastidious in this trimming. The okra can then be steamed, boiled, stewed with tomatoes, pickled, or even grilled.

Okra Fritters

Fritters are another popular okra dish; dozens of batter recipes are used in the South. This one combines a tempura batter with partially steamed okra.

If you're using frozen whole pods in this dish, allow them to thaw at room temperature in a colander, then proceed with the recipe as if they were parboiled.

> 1 pound fresh small okra pods, trimmed, or a 10-ounce
> 　package frozen whole okra, thawed
> peanut oil for frying
> salt and freshly ground black pepper to taste
> 1 egg yolk
> 1 cup ice water
> 1 cup unbleached all-purpose flour

If you're using fresh okra, place the trimmed okra in a saucepan with a tight-fitting lid and add just enough water to cover the bottom of the pot, about ⅓ cup. Cover tightly and steam over medium-high heat for about 5 minutes or until the water evaporates. Transfer the okra to a towel; pat dry and allow to cool. If you're using frozen okra, place it on the towel after it has thawed and pat dry.

Heat 2 inches of oil in a Dutch oven or deep skillet to 365°. Season the okra with salt and pepper.

In a wide bowl, thoroughly mix the egg yolk and ice water with a wooden spoon. Dump the flour into the liquid all at once, stirring quickly. The batter will be lumpy.

Holding the okra pods by the stem ends, drag them through the batter and drop into the hot fat, frying each one for about a minute or two, until it just starts to brown. As it is cooked, transfer each pod to a rack to drain until all the okra is fried. Do not crowd the pot; keep the oil at 365°.

Let everyone salt the okra to taste. If you salt it before it is served, it will become soggy. Be careful; these are hot!

Serves 4

Okra and Tomatoes

This simple dish is a true southern classic from Memphis to Miami. It is served most often over rice in the summer, when tomatoes are truly fruitlike and when tiny, finger-length okra is bright green and neither seedy nor stringy. I had always thought that every recipe for okra and tomatoes started with some oil or bacon grease and an addition of herbs and other seasonings until I found this perfectly delicious recipe in *The Savannah Cook Book,* first published in 1933. Modern tomato cultivars are rarely acidic; I usually omit the sugar.

> 1 pint okra
> 1 pint tomatoes
> 1 teaspoon sugar, optional
> 1 onion, chopped
> salt and pepper to taste

Cut up okra, peel tomatoes. Put in a saucepan without water, and add a teaspoon of sugar, a chopped onion, a little salt and pepper, and stew together for fifteen minutes.
Serves 8

Rice and Rice Pilaf

In some parts of the South, either rice or grits are served with every meal. Rice is still eaten daily in some of that land where it hasn't been grown in nearly 100 years. It holds sauces and gravies, is stuffed into tomatoes, fills out sweet puddings, and is found in breads, soups, and croquettes. More important, it is the center of the cuisine in the low-lying coastal plains of both South Carolina, where for 200 years its planting shaped the culture, and Louisiana, where it has been grown for about 100 years. Both the Carolina Huguenots and the Louisiana Catholics based their marvelous cuisines on a foundation of rice.

In *The Carolina Rice Kitchen: The African Connection,* Karen Hess takes a deep look into the evolution of rice cookery in South Carolina, tracing the path of the pilau. In the process she shows how those Frenchmen in America, previously unknown as rice cooks, came to cook pilau (pronounced PERloe, perLOE, or piLOE in South Carolina and known as jambalaya in Louisiana) on a daily basis.

Southern cookbooks old and new often call for a side dish of "rice pilaf," a name all but redundant in southern ricelands. Hess defines the dish (*pilaf* is the Turkish form of *pilau*): "In its most basic version, *long-grain* rice that has been washed and presoaked is added to simmering aromatic broth, usually in the proportion of two parts of liquid to one of rice by volume, then covered and cooked until 'nearly dry.'" Rice in the South is *always* cooked like the Persian pilau—steamed so that each grain is separate. Only the addition of some seasoning distinguishes pilaf, but the differences are subtle: a dish of plain steamed rice covered with stewed okra and tomatoes can be called *okra pilau.*

Plain steamed rice invites a host of accompaniments. Gumbo is always served on it; chili often is. The gravy that accompanies fried chicken is traditionally served over rice, not mashed potatoes, in the Deep South. Having been reared in rice country, I am always amazed when people tell me that they can't cook rice. Nothing could be simpler; I am even more astonished when I am served insipid parboiled or "converted" rice, especially in Louisiana and South Carolina restaurants. A recipe for rice—or rice pilaf—follows.

1 quart water

½ teaspoon salt

2 cups long-grain white rice (see Variations)

Put the water in a pot with a tight-fitting lid and a capacity of at least 2 quarts. Add the salt and bring to a boil, then pour in the rice. Stir once with a fork to distribute the rice evenly. Never touch it with a spoon and do not stir it again. Lower the heat a little and cover the pot, watching to see when it comes to a simmer. Adjust the heat so that the rice simmers (bubbles just barely break the surface)—and no more than simmers. Cook, covered, for 13 minutes, never lifting the lid. Turn off the heat and let it stand, still covered and untouched, for another 12 minutes.

Leave the pot alone until you're ready to serve the rice. At the point of serving, lift the lid and fluff the rice with a large fork, never a spoon: what you are trying to do is further separate the grains—which should be all but dry—from each other. Old southern black cooks tell me, "They should fall out of the pot like popcorn."

Serves 6

Variations

When you shop for the rice, you should look for rice that is the longest and whitest, all the same size, with no middlings (broken pieces). You can use an aromatic rice such as Texmati or basmati (see Ingredients and Sources) for interesting flavors. You can also use a brown rice, but you will have to increase the amount of water and the time by about as much as a half. Brown rice is not traditional, but many other variations are. Just remember to keep the ratio of liquid to rice 2 to 1.

The most common variation is the substitution of stock for the water. Even canned chicken broth will do, but be sure to use the lowered-salt version and don't salt the pot. If the rice is accompanying a meat or poultry dish, cook it in a stock quickly made with the trimmings of the main dish and some herbs and aromatic vegetables. If you don't have time to make a stock, you can still add a browned bone or wing tip to the rice, then pull it out before you serve.

I don't cook with brown rice, but if I am feeding vegetarians or I want a whole-grain flavor (but not the heaviness), I'll substitute some cracked wheat (see Ingredients and Sources, Flour and Wheat) for as much as half of the rice. Do *not* use bulgur, which is cracked wheat that has been precooked; it would overcook with the rice.

Grated lemon zest, pecans, chopped herbs, and tomatoes are delicious common additions. Sautéed onions are often added, as is sausage. Any cooked meat can be folded into the steamed rice as it is fluffed before serving. When rice is added to an almost cooked pot of beans, it becomes the famous pilau, hoppin' john. Black beans and rice is a similar dish.

The Best Grits

Southerners are great growers and lovers of corn; it is eaten fresh and plain, in puddings, and fritters and, when dried and ground, as grits, in breads, and as breading. Cornmeal mush, corn pone, corn dodgers, corn relish, corn liquor, corn bread, cornsticks, and corn stuffing are just a few of our many dishes based on this native American staple. It is eaten with gusto, even in the old rice-growing lands of the South.

Supermarket grits are processed hominy: corn that's been treated in an alkaline solution so that the hulls and germ float to the surface. Thus bleached, the corn is dried, enriched (some of the nutrients lost in the processing are added back in) and ground—too fine, to my taste. These tasteless, ashen grits are served as a matter of course in countless restaurants and homes throughout the South. It's no wonder outsiders don't like them.

When early colonists arrived in the South, the Native Americans made hominy by soaking their corn in a solution of lye made from wood ashes. Ashen grits were made to preserve the grain through the winter and spring, when temperatures often stayed in the 70s and 80s. This processing was of course unnecessary up north.

When I went looking for great grits, I tried more than two dozen mills before I found one that could consistently provide coarse-ground, whole-grain grits (see Ingredients and Sources, Corn Products). I now sell tons of the best grits I've ever eaten. They taste like freshly ground corn because they are just that; when cooked, they resemble creamed fresh corn, but are starchier. They can be used just like pasta or rice. Not only local home cooks and restaurateurs, but also cooks throughout the country have added real grits to their menus, so that old southern favorites like Lowcountry shrimp and grits have reentered the culinary vernacular as if they had never been missing.

Some people cook their grits for a long, long time. It's true that the longer they cook, the creamier they become. You can put them in a slow cooker overnight, and they'll be delicious. But you can easily cook grits in less than 30 minutes if you're willing to watch the pot and stir occasionally. Cooked grits can then be enriched with egg, poured into a well-seasoned cast-iron skillet or greased baking pan, and refrigerated. The chilled grits are then unmolded, cut into portions, dusted with flour or cornmeal, and panfried like polenta.

Basic recipes for grits and grits cakes follow. There's also an innovative variation on grits cakes from chef Frank Stitt. Be sure to see Fran Freeberg's version of shrimp and grits and Rob Ennis's Sautéed Oysters Over Grits Cakes in Chapter 2 and the recipe for Garlic Cheese Grits in Chapter 5 as well.

Basic Grits

Grits invite a host of accompaniments. Any sauce or gravy that you would put on pasta or rice is ideal. If you plan to serve the grits plain, a little stock made from trimmings from the main course is a welcome addition if stirred in near the end of the cooking.

> 1 quart water
>
> 2 tablespoons butter
>
> salt to taste
>
> 1 cup stone-ground whole-grain grits

Bring the water, butter, and salt to a boil in a stockpot. Gradually add the grits, return to a boil, then reduce to a simmer. Cook the grits, stirring occasionally so that they do not stick or form a skin, until creamy and done to your liking, about 25 minutes. Many people like to cook them much longer; if you do, you may have to add more water.

When the grits are almost done, you can turn the pan down to its lowest setting and cover it while you prepare the rest of the meal.

Basic Grits Cakes

1 recipe basic grits

2 eggs

2 tablespoons heavy cream

2 teaspoons water

¼ cup unbleached all-purpose flour, cornmeal, corn flour
  (see Ingredients and Sources), or fine dry bread crumbs

peanut oil for frying

As soon as the grits are done, put one of the eggs into a medium mixing bowl with the cream and stir well to combine. Quickly add some grits to the egg and cream, beating well with a wire whisk so that the egg doesn't curdle. Dump the mixture into the grits pot and whisk all together well.

Turn the grits out into a greased 9-inch cake pan and cool to room temperature. Refrigerate until firm.

When you're ready to cook, heat some oil in a heavy pan over medium-high heat. Preheat the oven to its lowest setting. Place a rack over a sheet pan and place it in the oven along with 4 appetizer plates or 2 dinner plates.

Remove the grits from the refrigerator and turn them out onto a cutting surface. Beat the remaining egg with the water in a pasta bowl to make a wash. Cut the grits into 8 wedges, then gently lift each one up and dip it in the egg wash, then in the flour. Sauté or deep-fry until golden brown, then transfer to the rack in the oven to drain and stay warm while you prepare the sauce.

Serves 4 as an appetizer, 2 as a main course

Baked Grits with Mushrooms and Country Ham

This is one of chef Frank Stitt's wonderful recipes. Frank combines the best of southern home cooking with classic French techniques to provide some of the most delicious fare in the South. Don't be daunted by the number of pots and pans you'll use here: The results are worth the effort. Of course, you can serve these timbales with any simple sauce.

These grits timbales are elegant, but the dish is very rich. Serve it as intended, as appetizers for a dinner party of six.

FOR THE GRITS:

> 1 quart water
>
> salt to taste
>
> 1 cup stone-ground whole-grain grits
>
> 2 tablespoons butter plus butter for greasing molds
>
> freshly ground white pepper to taste
>
> ¼ cup freshly grated Parmesan cheese
>
> 1 egg

FOR THE SAUCE:

> ½ cup dry white wine
>
> 2 tablespoons white wine vinegar
>
> 2 shallots, finely chopped
>
> 1 dried hot red pepper or ¼ teaspoon hot red pepper flakes
>
> 1 bay leaf
>
> 1 fresh thyme sprig
>
> fat, gristle, and bone trimmed from 2 thin slices of
>   country ham
>
> 1 tablespoon whipping cream
>
> 1 cup butter, 2 sticks, cut into cubes
>
> 2 tablespoons freshly grated Parmesan cheese
>
> salt, freshly ground black pepper, and fresh lemon juice to taste

FOR THE MUSHROOMS AND FINAL ASSEMBLY:

1 tablespoon olive oil

2 thin slices of country ham, trimmed and julienned

1 shallot, minced

1 garlic clove, minced

½ pound mushrooms—morels, chanterelles, shiitakes, or
   oyster mushrooms—cut into thick slices

fresh thyme sprigs for garnish

Preheat the oven to 350°. Grease six 4- to 6-ounce ramekins or custard cups and place in a baking pan. Put a pot of water on to boil while you prepare the grits.

Bring the water and salt to a boil, then slowly stir in the grits with a wooden spoon. Cook, stirring constantly, until thickened, about 12 minutes.

Pour into a large bowl and add the butter, pepper, and cheese. Using a heavy whisk, beat well, then add the egg and whisk until the mixture is blended evenly.

Pour the grits into the greased molds, then pour boiling water around them. Bake for about 25 minutes or until a knife inserted in the grits comes out clean.

While the grits are baking, prepare the sauce: Place the wine, vinegar, shallots, red pepper, herbs, and ham trimmings in a heavy sauté pan over high heat. Cook until only 1 tablespoon of liquid remains. Reduce the heat to low, stir in the cream, then whisk in the butter until it is all absorbed.

Strain the sauce into another container, then whisk in the cheese. Wipe out the sauté pan and reserve for the mushrooms. Correct the seasoning with salt, pepper, and lemon juice and set aside to keep warm while you unmold a timbale on each of 6 warmed salad or dessert plates and prepare the mushrooms: In a clean heavy sauté pan over high heat, add all of the ingredients except the garnish and sauté until just done—about 3 minutes.

Ladle the sauce around the grits, then divide the mushroom sauté among the plates. Garnish with thyme and serve immediately.
Serves 6

WINE:
Grand Ardèche from Louis Latour

Corn Pasta Lasagne with Fresh Tomato Sauce

Right up until World War II most meals and flours in the South were milled locally. Even as late as the 1960s in South Carolina, the cornmeal and grits in the large grocery stores were, for the most part, local. In the backwoods today, grits and cornmeal are still ground to order. Corn flour is the finest grind, traditionally used to dust fish and vegetables for frying.

I have my own label of grits, cornmeal, and corn flour ground from organically grown corn at Logan Turnpike Farm, near Blairsville, Georgia (see Ingredients and Sources). George and Cecilia Holland, who bought the mill in the mid-eighties, left full-time jobs in Atlanta to move to the mountains 100 miles from the city. "It's not your idea of the old mill by the mountain stream," Cecilia says, but in fact the setting could not be more bucolic: a breathtaking waterfall plunges through the rhododendrons not 100 yards from the mill, which does have old blue granite stones, though they are powered electrically.

This recipe for delicate corn-flavored pasta was Cecilia's idea. Sheets of it can be layered in lasagne; it can be filled with cheese, meat, or vegetables for ravioli; or it can be cut into fettuccine to be topped with your favorite sauce, especially one made with tomatoes or mushrooms, which complement the corn.

In the following recipe, which is perfect in the summer when fresh tomatoes are in, I use a light southwestern-style salsa rather than the traditional, heavier cooked tomato sauce. Since the lasagne is made as soon as the pasta is rolled, there's no reason to parboil the pasta. Assemble the salsa first, then make the pasta.

FOR THE SALSA:

2½ pounds vine-ripened Roma or plum tomatoes, chopped

½ cup chopped scallion

3 garlic cloves, minced

1 teaspoon salt

freshly ground black pepper to taste

1 jalapeño chili, seeded and chopped

¼ cup cilantro leaves

FOR THE PASTA:

²/₃ cup very fine corn flour (see Ingredients and Sources)

1 cup unbleached bread flour

2 eggs

2 teaspoons water

1 teaspoon salt

FOR THE LASAGNE:

1 pound fresh mozzarella, grated

1 cup freshly grated Parmesan cheese, about ¼ pound

In a large mixing bowl, toss all the salsa ingredients together and set aside.

Put ½ cup of the corn flour and the cup of bread flour in a food processor and pulse to blend. Add the other ingredients and blend until a ball of dough is formed. Dust a counter with the remaining corn flour and knead the dough until smooth. Work quickly and don't let the dough dry out, or it will crack when you roll it.

Roll the dough by hand or through a pasta machine until it is very thin, then cut into desired shapes. This recipe makes about 20 ravioli or 4 to 6 servings of flat pasta. For this lasagne, roll the dough into flat sheets 4 inches wide by the length of the pan you're using. I use an 8- by 11½-inch pan, so I roll them 11 inches long, but the size of the pan is not critical.

Cover a sheet pan with wax paper or parchment and put the pasta on it, not touching. Place another sheet of paper on top of the pasta and add another layer of pasta. Continue until all the pasta is covered.

Preheat the oven to 400°. Oil the baking pan and fill it with alternating layers of pasta, salsa, mozzarella, and Parmesan, in that order and finishing with the Parmesan.

Bake for about 25 minutes or until the lasagne is bubbly and beginning to brown. Let it cool for a few minutes before serving.
Serves 6

WINE:
Rioja—red or white

Tomatoes with Goat Cheese

The northern reaches of the South—the piedmont, foothills, and mountains—are dotted with new dairy farmers who are producing farmstead cheeses from their own herds of cattle and goats. Farmers' markets, gourmet shops, and natural foods stores now offer an array of their blue cheeses, fresh cream cheeses, and fresh and aged goat cheeses. Southern food writers and chefs have embraced the welcome additions to local dairy cases. Marion Sullivan is a South Carolinian who writes about food. Her recipe comes with the warning:"As with any really worthwhile fresh tomato recipe, this new southern version of the traditional old workhorse broiled tomato is meant to be made in the summer, when the fruit has perfect texture and taste."

> 2 vine-ripened tomatoes, cut in half
> 3 ounces cream cheese, 1 small package, at room temperature
> 3 ounces soft fresh goat cheese, 5 tablespoons, at room temperature
> ³/₈ cup dried bread crumbs, preferably from French bread
> 1 shallot, minced
> ¹/₈ teaspoon minced fresh thyme leaves
> salt and freshly ground black pepper to taste
> herbed olive oil

Preheat the oven to 350°. Seed the tomato halves, scoop out the pulp, and coarsely chop it.

Beat the cream cheese and goat cheese together. Fold in about three-quarters of the bread crumbs, the shallot, and the thyme, then fold in the tomato pulp. Season with salt and pepper. Fill the tomato halves with the mixture and sprinkle with the remaining bread crumbs. Place on a baking pan and drizzle lavishly with herbed olive oil. Bake until thoroughly warmed, about 25 to 30 minutes, and serve immediately.

Serves 4

Summer Pasta

This pasta dish that I learned to make when I lived in Italy is perfect fare during the summer tomato season. Raw tomatoes and basil are chopped and added to cooked pasta; hot garlic-flavored olive oil is poured over the dish to warm it all through. I've heard this dish called by several names in Italy, but most of them are too vulgar to print. Down South, we call it *summer pasta*.

It is essential that you use firm ripe tomatoes for this dish. The recipe serves two, but you can multiply it without fear.

> ½ pound fettuccine or other dried pasta
> ¼ cup extra-virgin olive oil
> 4 or 5 garlic cloves to taste, peeled
> 1 firm ripe tomato
> fresh lemon juice to taste, optional
> ½ cup firmly packed fresh basil leaves
> salt and freshly ground black pepper to taste
> freshly grated Parmesan cheese for serving, optional

While you cook the pasta, put the olive oil in a small saucepan over medium-high heat and add the garlic cloves. They will begin to sizzle in the oil after a moment or two. Continue to fry them while you prepare the tomatoes and basil. You want the oil to stay very hot, but you do not want to burn the garlic or it will impart a bitter flavor. Turn down the heat when they turn golden or move the pot off—or partially off—the heat.

Cut the tomato into large dice. You should have about a cup of chopped tomato. Taste it for acidity, and if it's not the perfect summer tomato, squeeze a little lemon juice over the pieces. Sprinkle the basil with a small pinch of salt and coarsely chop it. You should have 3 or 4 tablespoons.

Just before the pasta finishes cooking, put the oil back over high heat to get it very hot. When the pasta is cooked, drain quickly, then transfer it either to a large bowl or back into the empty pot in which it was cooked. Distribute the tomato and basil over the pasta, then pour the sizzling oil over the pasta through a sieve so as to catch the garlic, which you then discard.

Toss quickly together and divide among two pasta bowls. Let each diner season to taste with salt, pepper, and, if desired, Parmesan.
Serves 2

WINE:
A really young and fresh Italian white such as Frascati

Gilson's Tomatoes

Gilson Capilouto is from the Sephardic community of Montgomery, Alabama, where they cling to their Jewish cooking traditions. Her ancestors were dispersed during the Spanish Inquisition, and the diaspora took them to Brussels, Istanbul, and the Greek island of Rhodes. Her cooking draws heavily from the Mediterranean basin. On several occasions I've heard Gilson declare an old southern dish Sephardic, especially those with okra and tomatoes, favorites in the Carolina Lowcountry where she now lives.

Sun-drying tomatoes rarely caught on in the humid American South, but these slowly baked ones, found throughout the south of France, are becoming widely appreciated as the foods of the Mediterranean become better known. Gilson puts hers in a sterilized jar and tops them with olive oil to preserve the roasted tomato flavor. Refrigerated, they'll keep for about two weeks.

They are delicious warm or at room temperature as a side dish, spread on crusty bread, or pureed and heated as a pasta sauce. Their taste is somewhere between the finest sun-dried and best vine-ripened tomatoes you have ever eaten. When the tomatoes are gone use the infused oil on pasta.

large vine-ripened tomatoes
olive oil, about 1 teaspoon per tomato
salt and freshly ground black pepper to taste
minced garlic, about 1 clove per tomato
basil leaves, 2 to 4 per tomato
balsamic vinegar to taste

Preheat the oven to 300°. Cut the tomatoes in half crosswise and place them cut side up on a baking sheet. Drizzle the oil over the tomatoes, then season with salt and pepper.

Bake for about 1½ hours, then sprinkle with the garlic. Continue baking until the tomatoes collapse and begin to caramelize. It will take anywhere from 2 to 4 hours altogether.

In the meantime, sterilize a jar that will hold what you don't plan to use immediately by placing it in a simmering water bath. A dozen tomatoes will produce a pint.

When the tomatoes are done, transfer them with a metal spatula to the jar one by one, placing a layer of basil leaves on each tomato half. When all of the tomatoes are in the jar, put it in the refrigerator until they have released their water—about 45 minutes. Run a clean, small rubber spatula (or the tool made specifically for the task) between the tomatoes and the inside of the jar to release any air bubbles. Tap the jar once or twice on the counter to loosen any recalcitrant ones. Pour a layer of olive oil over the top of the tomatoes, then splash a bit of balsamic vinegar into the jar. Cap the jar and store in the refrigerator.

Green Tomato Chutney

Southern chutneys are traditionally made in the summer and fall with fresh fruits and vegetables, cooked with vinegar and seasonings, then "put up" for use in the winter and spring. Chutneys are akin to other sweet-and-sour southern condiments, and, as in India, they add spice and texture to plates of meats, vegetables, and grains. I can't imagine eating a plate of beans and rice—a very popular southern dish—without some artichoke or pear relish, some peach chutney, or, at the very least, some hot pepper vinegar. Chutneys, like relishes and salsas, are all similar. There are some basic proportions that work well, but the fruits and spices can be varied infinitely.

In my first book I gave explicit canning directions and recipes for chutneys and relishes that were larger, traditional quantities to be canned for winter use. This green tomato chutney can simply be put in a jar and kept in the refrigerator until it's gone. In Charleston green tomatoes are available year-round now thanks to the film *Fried Green Tomatoes*. Tourists in Charleston expect to find them on the menu, so a once seasonal dish has become a standby. But unless you order from a large food distributor, you'll probably have to make this chutney in season.

Peach or pear chutney can be made with the same formula, but you'll need to use unripe fruit. Many cooks substitute apples for some of the tomatoes, but I like the distinctive taste of the green tomato. Be sure to use hard, round, green tomatoes with no sign of red or white.

2½ pounds green tomatoes (or replace up to ½ pound
    tomatoes with apples), trimmed of stem end and cut into
    ¾-inch cubes, about 6 cups
1 cup raisins, about 6 ounces
1 cup chopped onion, about 1 medium
1½ cups packed light brown sugar
1 teaspoon salt
1¼ cups white or cider vinegar
1½ teaspoons mustard seeds
1 teaspoon cayenne pepper
2 tablespoons chopped crystallized (candied) ginger

Put all the ingredients in a heavy saucepan and bring to a boil. Reduce the heat and cook until thick, about an hour or so, then pour into sterilized jars and seal. Process in a boiling water bath for 10 minutes and store in the refrigerator.

Makes about 3 pints

Spicy Sautéed Rape Greens

Greens are often misunderstood outside the South, even among botanists. The scientific nomenclature is maddening. Rape, an unfortunate name in English, is seldom marketed as a vegetable outside Italy or China, though many southern African-Americans have grown it for the table for many generations. In Italian and French the names for most greens and turnips are confusingly similar; the Italian for rape translates as "turnip broccoli," though many of us now know that vegetable as broccoli raab.

Almost no white southerners grew up eating rape, because, like most Americans, they never cultivated a taste for the bitter. The traditional long simmering of greens in the South is, in fact, aimed to reduce bitterness. But not all greens are cooked forever. Collards are cooked for 2 hours, but turnip greens cook in about half an hour. Kale is steamed for a few minutes; spinach is sautéed in a matter of seconds.

In late summer, before the traditional fall greens arrive, rape appears at southern farmers' markets among the black growers. Bitterness has long been esteemed as admirable among Africans, the Chinese, and southern Europeans. The Reverend York Washington, an African-American who has been farming in South Carolina for sixty years, says, in his heavy Gullah accent, "Rape eats better than collards." The rape seeds that he sows are gathered from flowering plants each season and have been passed down through his family for decades. Though the plant that is now grown in the South is much larger than what is marketed as broccoli raab (*broccoletti di rapa* in Italy), southerners of Italian descent still recognize this dish as *broccoli di rapa alla romana.*

You may use either large, turnip-like rape leaves or the smaller, now trendy broccoli raab (or rabe) from the gourmet shops. Replace the olive oil with sesame oil and use rice vinegar instead of lemon juice, and the dish is Chinese. In the Sichuan province of China, it is a common side dish. Mikel Herrington, who grew up on a South Carolina farm, lived in Sichuan for two years. Though he doesn't remember rape from his childhood, he says its taste is redolent of Sichuan, where "everything is cooked in rapeseed oil."

A bunch of rape in the Deep South is likely to be as many as 20 mature plants, with leaves as big as turnip greens. It will weigh, stems and all, about 4 pounds. Oriental grocers are good sources for rape; a bunch of smaller plants will yield 6 to 8 cups of trimmed leaves, weighing about a pound.

1 pound rape or broccoli raab leaves, trimmed of the tough stems and any yellow spots and cut or torn into pieces

1 gallon water

2 garlic cloves, minced

3 tablespoons olive oil

¼ teaspoon hot red pepper flakes

salt and freshly ground pepper to taste

1 lemon

Plunge the rape into the rapidly boiling water and cook for 2 or 3 minutes, until all the leaves are completely wilted. Place a colander inside a large bowl and lift the rape from the water into the colander to drain.

In a large sauté pan with a lid, sauté the garlic in the oil over medium heat for a few minutes. Do not let it brown. Add the pepper flakes and wilted rape, toss together well, then cover the pan and lower the heat to simmer for 10 minutes. If there is not enough liquid clinging to the leaves, add up to ¼ cup from the cooking water that has drained from the leaves into the bowl under the colander.

After 10 minutes, lift the lid and season with salt and pepper. Serve the greens with a fork either hot or at room temperature, squeezing the juice from the lemon onto the greens just before serving.

Serves 4

Creamy Spinach

Creamed spinach is an old southern favorite—heavy with butter, cream, and flour. In this lightened version I've added some shallots and garlic for flavor, replaced the cream with yogurt, and freshened it with a bit of mint.

> 1½ pounds fresh spinach
> 1 shallot, minced
> 1 garlic clove, minced
> 2 tablespoons olive oil
> 1 cup plain yogurt
> salt and freshly ground black pepper to taste
> 1 tablespoon minced fresh mint leaves

Wash the spinach well, trim it, and chop or tear it into pieces, letting them fall into a large saucepan. Add the shallot and garlic and cook over medium heat, covered, for about 5 minutes. Shake the pan occasionally so that the vegetables do not stick.

Drain the vegetables well, then add the olive oil and continue to cook for 3 minutes, stirring constantly. Remove from the heat, stir in the yogurt, and season with salt and pepper. Fold in the mint and serve immediately.
Serves 4

Beets with Their Greens

Southerners like to use beets pickled, as a relish or garnish for other foods. I love to bake beets whole until they give to the touch, peel them, slice them, and splash with balsamic vinegar; but when fresh young beets with their tops are available, I cook them with their greens. Use only small and fresh beets with bright greens for this recipe.

> **2 bunches of small beets with their greens attached, about**
> **   2½ pounds**
> **3 tablespoons butter**
> **salt and freshly ground black pepper to taste**

Rinse the beets and greens under cold running water, then fill the sink with enough water to cover the plants. Cut the roots from the tops, peel the roots, and cut into ¼-inch slices. Shake the leaves around in the water to free them of any grit, changing the water as many times as necessary. Cut any tough stems from the leaves.

Put the beet slices in a heavy saucepan and add about half the butter and a little salt and pepper. Add the greens, the remaining butter, and a little more salt and pepper. Cover and cook over medium heat until the beets are tender, about 5 to 10 minutes.

Serves 4

Grilled Fruits and Vegetables

When I say that I grill everything, I'm hardly exaggerating: bananas, pineapple, grapefruit, underripe peaches and pears, green and red tomatoes, leeks, cabbage, onions, garlic, eggplant, squash, peppers, and bread, not to mention all the fish, fowl, meats, and game.

Nearly all of these foods are prepared in basically the same way: lightly oiled and seasoned, then grilled to taste. Some of them appear elsewhere in this book as part of other recipes. (See instructions for grilling eggplant, fennel, and tomatoes with the frittata recipe in Chapter 5.) A few notes on my mixed grill follow. I recommend a medium flame for most vegetables unless you're searing the skins of peppers to peel them.

Hard-skinned fruits:
Don't peel bananas, pineapples, or grapefruits, though you should quarter the pineapples and grapefruits lengthwise. All are good with fish; the pineapple is good with pork. You can put them directly on the grill; oiling the fruits is optional.

Soft-skinned fruits:
Don't peel peaches or pears, but lightly baste them with a tasteless oil and cook them just to warm through.

Tomatoes:
Green tomatoes are just as good grilled as fried. Cut them into 1/2-inch slices, oil and season them with salt, pepper, and cayenne to taste, and grill until they just begin to soften and are warmed through. You can also dust them in seasoned corn flour as if you were frying them if you want a crispy coating.

Red ripe tomatoes are delicious grilled. Cut the tomatoes in half crosswise and place them on a plate, cut sides down. Oil the skin sides and place the oiled sides down on the grill. Cook until the skin starts to pull back, drizzle some more oil on top, then turn to cook on the other side *or* drizzle some seasoned bread crumbs, grated cheese, or minced basil leaves on the tops, then cover the grill and cook for a few more minutes just to warm through.

Onions, leeks, and garlic:

Grill whole onions just as you do red tomatoes, slicing them unpeeled in half crosswise. Oil the skin sides, place them oiled sides down on the grill, and cook until they begin to give to the touch. Drizzle oil on the cut sides and turn to finish the cooking. Trim after grilling but before serving. Sweet onions are particularly good this way.

Split leeks lengthwise down to—but not into—the base. Wash well under running water until there is no sign of grit, then shake off the excess water. Oil well and season with salt and pepper. Grill until the leek softens and is slightly charred all over. Remove from the grill and slice off the base and the outer leaves and discard.

Whole heads of garlic can be roasted either on a covered grill or down in the coals. They will take about 30 minutes, depending on the heat. Oil them lightly. If you place them down in the coals, wrap them in aluminum foil.

Corn on the cob:

Carefully pull back the corn husks without removing them from the ear of corn. Pull away the silk, then lightly oil the corn kernels. Pull the husks back up around the corn and grill until done to your liking. Many new varieties of corn are so sweet that they really don't need to be cooked, just warmed through. Don't let corn dry out!

Cabbage:

Quarter small cabbages or cut larger ones into eighths. Don't bother to remove the outer leaves. Oil the cabbage, season it with salt and pepper, and grill on each side until it just starts to become translucent and is richly branded by the grill.

Tuscan-Style Beans

Dried beans have been a staple in the South since time immemorial, traditionally cooked with pieces of cured pork. The minuscule amount of fat that a smoked ham hock adds to a pot of beans probably wouldn't hurt anyone, but many people shy away from cooking the old way regardless. This is a perfectly delicious way to serve beans, even if you're a traditionalist like me—and it's something you can serve your friends who won't eat pork.

Hundreds of varieties of beans have always been grown in the South, some of them hard to find outside the region. Other parts of the country have their own special varieties as well. Phipps Ranch in Pescadero, California (see Ingredients and Sources, Dried Beans), grows dozens of varieties organically. All of its harvesting and sorting is done by hand, and the beans are always the most recent "vintage." Use whatever bean you prefer, but be mindful that freshness and variety determine cooking times.

1 cup dried beans, about ½ pound, rinsed and picked over

6 cups water

3 garlic cloves, unpeeled

1 fresh thyme sprig

1 teaspoon salt

3 tablespoons olive oil

**1½ cups peeled, seeded, and chopped tomatoes, about
  3 medium**

2 tablespoons chopped fresh basil

1 tablespoon fresh lemon juice

Soak the beans in water overnight. Drain and rinse the beans, then place them in a stockpot with the 6 cups water, the garlic, thyme, and salt. Simmer for 1 to 1½ hours or until tender. Drain the beans.

Warm the olive oil in a sauté pan over medium heat. Slip the cooked garlic out of its skins and add it, the tomatoes, and 1 tablespoon of the basil to the oil, stirring well. Cook until most of the liquid has evaporated and the flavors have mingled.

Add the beans and heat just through, carefully mixing with the tomatoes, being careful not to break the beans. Finish the dish with the lemon juice and remaining basil. Serve warm or at room temperature, but don't leave them out for long if it's warm; beans turn quickly.

Serves 6

Creamed Peas with Pearl Onions and Mint

Fresh green peas are a sure sign that spring has arrived. Delicious with potatoes, mushrooms, or onions, they can accompany any simple roast meat, fowl, or fish. Nearly all the good recipes for English peas have been around for centuries, though today's varieties will cook in less time.

When fresh peas arrive at the market, I can't resist pairing them with pearl onions and cream. The addition of mint, found in nearly every southern yard, is classic; Elizabethan and Jacobean cooks invariably included it.

Freshly shelled peas fade rapidly. If you can't cook them immediately, it's better to use frozen peas.

> **10 ounces pearl onions**
>
> **2 cups freshly shelled or frozen green peas, about 2 pounds in the shell**
>
> **1 teaspoon sugar**
>
> **1 cup whipping cream**
>
> **½ teaspoon salt**
>
> **2 tablespoons finely cut mint leaves, plus a few leaves for garnish**

Drop the whole onions into boiling water for 3 minutes, then transfer them with a slotted spoon to a colander. Rinse them well under cold water, slice off the base of each onion, and pop it out of its skin. Set aside.

Rinse the peas well and remove any that show any sprouts or bruises. Put them and the sugar in the boiling water and cook until just tender, about 5 minutes depending on the size and age of the peas. Drain in a colander.

Put the cream, salt, and mint in a pan with the peeled onions. Bring to a boil and cook for 1 minute. Add the peas to heat through. Serve immediately.
Serves 4

Sugar Snaps with Lemon Thyme Butter

Sugar snaps are delicious, but must not be overcooked. Lemon thyme is now widely available in supermarkets—it's also easy to grow and is a perfect complement to quickly cooked dishes such as this one. A pound of sugar snaps will give you four servings, but don't buy them until the day they're to be cooked. Freshness is everything in this dish.

> **1 pound sugar snap peas**
>
> **2 tablespoons butter**
>
> **salt and freshly ground black pepper to taste**
>
> **3 fresh lemon thyme sprigs**

Snap off the stem ends of the peas and remove the strings from both sides. Blanch the peas by plunging them into a large pot of boiling water for 1 or 2 minutes. Drain and set aside.

Melt the butter in a sauté pan over medium-high heat. Add the peas, salt and pepper, and thyme. Stir-fry quickly for about 3 minutes, just long enough to heat through. Taste one to be sure they're cooked and warmed through. Turn off the heat. Lift the thyme sprigs one at a time, holding each over the pan as you run your thumb and index finger down the stem to release the leaves. Stir well to distribute the leaves among the peas and serve immediately.

Serves 4

Green Beans with Pecans

Pecans are considered a luxury item outside the South, but we use them with abandon as snacks, in salads and stuffings, as breading, in desserts, and with vegetables. The following buttery recipe is a year-round favorite.

> **1 pound tender young green beans, stemmed but with the tender young green tips intact**
>
> **2 tablespoons butter**
>
> **⅓ cup pecan halves**
>
> **1 shallot, finely chopped, or ¼ cup finely chopped onion**
>
> **salt and freshly ground black pepper to taste**
>
> **dash of cayenne pepper, optional**

Plunge the beans into a large pot of rapidly boiling water and cook them, uncovered, until just tender, about 3 to 5 minutes. Taste them frequently and do not overcook. When they lose their raw flavor, immediately pour them into a colander to drain.

Melt the butter in a large skillet over medium heat. Sauté the pecans in the butter for 5 minutes, then add the shallot and continue cooking for 5 minutes. Just before serving, add the beans. Season with salt and pepper and, if desired, the cayenne. Toss the beans, nuts, and shallot together well, turn off the heat, and cover for a moment to warm the beans through and blend the flavors.

Serves 4

Black Beans and Rice

Throughout the South, beans and rice are served as a side dish. From South Carolina's hoppin' john to the *moros y cristianos* of Cuban immigrants in Florida, this is typical southern fare. If you can find fresh epazote, use it—this Mexican herb minimizes the gas beans produce. Serve this with the Cuban- and Mexican-inspired pork roast in Chapter 3, garnished with Mango Relish (Chapter 7).

> 1 cup dried black beans, about ½ pound, rinsed and
> picked over
> 5 cups water
> 1 small onion, chopped
> 1 dried hot red pepper, optional
> 1 strip of bacon
> 1 cup long-grain white rice
> 1½ teaspoons salt
> 2 epazote sprigs, if available

About 4 hours before you plan to eat, place the beans, water, onion, pepper, and bacon in a heavy saucepan and simmer gently, covered, for 3 hours or until 2 cups of liquid remain. After 3 hours, add the rice, salt, and epazote, bring to a simmer, cover, and cook over low heat for about 20 minutes, never lifting the lid.

Remove from the heat and allow to steam, still covered, for another 10 minutes. Remove the cover, lift out the epazote and bacon and discard, fluff with a fork, and serve.

Serves 6

Easy Bean Cakes

The next time you have leftover beans—lima, pinto, garbanzo, black, or black-eyed peas—make these panfried bean cakes and serve them as a side dish or with a salad for lunch. People love them. If you don't have home-cooked beans, use a 1-pound can of black beans, but make sure it contains nothing but beans, water, and salt and rinse the beans well.

You can serve them with a puree of roasted red peppers, with herbed mayonnaise or tartar sauce, with any of the relishes in this book, or with bottled hot pepper sauce.

> 2 cups cooked and drained beans or a 1-pound can black beans, drained
> 1 egg, separated
> 1 teaspoon dried mixed herbs such as herbes de Provence or Italian seasoning or 1 tablespoon chopped fresh herbs of your choice
> 4 scallions, white and some green, chopped
> 1 garlic clove, minced
> ¼ cup chopped roasted red bell pepper or ¼ cup sliced pimientos with their juice, 1 small jar
> 1 jalapeño chili, seeded and chopped, or bottled hot pepper sauce to taste or hot chili powder to taste
> ¼ teaspoon cumin, preferably freshly ground (omit if you use chili powder)
> salt and freshly ground black pepper to taste
> ¾ cup fine very dry bread crumbs
> 3 tablespoons peanut oil or clarified butter

Mash the beans in a mixing bowl with a large fork, a potato masher, or your hand, but do not use a blender or food processor. Add the egg yolk and mix well, then add the remaining ingredients except the egg white, bread crumbs, and oil. Fold in ½ cup of the bread crumbs.

Beat the egg white to soft peaks and fold it into the cakes.

Heat the oil in a skillet over medium-high heat. Form the bean

mixture into 3 large burgerlike patties or 6 smaller ones and place each down in the bread crumbs, coating both sides well. Fry the bean cakes until golden all over, about 2 minutes on each side.
Serves 6 as an appetizer or 3 for lunch

Carrots in Ginger Ale

The South is home to many soft-drink manufacturers. Recipes for cakes made with Coca-Cola and salads made with 7UP are not uncommon. Coke was first made in Atlanta over 100 years ago, but old-fashioned ginger ale, sarsaparilla, and cream sodas had been around for nearly 100 years before that. North Carolina gave us Pepsi-Cola, Texas gave us Dr Pepper, and 7UP came from St. Louis.

Several old-fashioned soft drinks are available locally, notably South Carolina's Blenheim Ginger Ale (see Ingredients and Sources), which was introduced in 1903. Made from water from a mineral spring behind the old bottling plant in Blenheim (a town of 200 residents), its taste is an acquired pleasure. Traces of 22 minerals, including sulfur, are countered with the strong bite of imported gingers. Number 5, the Extra Pale, is strong; Old Number 3, which locals call "Old Hot," is a potent reminder that ginger is used in various pharmaceutical stimulants and carminatives as well as in the kitchen.

Use whatever ginger ale you can get. If you want a spicier flavor, add a piece of fresh ginger or some dried and ground ginger to the carrots as they are cooking. This recipe is simplicity itself.

PER PERSON:

> 1 large carrot, peeled, quartered lengthwise, and cut into 2-inch pieces
> ½ cup ginger ale, preferably a potent one such as Blenheim's
> ½ tablespoon orange marmalade

Place all the ingredients in a saucepan and boil over high heat until the carrots are cooked but still firm and the liquids have reduced to a glaze, about 10 minutes. Serve immediately.

Peanut Butter Hummus

Batik artist Mary Edna Fraser is typical of the new breed of southerner with international tastes, but she is often hard-pressed to get her young daughters to eat the things she prefers. "I make hummus with peanut butter instead of tahini, and the kids love it," she told me. Serve it as a dip with toasted pita bread and crudités, and the adults will, too.

You can use canned chick-peas here.

1 pound cooked or canned chick-peas (garbanzo beans)

⅓ cup natural peanut butter (100 percent peanuts)

juice of 1 or 2 lemons to taste

1 or 2 garlic cloves to taste, peeled

salt to taste

3 tablespoons olive or peanut oil plus olive oil to cover

If the chick-peas are canned, boil them over medium heat for 5 minutes, then drain well. Put all of the ingredients in a blender and blend until perfectly smooth, adjusting the flavor by varying the lemon juice, garlic, salt, and oil. Put in a bowl and cover with a thin layer of olive oil, then serve as a dip.

Makes about 2 cups

CHAPTER
7

Fresh Relishes and Salads

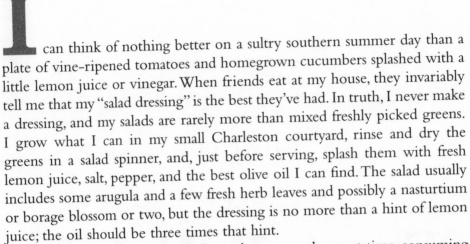

I can think of nothing better on a sultry southern summer day than a plate of vine-ripened tomatoes and homegrown cucumbers splashed with a little lemon juice or vinegar. When friends eat at my house, they invariably tell me that my "salad dressing" is the best they've had. In truth, I never make a dressing, and my salads are rarely more than mixed freshly picked greens. I grow what I can in my small Charleston courtyard, rinse and dry the greens in a salad spinner, and, just before serving, splash them with fresh lemon juice, salt, pepper, and the best olive oil I can find. The salad usually includes some arugula and a few fresh herb leaves and possibly a nasturtium or borage blossom or two, but the dressing is no more than a hint of lemon juice; the oil should be three times that hint.

On the other hand, salads can be among the most time-consuming meals to prepare, especially if they are to be the main course. Many cooked meats, seafoods, and vegetables are delicious cold, but each ingredient should be cooked separately so that it does not lose its identity on the salad plate. The radishes in this chapter are often part of a larger salad, perhaps with leftover chicken, roasted and peeled peppers, boiled potatoes and eggs, blanched green beans, on a bed of arugula.

I was not reared in what I like to call the Mayonnaise Belt, though I know many southerners who were. I'll occasionally whip together some homemade mayo for pimiento cheese or potato salad, but I've never been fond of cold chicken or pasta in mayonnaise. My friend Richard Perry grew up in Mobile and Williamsburg. His spicy shrimp and asparagus marinate overnight in a heavily dilled mayonnaise. A traditional pickled shrimp recipe is included as well.

Relishes are of two sorts in the South: one, like salad, is mostly raw fruit and vegetable combinations that add color and flavor to meat and vegetable dishes. In the Southwest it's mostly called salsa—sauce, implying salsa cruda, or raw sauce. I include them here with the salads because I often serve them as side dishes. You will note that the recipes are similar. You can substitute just about any fruit for the mango in that relish and it will taste fine. Relishes are simple to make and easy to season to taste; these recipes more than any in this book are infinitely variable. Don't hesitate to make substitutions or to experiment. A relish made with bananas, for example, is excellent with lean fish; grapefruit pairs well with oily ones.

The second type of southern relish is a cooked condiment that is canned for use throughout the year so that when fresh fruits aren't available the pantry still provides accompaniments for roast meats and for beans and rice. Pear relish, chowchow, artichoke relish, and pickles fall into this category. They are usually sweet-and-sour combinations that are more closely related to Indian chutneys.

Fresh Relishes

Think of these recipes as guidelines. Mangoes or tomatoes can be added to the black beans; lemon can replace lime; oil can be included or not; herbs and spices can be altered at will. With the addition of oil, most of these relishes can serve as vinaigrettes for topping salads or fish; some are delicious heated, like the tomato-basil vinaigrette paired with tuna in Chapter 2.

These relishes are lighter than the traditional sweet, canned relishes of the Old South.

Black Bean Relish

This relish can be served as a side dish or alongside bean cakes, crab cakes, rice dishes, and roasted or grilled meats. Another bean or black-eyed peas can be substituted for the black beans. Cilantro is most often called for in this sort of relish, but I like to substitute basil, parsley, or dill, depending on the dish the relish will accompany.

1½ cups cooked and drained black or other beans, well
   rinsed if canned
½ cup chopped scallion or shallots
1 medium jalapeño chili, seeded and chopped
½ cup chopped red bell pepper, about ½ large
2 tablespoons finely chopped fresh herb of your choice
1 tablespoon extra-virgin olive oil
2 tablespoons fresh lemon juice
salt and freshly ground black pepper to taste

Toss all the ingredients together, seasoning to taste. Allow to sit at room temperature for 30 minutes, then taste for seasoning again.
Makes 2 cups to serve 4 as a side dish or 6 to 8 as a garnish

Mango Relish

This relish complements roast pork or fish served with rice and beans and stands as a side dish on its own. Serve big mounds of it.

2 mangoes, peeled, pitted, and cut into large dice

1 orange, peeled, seeded, sectioned, and cut up

1 cup chopped scallion, white and tender green parts only, or sweet onion such as red or Vidalia

1 jalapeño chili, seeded and chopped

½ cup chopped red or green bell pepper, about ½ large

¼ cup fresh lime juice

1 teaspoon cumin seeds

salt to taste

1 scant teaspoon sugar, optional

¼ cup fresh cilantro leaves

Combine the mangoes, orange, scallion, chili, bell pepper, and lime juice in a nonreactive container. Toast the cumin seeds in a skillet for just a moment or two over high heat, until they begin to jump around in the pan and give off little whiffs of smoke. Do not burn them.

Transfer the cumin seeds to a mortar or spice mill and grind fine. Add to the relish, toss well, and season with salt. If the onions are not sweet or the mangoes not very ripe, you may want to add a little sugar to the relish. Toss in the cilantro and serve immediately. The relish will keep for several days in the refrigerator.

Serves 6

Jícama-Onion Relish with Fresh Fruit

I don't know whether my backyard or the local grocery store is more illustrative of the new flavors of the South. Where I once had a mulberry tree (mutilated by a hurricane) and a few herbes de Provence in my yard, now there are bananas, lemongrass, several varieties of mint, cilantro, arugula, Mexican tarragon (*Tagetes lucida*), cardamom, and ginger lilies. The supermarket regularly carries Asian vegetables, Mexican peppers, melons from God-knows-where, and several Caribbean root vegetables, such as jícama.

Jícama is available year-round and is versatile in the kitchen. It retains its crunchy texture even after cooking, but it quickly absorbs other flavors, making it particularly well suited to salads of bright summer flavors. The traditional Latin American seasoning is lime, chili, and salt, but this recipe is more typical of the flavors favored by new southern chefs. You can make this relish (which is delicious alone as a salad) with soft or hard fruit, but you will want to eat it before the fruit breaks down in the lime juice. I like to make the salad in May and June, when sweet southern onions are available.

> 1 jícama, about 1 pound
> 2 pears, apples, bananas, or mangoes
> 2 jalapeño chilies, seeded and minced
> ¼ cup fresh lime juice
> 1 lemongrass stalk, white part only, as finely minced
>   as possible
> 1 small onion, preferably Vidalia or Wadmalaw, chopped
> 1 garlic clove, minced
> salt to taste
> 1 scant teaspoon sugar, optional
> ¼ cup loosely packed cilantro leaves
> ¼ cup loosely packed fresh mint leaves
> oil, optional

Peel and grate the jícama into a mixing bowl. Add the fruit, sliced. Add the jalapeños, lime juice, lemongrass, onion, garlic, and toss well. Add salt and, if your onions are not sweet, sugar. Just before serving, add the cilantro and mint and toss again. If you're serving the relish as a salad, add a little oil if you wish.

Serves 8

Grapefruit Relish

I serve this relish with fish that has been grilled or baked with grapefrui quarters. The contrast of the raw and the cooked, the cool and the warm is intriguing.

> **1 grapefruit, peeled, sectioned, and cut up, about 1 cup**
> **½ cup chopped mild onion or scallion, about ½ medium onion**
> **1 jalapeño chili, seeded and chopped**
> **¼ cup loosely packed fresh mint leaves, finely chopped**

Combine the ingredients and allow to sit for about 30 minutes.

Serves 4

Moravian Coleslaw

No fried chicken or barbecue restaurant in the South is without its coleslaw. There are just as many recipes for slaw as there are for the chicken and hog. Slaw might not seem particularly southern, but Germans were early settlers in the Carolinas. The recipe that follows is, in fact, from Old Salem, the Moravian village in Winston-Salem, North Carolina. Many recipes call for mayonnaise, celery seeds, caraway seeds, and other binders and flavorings. Add them to taste if you will. This version is good as long as you keep it. The amount of liquid may seem like a lot, but the sugar and vinegar preserve the cabbage. Serve the slaw with a slotted spoon to drain off the excess.

> 2 cups water
> 2 cups white vinegar
> 2 cups sugar
> 3 pounds green cabbage, grated, about 1 large head
> 2 medium white onions, finely chopped
> 1 green bell pepper, finely chopped
> 1 carrot, peeled and grated
> 1 tablespoon salt
> 1 tablespoon mustard seed, optional

Combine the water, vinegar, and sugar in a saucepan and bring to a boil. Set aside to cool. When cool, pour over the remaining ingredients. Mix well and refrigerate for at least 24 hours before serving.
Serves 12

Radish Salad

Radishes of varying sizes and shapes are grown throughout the world. They are pickled, sautéed in butter, stir-fried, and stewed. The French make a hearty sandwich of bread, butter, and salted radishes; the British (and, regionally, some southerners) serve prissy little radish and cucumber sandwiches at tea. Most Americans, though, simply toss the little cherrylike radishes that are commonly available into salads or serve them on the crudité tray with a bowl of salt to dip them in.

Try this simple marinade, then feature them as the main part of a salad. You'll be surprised at how refreshing it can be. Be sure to use the best oil you can find.

> 1 bunch of radishes with their greens or a 4- to 6-ounce
>   package trimmed radishes
> 2 teaspoons fresh lemon juice or vinegar of your choice
> freshly ground black pepper to taste
> 2 tablespoons extra-virgin olive oil
> salt to taste
> mixed greens

There are 3 ways to go about this recipe. You decide which method is best for you and the radishes that you have.

Garden radishes:

I make this salad only when I've just returned from the farmers' market and there is still dirt clinging to the radishes. About an hour before you plan to eat, wash, trim, and pat the radishes dry. Thinly slice them and toss them with the lemon juice or vinegar, pepper, oil, and salt. Place them in the refrigerator until just before serving on clean, dry mixed greens.

Store-bought radishes:

The second and third methods give you a little leeway in case your radishes aren't just picked. All of the ingredients are the same, but you may want to salt the sliced radishes first and let them drain for a while in a colander or sieve to freshen them before you marinate them in the oil. Leave the lemon juice or vinegar out of the marinade as well until serving time.

Quick method:

When you not only don't have the freshest radishes, but also don't have much time, do this: slice the radishes and add them to the oil and pepper, leaving out the salt and lemon juice until serving.
Serves 2

Salad of Roasted Peppers, Onion, and Endive

This is one of those salads that can double as a condiment. Simply leave out the endive and it's a perfect complement to omelets (Chapter 5) and grilled foods. Blanching the onion cuts its harshness.

> **1 large onion, thinly sliced into rounds**
> **2 tablespoons extra-virgin olive oil**
> **¼ teaspoon salt**
> **¼ teaspoon hot red pepper flakes**
> **3 red bell peppers**
> **½ lemon**
> **1 head of Belgian endive, washed, drained, and separated into leaves**

Place the onion slices in an empty heatproof container and cover with boiling water. Let the water sit on the onion rounds for just a moment, then drain well. Sprinkle the onion with the olive oil, salt, and red pepper flakes. Refrigerate.

Meanwhile, roast the bell peppers by applying direct heat to them—preferably an open flame, but you can place them in a pan under an oven broiler as well. Roast them until the skin blisters and turns black, turning them with tongs as the skin chars. Burn only the skin, not the pepper flesh. Place the blackened peppers in a paper bag with the top folded down or in a bowl with a plate set on top. Leave them for about 10 minutes so that the charred skins steam away from the flesh.

When they have cooled somewhat, place them on a cutting board. Peel away the skins, then seed them by pulling the stem end away from the pod. Most of the seeds will pull out from the pepper with the stem.

Slice the peppers and toss with the onions. Just before serving, splash with the juice of about ½ lemon, correct the seasoning, and serve over a bed of crisp leaves of Belgian endive or as a condiment alongside other dishes. *Serves 3 or 4*

Smoked Avocado Guacamole

The rest of the country may not consider the west coast of Florida southern, but the young people who grew up there certainly think of themselves as southerners, even as their hometowns are overrun with Yankee retirees. Florida has long had heavy tropical and Latin influences in its cooking, but it took a group of young chefs in St. Petersburg to start smoking fruits and vegetables as well as the traditional mullet.

Chef Mark McDonough agrees with me that electric smokers are the easiest and most efficient ones to use. "You want to add the smoked flavor to the avocados without cooking them," says Mark, "so you can add them when you're near the end of smoking something else."

To smoke avocados, shrimp, and garlic—all unpeeled and whole—place them on the smoker for about 10 minutes. Unplug the smoker and let them stay for another 20 to 30 minutes. You'll have to experiment to find out which wood flavoring suits your own palate and exactly how long the avocados (or shrimp or garlic) will take on your smoker. Use the smoked avocado and shrimp in traditional salads such as this guacamole. Use the garlic in any cooked dish calling for garlic in which smokiness would be agreeable—beans, for instance.

The secret to a delicious guacamole is to assemble it at the last moment.

2 smoked avocados, peeled and pits removed

1 small onion, chopped

2 medium vine-ripened tomatoes, peeled, seeded, and chopped

1 jalapeño chili, seeded and minced

juice of 2 limes

salt to taste

¼ cup loosely packed cilantro leaves

Crush the avocado flesh roughly in a bowl with a large pestle or wooden spoon. Add the onion, tomatoes, chili, and lime juice and mix with the avocado, taking care not to make mush of the avocado or tomato pieces. Season with salt, then tear the cilantro leaves into 2 or 3 pieces each and toss with the guacamole one last time. Serve immediately with chips or atop a bed of lettuce.
Makes about 2 cups

Cucumber-Yogurt Salad

With its vibrant history of merchant ships and the heavy English influence of colonial days, the South has long revered the foods of India. Curries and rice dishes such as chicken country captain are favorites both here and on the subcontinent, and the vast array of chutneys, relishes, and pickles that accompany them appear virtually the same in both cuisines. Many side dishes, such as this one inspired by an Indian raita, are meant to complement the main dish, though I like this alone as well.

I puree leftovers of this dish with the Light Tomato Soup in Chapter 1 and serve it cold, garnished with a little dill. The dill is a refreshing touch, and raitas from northern India often include it. You can use cilantro or mint or both if you prefer.

2 large cucumbers

salt

2 garlic cloves, minced

1 tablespoon olive oil

1 cup plain yogurt

¼ cup loosely packed fresh dill leaves

Peel the cucumbers and slice in half lengthwise. Scoop out the seeds and cut the halves into several strips. Place them in a colander and sprinkle heavily with salt. Allow them to drain for about 30 minutes.

In a very small pan over medium heat, cook the garlic in the oil for about 2 minutes. Do not let it brown. Add to the yogurt and stir in well. Add the dill leaves, with no stems, and mix in well.

Wipe the cucumbers dry with a paper or cloth towel, then dice them. Add them to the yogurt and mix well. Refrigerate for an hour before serving.
Serves 3 to 4

Tabbouleh

Tabbouleh, the traditional Middle Eastern salad of cracked wheat, cucumbers, parsley, and mint, is widely popular in the South, where its cooling effect is welcomed in the 100-degree summers. Bulgur is cracked wheat that has been precooked; it needs to soak only a little to rehydrate. The following recipe is a traditional one from the Palestinian community in Jacksonville, Florida.

> 1 large cucumber, optional
> salt
> ½ cup fine bulgur
> 2 large or 3 medium vine-ripened tomatoes, diced
> 1 cup finely chopped scallion
> 3 cups finely chopped parsley, preferably flat-leaf
> juice of 3 lemons
> ½ cup extra-virgin olive oil
> ¼ cup finely chopped fresh mint or 2 tablespoons dried, crumbled
> freshly ground black pepper to taste

Peel the cucumber, halve it along its width and length, scoop out the seeds with a spoon, and cut each quarter into 4 or 5 strips. Place them in a colander or sieve and sprinkle with a tablespoon of salt. Set aside to drain.

Soak the bulgur in cold water for about 10 minutes, then thoroughly drain it in a colander lined with damp cheesecloth. Wrap the bulgur in the cheesecloth and squeeze out any excess water. Place the bulgur in a large bowl and toss gently with the remaining ingredients. Refrigerate for about an hour so that the bulgur can absorb the juices.

Remove the tabbouleh from the refrigerator. If the mixture is too juicy, put it in a colander and drain off some of the liquid. Dice the reserved cucumber, which should be well drained by the time you're ready to serve, pat it dry with towels, and mix into the salad. Season to taste with salt and pepper.
Serves 4

Potato Salad

You find this composed salad at every southern picnic. It accompanies fried chicken, sandwiches, burgers, barbecue, and fried fish. The distinctive southern touch is the sweet pickle, sold throughout the South as "sweet salad cubes." If you can't find them locally, buy any sweet cucumber pickles and mince them. Most versions call for a lot more mayonnaise than this simple recipe does. I also leave the potatoes unpeeled, cut into large wedges.

2 pounds waxy or new potatoes, well scrubbed but
    unpeeled, cut into 1½-inch wedges, boiled, and cooled
3 hard-cooked eggs, peeled and chopped
1½ cups minced celery, about 3 large ribs
1 cup finely chopped scallion or mild onion
½ cup blender mayonnaise (see Pimiento Cheese recipe
    in Chapter 5)
1 heaped tablespoon prepared mustard
½ cup sweet pickle cubes with juice
salt, freshly ground black pepper, and cayenne pepper to taste
1 to 2 tablespoons chopped fresh herbs of your choice to
    taste, optional
paprika, optional

Combine all the ingredients except paprika. It's traditional to dust the top of the salad with paprika.

Serves 6 to 8

Spicy Shrimp and Asparagus

My friend Richard Perry has worked as a troubleshooter in some of the South's finest restaurants. Wherever he goes, this simple recipe of his ends up on the menu and stays there long after he leaves the restaurant standing on its own two feet.

It's nothing more than cooked shrimp and asparagus in a spicy mayonnaise, but people love it. Make it a day ahead so the flavors can mingle. Serve it as an appetizer or as lunch.

> 2 pounds fresh shrimp
> crab or shrimp boil, such as Old Bay Seasoning
> 2 pounds fresh asparagus
> 2 cups blender mayonnaise (see Pimiento Cheese recipe
>   in Chapter 5, noting the changes below)
> 1/4 cup coarse prepared mustard, not Dijon style
> 2 tablespoons, more or less, bottled hot pepper sauce such
>   as Texas Pete or Crystal
> 1 to 2 cups loosely packed fresh dill leaves to taste
> fresh lemon juice to taste

Have ready a bowl of ice cubes. Drop the shrimp into a large pot of highly seasoned boiling water until the shrimp are just done—no more than 3 minutes. Drain them, then plunge the shrimp into ice to stop the cooking. Peel the shrimp when they're cool enough and set aside in the refrigerator.

Add the asparagus to a pot of boiling water and cook, covered, until just done, 5 to 10 minutes, depending on the size of the stalks. Test them frequently, and the instant the tips become tender, remove them from the heat, drain, and spread out on a kitchen towel to cool.

Make the mayonnaise as described, doubling the amounts, omitting the lemon juice, and adding the 1/4 cup prepared mustard while the mayonnaise is still in the blender. Add the hot sauce and dill and blend until well incorporated.

Cut the asparagus into 2-inch pieces and toss gently with the shrimp and mayonnaise. Refrigerate overnight. The next day, correct the seasoning with salt, pepper, and lemon juice, and serve over salad greens.
Serves 8 as an appetizer or 4 for lunch

Pickled Shrimp

The best salad I know is a good mound of these atop fresh greens or avocado slices. There are two secrets to this recipe: the quality of the olive oil and the quantity of bay leaves—which may seem extravagant.

On the coast of South Carolina, where I live, many people grow bay. My friend Billie Burn, author of *Stirrin' the Pots on Daufuskie,* sends me prunings every year from her home on that barrier island. Go to your natural foods store and buy bay leaves in bulk. They'll be fresher and a lot less expensive than those bottled ones in the grocery store.

1 tablespoon salt

1 cup extra-virgin olive oil

⅓ cup fresh lemon juice

1 teaspoon mustard seeds

1 teaspoon celery seeds

2 garlic cloves, minced

2 pounds small to medium shrimp, 45 to 50 per pound, cooked and peeled (Chapter 2)

25 to 30 bay leaves

1 medium onion, thinly sliced

Sterilize a quart jar in a pot of boiling water and set aside. Combine the salt, oil, lemon juice, mustard and celery seeds, and garlic and set aside. Place about 15 shrimp in the jar, then add a layer of about 4 bay leaves, then a layer of onion slices. Continue making layers until the jar is filled and all the ingredients are used. You'll have to pack the jar fairly tightly to get them to fit. You may have to push down on the ingredients a little. (I use a tall, narrow olive or capers jar.)

When the jar is full, stir the oil mixture well and pour slowly into the jar. Use a fork or a spatula to run down the sides to release air bubbles and to make sure the jar fills. If well packed, the jar will hold all the ingredients perfectly. Put the lid on the jar and turn it over to make sure everything is coated with oil and the air bubbles are out. Open the jar again and push the ingredients down again so that they are covered with a film of oil.

Refrigerate for at least 24 hours before serving. When you remove shrimp from the jar, be sure to use a clean fork, never a finger. Before returning the jar to the refrigerator, make sure the remaining ingredients are covered with a film of oil and they will last easily for 2 weeks if you can keep out of them!

Makes 1 quart

Tomato, Sweet Corn, Fried Okra, and Smoked Bacon Salad with Chive Dressing

When Birmingham chef Chris Hastings gave me the recipe for his signature salad, he admitted, "This salad is neither short nor terribly easy." I took one look at all the ingredients and knew that I wouldn't prepare it. Shortly thereafter, there was a spring hot spell in Charleston. I went to the farmers' market and found delicious tomatoes, okra, and corn from Florida; I pulled butter beans from my freezer that I had put away the summer before. Then I went back to Chris's letter:

> *Of all the tomato salads I have seen, made, eaten, and hope to find, this one is my favorite. It combines the best of our southern summer vegetables in an unusual way. The common ingredients are not too dissimilar from succotash, but oh so different: old southern flavors with a little fine tuning and a lighter hand.*

I realized that I would be cooking all of those vegetables to go with dinner anyway, so I put a chicken and some new potatoes in the oven to roast and went about making this "salad" to round out our early summer meal. Though it's a bit fussier than the cooking I usually do, and it does make

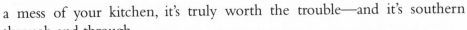

a mess of your kitchen, it's truly worth the trouble—and it's southern through and through.

I've made this salad with one tomato, although Chris includes four kinds. What's most important, he says, is quality: Try to get organically grown, but at least good local tomatoes.

FOR THE CHIVE DRESSING:

a handful of chives

1 egg yolk

2 large garlic cloves, finely minced

juice of 1 small lemon

salt and freshly ground black pepper to taste

1 cup olive oil

¼ cup crème fraîche (Chapter 6)

FOR THE SALAD:

2 large Beefsteak or other big red slicing tomatoes

2 large Golden Delight or other yellow slicing tomatoes

2 Big Rainbow or other flavorful, deeply lobed tomatoes

½ pint Sweet 100 tomatoes or other cherry tomatoes

30 very small okra pods

¼ cup buttermilk

¼ pound fresh or home-frozen butter beans

¼ cup chopped onion

salt to taste

1 small fresh thyme sprig

¼ pound old-fashioned smoked bacon, finely sliced into 24 slices, or 13 slices of any good smoked bacon, cut in half

3 ears of fresh sweet corn such as Silver Queen, shucked

2 scallions, both white and green parts, thinly sliced

scant ½ cup balsamic vinegar

¼ cup olive oil

¼ **cup extra-virgin olive oil**

freshly ground black pepper to taste

¼ **cup corn flour (see Ingredients and Sources)**

¼ **cup cornmeal**

¼ **cup all-purpose flour**

1 quart vegetable oil

Preheat the oven to 400°.

First make the chive dressing: Finely chop the chives and put them in a small bowl. Add the egg yolk, garlic, lemon juice, and salt and pepper. Mix well.

Vigorously whisk in the olive oil, creating a smooth dressing. Whisk in the crème fraîche. If the dressing is too thick, whisk in a splash of water. You should have 1¼ cups.

For the salad, wash and core the tomatoes and set aside at room temperature. Trim the okra stems and place the okra in a small bowl with the buttermilk. Toss every so often to keep them coated.

Put the butter beans and chopped onion in a saucepan, cover with salted water, add the thyme and the bacon trimmings from the old-fashioned bacon (or the 13th slice from the presliced), and simmer until just tender, about 20 minutes. Set aside.

Place the bacon slices on a sheet pan and bake in the preheated oven until golden brown and crisp, about 15 to 20 minutes.

Place the corn in a pot of boiling salted water. Remove as soon as it is tender (just a few minutes), then shave the corn kernels from the cobs into the butter beans.

Place the scallions in a small bowl, then add the balsamic vinegar. Make a vinaigrette by whisking in the olive oils. Season with salt and pepper. Add 3 tablespoons to the corn and butter beans.

Combine the corn flour, cornmeal, and all-purpose flour in a medium bowl. Season generously with salt and pepper and toss well. In a large pot, heat the vegetable oil to 350° over medium-high heat.

While the oil is heating, slice the tomatoes (except the Sweet 100s), season with salt and pepper, and splash well with the vinaigrette. Arrange the tomato slices attractively on 6 plates. Put a few of the whole small tomatoes on each plate.

Drain the okra from the buttermilk, toss them in the cornmeal mix, and shake off the excess. Fry in the oil for a few minutes until golden brown, working in batches if necessary. Drain on racks.

Using a slotted spoon, scatter the corn and bean mix over the tomatoes. Add a pile of fried okra to each plate, then top each salad with 4 slices of bacon, forming a square.

Drizzle the chive dressing over each dish and serve immediately.

Serves 6

WINE:
Crisp Chenin Blanc, Vouvray or one from a cool area like Oregon

Hoppin' John Salad

Hoppin' John, the beans and rice pilau that we southerners eat on New Year's for good luck, is usually cooked with a piece of seasoned pork and served hot with rich corn bread and greens. This cold version is welcome any time of the year. Vinaigrettes are classically made in the proportion of three parts oil to one part acid, but I find that this salad calls for more lemon juice than usual.

> **2 cups cooked and drained small southern beans such as black-eyed peas**
>
> **3 cups cooked long-grain white rice**
>
> **½ cup chopped red onion, about ½ medium**
>
> **¼ cup chopped celery**
>
> **1 jalapeño chili, seeded and finely chopped**
>
> **½ cup loosely packed fresh herbs such as parsley, mint, and chervil**
>
> **1 garlic clove, peeled**
>
> **½ teaspoon salt**
>
> **juice of about 2 lemons to taste**
>
> **¼ cup olive oil**
>
> **freshly ground black pepper to taste**

Toss the beans, rice, onion, celery, and chili together in a large mixing bowl. Place the herbs and garlic clove on a cutting board and sprinkle with the salt. Chop very finely. You should have 3 or 4 tablespoons of garlic–herb mixture. Add to the beans and rice and toss. Add 1 or 2 tablespoons of lemon juice to the olive oil and whisk together, then pour over the salad, tossing well. Correct the seasoning with lemon juice, salt, and pepper.

Serves 8 to 10

Wine:
Gewürztraminer

Breads

Most of the breads associated with the South are quick breads leavened with baking powder—biscuits and corn bread—or crackerlike party foods such as cheese straws and benne wafers. Bill Neal's excellent *Biscuits, Spoonbread, and Sweet Potato Pie* delves deeply into the history and folklore of traditional southern baking, with some 300 recipes. Here are a few basics and some contemporary variations. If I had to, I probably *could* live by my corn bread alone.

Biscuits

A lot has been written about the lowly southern biscuit, a chemically leavened quick bread that developed as a real convenience with the availability of baking powder in the nineteenth century. As I wrote in *Hoppin' John's Lowcountry Cooking,* the perfect biscuit is largely in the choice of flour. Anyone can make a good biscuit with soft southern flour (see Ingredients and Sources).

The flakiest biscuits are made with fresh lard, which I prefer. I make it myself by melting fresh pork fat and straining it. It keeps for a long time refrigerated. It has close to half the saturated fat (cholesterol) of butter. I avoid commercial shortenings and, for that matter, all processed foods, because it's hard to know exactly what you're getting. Recent USDA studies show that vegetable shortenings have three milligrams of saturated fat per tablespoon (lard has five), but because they're partially hydrogenated they contain damaging trans fats that actually raise cholesterol. Pass the butter, please!

It's a good idea to weigh the flour and shortening you use when baking and to maintain a ratio of four to one for both biscuit and pie doughs. Avoid touching any dough other than yeast breads with your hands; you'll just toughen it. Use your fingertips and work lightly.

Good biscuit recipes are in any southern cookbook; these are newfangled variations. If you omit the orange and sugar from the Orange Biscuits, you'll have a classic southern biscuit.

Orange Biscuits

Southern biscuits are nothing more than English scones without the sugar. In this version a sugar cube soaked in orange juice glazes a biscuit flavored with orange peel. These are wonderful for breakfast, but they go well with Oeufs en Gelée (Chapter 5) at lunch, too.

> 1 orange
>
> ³/₄ pound soft southern flour (see Ingredients and Sources), about 3 cups, plus a little for dusting
>
> 1 teaspoon baking soda
>
> 1 teaspoon cream of tartar
>
> 1 teaspoon salt
>
> 3 ounces chilled fresh lard or other shortening, about ¹/₂ cup
>
> ³/₄ cup buttermilk
>
> 10 sugar cubes

Preheat the oven to 425°. Grate the zest from the orange into a large mixing bowl. Squeeze the juice into another container and set aside.

Sift the flour, soda, cream of tartar, and salt together into the mixing bowl with the orange zest. Cut in the lard with a pastry blender or 2 knives until it is uniformly incorporated into the flour and there are no large clumps. Working swiftly, fold in the buttermilk a little at a time with a rubber spatula until it is just blended in smoothly.

Dust a counter lightly with some flour and scoop up the dough onto the counter with the spatula. *Lightly* work the dough, working only with the fingertips, until it is blended evenly. Roll it out about ¹/₂ inch thick and cut into ten 2-inch biscuits, using a metal biscuit cutter dipped in flour and a quick, clean motion. Do not twist the biscuit cutter; you should be punching the biscuits out of the dough. Place the biscuits close to each other on a baking sheet.

Dip the sugar cubes one at a time in orange juice and press each into the top of one of the biscuits.

Bake for 10 to 15 minutes or until the biscuits are lightly browned. The melted sugar can burn the roof of your mouth, so be sure to have your diners spread it around a little before eating them. These biscuits should be eaten hot, but if carefully wrapped, they can be reheated later.

Makes 10 biscuits

Tomato Biscuits

I found this recipe in a cookbook sponsored by the Orangeburg (my hometown), South Carolina, PTA in 1948. The biscuits are a beautiful coral color and a delight on the palate. Omit the salt if you're using a heavily salted canned juice or if you plan to serve them with slivers of country ham.

> **2 cups soft southern flour (see Ingredients and Sources), plus some for dusting**
>
> **1 teaspoon cream of tartar**
>
> **¹/₂ teaspoon baking soda**
>
> **¹/₂ teaspoon salt**
>
> **1 heaped tablespoon (4 teaspoons) cold fresh lard or other shortening**
>
> **³/₄ cup tomato or mixed vegetable juice such as V-8**

Preheat the oven to 425°. Sift the dry ingredients into a mixing bowl. Cut in the shortening with a pastry blender or 2 knives until it is uniformly incorporated into the flour. Pour the juice into the flour mixture and blend in quickly with a rubber spatula until smooth.

Dust a counter with flour and scrape the dough out onto it. Dust your hands with flour and lightly work the dough until it is smooth and not sticky. Roll it out about ¹/₂ inch thick and cut with a floured biscuit cutter into 2¹/₂-inch biscuits. Place on a baking sheet and bake for about 10 minutes or until lightly browned.

Makes 10 to 12 biscuits

Goat Cheese Biscuits

These cocktail biscuits are very delicately flavored cream biscuits, with just a hint of chèvre (see Ingredients and Sources). They're perfect with a glass of sherry. Serve them with herbed butter (recipe follows).

2 cups sifted unbleached all-purpose flour, preferably southern (see Ingredients and Sources)

2 teaspoons baking powder

$1/2$ teaspoon salt

3 ounces mild goat cheese, 5 tablespoons

$5/8$ cup whipping cream

Preheat the oven to 425°. Sift the dry ingredients together into a mixing bowl, then cut in the goat cheese with a pastry blender or 2 knives. Add the cream, blending with a spatula. Turn the dough out onto a lightly floured surface and roll out $1/2$ inch thick. Punch biscuits out with a floured $1^{1}/_{2}$-inch biscuit cutter and place, not touching, on a baking sheet. Bake for 10 to 15 minutes. Serve warm or at room temperature with herbed butter. *Makes 24 biscuits*

HERBED BUTTER

This butter is a variation of the classic maître d'hôtel butter traditionally used on grilled fish and meats. Rosemary and thyme accentuate the flavor of the goat cheese in the biscuits. The butter can be frozen for later use. It is especially good with grilled lamb and with other meat and poultry dishes with strong garlic and wine seasonings.

$1/2$ teaspoon salt

freshly ground black pepper to taste

1 tablespoon parsley leaves

$1/2$ teaspoon fresh rosemary leaves

$1/2$ teaspoon fresh thyme leaves

$3/4$ cup butter, $1^{1}/_{2}$ sticks, softened

1 teaspoon fresh lemon juice

Put the salt, pepper, and herbs in a blender and blend for about 20 seconds. Add the butter and the lemon juice and blend again until well mixed. Fill a ramekin with the mixture and serve at room temperature. *Makes ³/₄ cup*

The Best Corn Bread

This is the corn bread recipe from my first book, *Hoppin' John's Lowcountry Cooking,* but it bears repeating here. It is, quite simply, the best—truly southern, using no wheat flour or sugar, with a golden brown crust from the sizzling cast-iron pan. The recipe is really Appalachian, but throughout the country good cooks have discovered the magical combination of freshly ground cornmeal and a well-seasoned skillet. This is my most often requested recipe. It has run in dozens of newspaper and magazine articles, including *The New York Times Magazine* and *Vogue.* A week doesn't go by that someone doesn't call and tell me, "It really *is* the best!"

To obtain a golden brown crust, you will need a 9- or 10-inch well-seasoned, never-washed cast-iron skillet. If you don't have one, go buy a new one and wash it once. Render some fresh lard in it by slowly melting it either on top of the stove or in a low oven. Wipe it out and never put soapy water in it again.

Serve this corn bread with fish stews and rice dishes, gumbos, greens, and salads. It is also delicious for breakfast with sorghum or cane syrup. Many southerners dunk leftover corn bread in a cold glass of buttermilk, but today's cultured buttermilk just ain't the same thing. Most people will want more than one slice.

A few variations of the recipe follow.

1 egg
2 cups buttermilk
1³/₄ cups stone-ground whole-grain cornmeal (see note)

1½ to 2 teaspoons strained bacon grease

1 scant teaspoon baking powder

1 scant teaspoon salt

1 scant teaspoon baking soda

Mix the egg into the buttermilk in a mixing bowl, then add the cornmeal and beat it well into the batter, which should be thin. Put enough bacon grease in the skillet to coat the bottom and sides with a thin film, then put it in a cold oven and begin preheating the oven to 450°. When the oven has reached 450°, the bacon grease should be just at the point of smoking. Add the baking powder, salt, and soda to the batter, beat in well, and pour the batter all at once into the hot pan. Return to the oven to bake for 15 to 20 minutes or until the top just begins to brown. Turn the loaf out on a plate and serve with butter.

Makes about 8 slices

Variations

Jalapeño Corn Bread:

Add 1 seeded and chopped jalapeño pepper to the batter before baking.

Confetti Corn Bread:

Place ¼ cup each chopped red and green pepper, scallions, and corn kernels in a kitchen towel and squeeze out all the excess moisture before adding them to the batter.

Hushpuppies:

Add ½ cup chopped onion to the batter, then add ¼ to ½ cup corn flour (see Ingredients and Sources) or unbleached all-purpose flour to thicken the batter so that it can be spooned. Drop by teaspoonfuls into 365° deep fat and fry until golden, about 3 minutes. Makes about 4 dozen.

Crostini:

Allow the corn bread to cool, then wrap in aluminum foil and refrigerate for a couple of days if you wish. Preheat a gas grill to medium-high or build

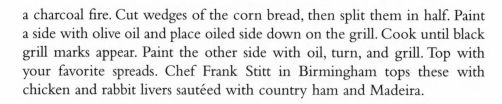

a charcoal fire. Cut wedges of the corn bread, then split them in half. Paint a side with olive oil and place oiled side down on the grill. Cook until black grill marks appear. Paint the other side with oil, turn, and grill. Top with your favorite spreads. Chef Frank Stitt in Birmingham tops these with chicken and rabbit livers sautéed with country ham and Madeira.

NOTE:
This recipe is foolproof, but if you want your corn bread to taste like mine, order my freshly stone-ground, whole-grain cornmeal (see Ingredients and Sources).

Corn Cakes

These fritters are one of an infinite variety of corn breads found in the South. They're particularly good with the Duck Etouffée in Chapter 4, but if you're serving them with that dish or other spicy food, leave out the jalapeño.

2 cups corn kernels, either blanched
    fresh (see note) or defrosted frozen
½ cup finely chopped scallion, white and some
    of the green
½ cup finely chopped peeled red pepper or
    canned pimiento
1 jalapeño chili, seeded and finely chopped, optional
½ teaspoon ground cumin
1 teaspoon salt
2 eggs, separated
½ cup whipping cream
2 tablespoons melted butter, plus butter for frying
2 cups corn flour or masa harina (see Ingredients
    and Sources)

Preheat the oven to its lowest setting and place a plate or two inside to warm. In a large mixing bowl, combine the corn, scallion, red pepper, chili, cumin, and salt. Mix the egg yolks with the cream and add to the vegetables, mixing well. Add the butter and mix well, then mix in the corn flour.

Beat the egg whites until they hold soft peaks, then fold into the mixture. Melt some butter in a large frying pan over medium heat, then add 3 large spoonfuls of the batter at a time to the pan, flattening them out into patties about 3 inches wide and ½ inch thick. Fry for about 2 or 3 minutes on each side, then transfer to a plate kept warm in a low oven while you fry the remaining cakes.
Makes 12 cakes

NOTE:
To blanch fresh corn, simply place freshly shucked ears in a pot of boiling water, cover, and turn off the heat. Let them sit for at least 10 minutes in the water.

Real Bread

What anyone knows of breadmaking is learned through experience. Making real bread—bread with a good crust and crumb and an earthy flavor of grain—is neither difficult nor time-consuming. It involves few skills and the one virtue of patience. Real bread—bread made from flour, water, yeast, and salt (and nothing more)—for so long a rarity in America, has finally resurfaced on our tables. Bakeries are once again making honest loaves of what we have come to call European-style breads, even as those breads become harder to find in Europe.

For years, bakeries that produced real bread were all but nonexistent except in a few large cities; they were even rarer in the South, where we have clung to our quick breads leavened with baking powder. Home bakers faced a next-to-impossible task finding a very hot oven, the flour, good yeast, and even a good book to guide them. Elizabeth David's *English Bread and Yeast Cookery,* published in England in 1977, was virtually the only text available on the subject for 15 years; while comprehensive, it focused solely on the breads of England. Most of the written word on real bread that has influenced my baking over the years has come from the hand of Karen Hess, who prepared the American edition of David's work and who continues to urge a restoration of the historical loaf of real bread—the classic yeasted white loaf—to the American table.

Offering a recipe for real bread is perhaps a perfunctory gesture because, as Karen Hess has demonstrated repeatedly, the only recipe one needs to make genuine bread is Mary Randolph's, from *The Virginia House-Wife* (1824), the facsimile edition of which was annotated with historical notes and commentaries by Hess in 1984. The recipe produces a classic, hearty white bread with dense crumb and thick crust. Here is my wording of the recipe, using Hess's brilliant instructions for simulating the conditions of a wood-fired brick oven at home. I offer just one difference in technique: directly mixing the dough rather than using the sponge method.

The recipe specifies several items that you probably don't have in your kitchen, but I've included it anyway because it really does produce a loaf that is as close to the real thing as possible. I use the best unbleached white flour I can find, fresh yeast, fine sea salt, and spring water. I advise you to do the same. If you can't find fresh yeast at your natural foods store, go to the best baker in town and ask him to sell you some; it costs pennies and keeps well in the freezer for months. You should weigh the flour and yeast. The flour that Mary Randolph used would have been soft flour, but do *not* use an overprocessed one. Use unbleached all-purpose or bread flour; I like to use about ½ cup whole-wheat flour as part of the mix. The amount of yeast is slightly more than what Karen Hess uses, but her overnight sponge requires less yeast.

I mix and knead my loaves by hand. Most important, no matter how the dough is mixed, is time: you must be patient and allow for a slow rise. Because my counters are too tall for me to work at comfortably, I place my mixing bowl (I use a large ceramic bowl from an antique washbasin) atop a bar stool fitted with a cushion. The bowl is the right height for me, and the padding atop the stool keeps the bowl from slipping and allows it to give a little with the kneading. It's really a very comfortable way to knead bread.

The brick oven is simulated with an overturned flowerpot that has the shape of a domed beehive. It is 6 inches across the base, and the top has a diameter of 13 inches. It fits upside down perfectly on a 13-inch pizza stone. An 8-inch clay tray with a deep rim into which the pot sits snugly acts as a cap. I use welder's gloves on my hands and long sleeves on my arms when opening and closing the oven. A pizza peel, available at restaurant supply houses, is helpful as well.

Of course you can bake this bread with dry yeast (¹/₄ teaspoon is plenty) and without the flowerpot. For a good crust, though, you should at least use the superheated pizza stone and mist the inside of the oven with water at 20-minute intervals. Otherwise follow the recipe.

All the ingredients should be at room temperature.

1¹/₂ cups spring water
¹/₂ ounce fresh compressed yeast
1 tablespoon pure salt
20 ounces flour, about 4 cups

Warm the water to no more than 115°. Mix in the yeast and allow it to sit for about 10 minutes to proof. It should have a fresh, not sour, aroma.

In a large mixing bowl, add the salt to the flour and stir to combine. Make a well in the center. Pour the water and yeast mixture into the well and stir with a wooden spoon until it becomes too stiff to stir. Then, using your hands, continue to mix the dough. It will take about 10 minutes. When it is thoroughly blended, mixing becomes kneading.

Knead until the dough is smooth and elastic, 5 to 10 minutes. Shape the dough into a ball, wipe the rim of the bowl clean with a damp towel, and cover with plastic wrap and then a towel. Place in a draft-free spot until the dough has doubled in volume. This may take anywhere from 4 to 8 hours: your choice of yeast, flour, salt, and water—all variables—are further varied by room temperature and the natural yeasts in the air. (Carol Field, an authority on Italian baking, told me that her San Francisco kitchen became so filled with wild yeasts that she could make bread from flour and water!)

When the dough has doubled, remove it from the bowl to a lightly floured surface. Punch it down and knead it for a few minutes until smooth again. Shape it into a ball, leave it on the counter, and place the mixing bowl upside down over it.

Open the oven and remove all but the bottom rack, placed on the lowest position. Place the pizza stone with the overturned flowerpot on it and preheat the oven to 500°. Place the clay tray in the sink filled with water to soak. Karen Hess suggests practicing all maneuvering beforehand, with a cold oven.

When the dough has risen by about a third and the oven has preheated, work quickly but methodically to get the dough into the simulated kiln. Open the oven and, using welder's gloves, remove the flowerpot from the oven. Quickly slash a tic-tac-toe pattern in shallow cuts with a razor blade on the top of the dough (slashes allow the bread to expand). Slip the pizza peel up under the dough and transfer it to the pizza stone with a flick of the wrists. Cover the dough again with the flowerpot, then put the soaked clay tray on top of it all. Immediately close the oven door and turn down the heat to 400°.

Bake the bread for a good hour, turning down the heat again to 350° after about 30 minutes to simulate the falling heat of a wood-fired oven. You can check the bread at 50 minutes to see how it is, removing the flowerpot. It may well be done. A rap on the bottom of the loaf with the knuckles should resound as if hollow. If the rap produces a dull thud, let it bake some more.

Let the bread cool completely before cutting and cut with a serrated bread knife. Store in paper, not plastic.

Makes a 2-pound loaf

Damon's Sally Lunn

Damon Fowler of Savannah is a culinary historian and food writer who has made commendable efforts to restore classical southern cooking to its former glory. This recipe for authentic, old-fashioned Sally Lunn, from his *Classical Southern Cooking,* contains no sugar or baking powder. It is the classic English variation of brioche that has been served at tea for centuries. Damon puts the dough into a circular cake pan or makes a dozen large rolls. I like to put it in a regular loaf pan, then use the rich bread for sandwiches. Damon suggests, "If you can get good cream, try Elizabeth David's recipe: omit the butter and substitute heavy cream (minimum 36 percent milk fat) for the milk." I like to add some freshly ground black pepper.

You'll need to start this recipe early in the day (or early afternoon if it's for dinner) because the dough needs time to rise.

> **1 cup milk**
> **¼ teaspoon preservative-free active dry yeast**
> **3 eggs**
> **20 ounces unbleached all-purpose flour, about 4 cups, plus**
> **flour for dusting**
> **1 teaspoon salt**
> **4 tablespoons butter, ½ stick, at room temperature**
> **freshly ground black pepper, optional**

Six to 8 hours before you plan to serve it (Damon suggests before you go to work) or the night before, scald the milk and let it cool slightly to around 90°.

Add the yeast and let it dissolve. Break the eggs into a bowl and beat them lightly. Stir the milk and yeast into the eggs.

Put the flour and salt in a large mixing bowl and mix well. With a large fork, work in the butter until the mixture resembles coarse meal. Make a well in the center and pour in the milk and egg mixture. Mix the liquid in well with the fork until the dough is smooth, then turn it out onto a lightly floured surface.

Knead the dough lightly for about 5 minutes, then gather it into a ball. Wipe out the bowl and return the dough to it. Cover with a damp linen kitchen towel folded double or plastic wrap and set it aside to rise, about 4 to 6 hours or overnight.

When the dough has doubled in bulk, lightly punch it down and knead it again lightly for about 1 minute, working in some pepper if desired.

Lightly grease and flour a loaf pan, a Bundt or tube cake pan, or large muffin tins.

Dust the dough with flour and roll it into a log that will fit into the loaf pan (or a longer one for the tube pan or 12 equal balls for rolls). Place in the pans (gently pressing the ends together if you're using the tube pan), cover with a damp towel, and set aside until it has doubled once again, about 1 to 2 hours.

Position a rack in the lower third of the oven and preheat to 400°. Bake the Sally Lunn until the top is a light gold and the crumb is cooked through, about 30 minutes for the loaves or 20 minutes for the buns.
Makes 1 loaf

Arabic Bread

Florida is rarely thought of as southern, though the northern part of the state shares history, geography, and culture with the rest of the Old South. Jacksonville, with its stately live oaks, meandering rivers, and barrier islands, resembles the neighboring Georgia Lowcountry. Not far south of the city is the "frost line" that divides the subtropical from tropical Florida, the very "southern" northern part of the state with the vacation playground for which the southern half of the state is best known.

Jacksonville is a huge city—the largest incorporated city in the United States in terms of physical size. It spreads from the state line in the north to the ocean in the east, through rolling farmland and subtropical swamp. The city center is home to many insurance companies; their headquarters are dramatic modern office buildings that rise up from the St. Johns River in stark contrast to the sleepy live oaks and palmettos that hug the banks of the river in suburban areas.

Many of those suburbs are neighborhoods built in the 1920s, when the pride in the state's Spanish heritage was at an all-time high. Houses are tiled and stuccoed. Many churches and buildings in shopping districts resemble the Spanish-motif structures built in southern California at the same time. It was during that building craze that Middle Easterners began moving to Jax and opening their restaurants and sandwich shops. From Syria, Lebanon, and Palestine they have continued to come to the city so that it now has a larger percentage of Middle Easterners than any other American city. Pita is the daily bread of many of the city's inhabitants. It has even replaced Sunbeam (the Wonder bread of the South) in the convenience stores.

Joe Assi is a Lebanese baker who has provided the city with khubz, or Arabic bread, for 30 years. Though he used to make 12,000 loaves of bread each day, he has reduced his daily output to only 2,400 loaves. "There are other bakers now, I am thankful," he told me from his colorful Gold Room restaurant on Beach Boulevard.

Most of us know this type of bread as pita, though Joe Assi and his wife never called it that. If there is no pita baker in your neighborhood as there is likely to be in Jacksonville, try making it at home. It's easy, delicious, and makes wonderful sandwich bread. Several fast-food chains in Jacksonville use this pocket bread to hold "sheikburgers" and "desert riders." Pita is especially good for picnics and is often served with tabbouleh, hummus, and baba ghanouj, traditional accompaniments that are now widely favored in the South.

> ½ ounce fresh compressed yeast or 1 teaspoon
> preservative-free active dry yeast plus ¼ teaspoon sugar
> or honey
> 1¼ cups warm water, 110° to 120°
> 1 pound unbleached all-purpose flour, about 3½ cups, plus
> flour for dusting
> 1½ teaspoons salt
> olive oil

Dissolve the yeast (and, if you're using dry yeast, the sugar or honey) in about ¼ cup of the water. Leave in a warm place for about 10 minutes to proof; it should be slightly bubbly.

In a warmed large mixing bowl, mix the flour and salt. Make a well in the center, pour in the yeast, and mix in thoroughly. Gradually add the remaining warm water as you knead the dough until it is elastic and smooth, about 15 minutes. It should be firm enough to roll with a rolling pin and should no longer stick to your fingers. Rub a little olive oil over the top of the dough so that it does not dry out and cover the bowl with a blanket or towel. Leave in a warm place to rise for about 2 hours or until it is doubled in size.

Punch the dough down and knead again for a few minutes to make the dough uniformly smooth again. Cut the dough into 6 equal parts, then shape into 6 balls. Roll the balls on a floured surface into circles ¼ inch thick and 6 or 7 inches in diameter. Dust with flour and cover with the towel or blanket again, allowing to rise for 45 minutes to 1 hour. Meanwhile, preheat the oven to 500° and oil 2 baking sheets.

Bake the bread for 5 to 7 minutes until the bottom is light brown, then broil the tops for 30 seconds, until light brown. Remove from the oven and immediately wrap in towels. Serve warm or cool.

Makes 6 loaves

Anchovy Puffs

Here's another recipe from *Orangeburg's Choice Recipes,* a cookbook assembled in 1948 as a fund-raiser for my hometown's PTA. These are an easy, delicious appetizer to serve at a cocktail party or with a glass of wine before dinner.

> **½ cup butter, 1 stick**
> **3 ounces cream cheese, 1 small package**
> **1 cup unbleached all-purpose flour, plus flour for dusting**
> **anchovy paste in a squeeze tube**

Cream together the butter and cream cheese. Mix in the flour, wrap the dough in plastic, and refrigerate for at least an hour to chill well.

About 15 or 20 minutes before you're ready to serve them, preheat the oven to 400°.

Remove the dough from the refrigerator and dust a counter and a rolling pin with flour. Roll the dough out very thin into a square about 14 inches wide. Cut the dough into 2-inch squares; you should have about 4 dozen of them.

Squeeze a dime-size bit of anchovy paste onto the center of each square, then fold a corner of each square diagonally across the paste to meet the opposite corner, forming triangles. Transfer the triangles to baking sheets, lightly pinching them together as you do.

Bake for 10 minutes. Serve warm.

Makes about 48 triangles

WINE:
Zinfandel—a fresh and fruity style like Seghesio's

Blue Cheese Walnut Crackers

Benne wafers and cheese straws have long graced the tables of southern cocktail parties. The combination of butter, flour, cheese, and nuts is well proven. I developed these for a party, but serve them with soups as well.

> 2½ cups unbleached all-purpose flour
> 1½ teaspoons salt
> 1 stick butter, ½ cup, softened
> ¾ pound blue cheese, crumbled
> 1 cup chopped walnuts

Preheat the oven to 350°. Sift together the flour and salt. Cream the butter in a mixing bowl, then work in the cheese. Add the dry ingredients, then the nuts, mixing it all well together. Don't worry if the dough seems too dry; work it in your hands until it comes together in a ball.

Pinch off 1-inch pieces of the dough and roll them between your palms to form little balls, then flatten each out to a circle about 1½ to 2 inches in diameter. Place on baking sheets and bake until golden brown, about 20 to 25 minutes.

Makes about 5 dozen crackers

Banana Pecan Pancakes

Most southerners forgo traditional breakfasts these days, but we all enjoy an occasional old-fashioned eye-opener of pancakes drenched in good cane syrup with bacon or sausage. These buttermilk pancakes are made special with the addition of fruit and nuts, and they make sense as a hearty breakfast.

        2 cups unbleached all-purpose flour
        1 teaspoon baking soda
        ¹/₂ teaspoon salt
        2 eggs, separated
        2 cups buttermilk
        2 tablespoons melted butter
        ¹/₄ cup chopped pecans
        1 or 2 bananas, peeled

Preheat the oven to its lowest setting. Preheat a well-seasoned griddle to medium-hot. Meanwhile, sift the flour, soda, and salt. In a small mixing bowl, beat the egg whites until they form soft peaks. In a large bowl, mix the yolks with the buttermilk, then stir in the sifted ingredients. Stir in the butter and nuts and mix well. Fold in the egg whites.

Ladle batter onto the hot griddle in circles about 4 inches in diameter and ¹/₄ inch thick. Slice the banana a little thinner than the pancake and place about 4 slices on each pancake. Cook until the pancakes are full of holes and have begun to brown on the edges. Turn and cook on the other side. Transfer the pancakes to a plate and place in the warm oven while you cook the rest of the pancakes.

Serve immediately with butter and syrup, with breakfast sausage or bacon on the side.

Serves 4

Waffles with Creamed Chicken

When I was growing up, my mother cooked three meals a day, six days a week. On Sundays, there was breakfast and a huge "dinner" in the middle of the day. We were left to fend for ourselves on Sunday night. Waffles have always been, since childhood, one of my favorite Sunday night suppers. Dried beef or virtually any leftovers such as chicken and turkey are used in this simple and comforting dish. Though usually made with a béchamel-like sauce, this easy version to serve two is made with leftover chicken and stock. You can easily multiply the recipe.

I often make a big pot of stock on rainy Sundays with an entire large stewing hen. I quickly assemble this meal on Sunday night, then use the remaining meat and broth throughout the week in soups and stews.

FOR THE WAFFLES:

> **2 eggs, separated**
>
> **1 cup unbleached all-purpose flour**
>
> **1 teaspoon baking powder**
>
> **½ teaspoon baking soda**
>
> **pinch of salt**
>
> **1 cup buttermilk**
>
> **4 tablespoons melted butter, ½ stick**

FOR THE CHICKEN:

> **2 tablespoons butter**
>
> **1 cup chopped onion, about 1 medium**
>
> **1 cup finely sliced mushrooms**
>
> **2 cups cooked, boned, and cut-up chicken**
>
> **¼ cup dry white wine, preferably the one you'll drink with this meal**
>
> **1 cup whipping cream**
>
> **1 cup chicken stock**
>
> **salt and freshly ground pepper to taste**

Preheat the waffle iron. Beat the egg whites until they form soft peaks. Set aside. Sift the dry ingredients together into a bowl. Add the egg yolks to the buttermilk and mix well, then add the liquid to the dry ingredients, mixing well. Stir in the melted butter, then fold in the egg whites. Follow the manufacturer's instructions on your waffle iron to make 4 large waffles. Preheat the oven to its lowest setting and place 2 dinner plates inside to warm. Transfer the waffles to the plates in the oven while you prepare the creamed chicken.

Melt the butter in a heavy skillet over medium heat. Add the onion and cook until it's becoming transparent, about 10 minutes. Add the mushrooms and cook until they've given off nearly all of their liquid, about 10 to 15 minutes. Fold the chicken meat into the mixture and toss well. Remove and set aside.

Add the wine to the pan and deglaze it, scraping up any little bits of flavor or scorched butter. Raise the heat and cook until the wine all but evaporates, then add the cream and the stock all at once. Continue to cook over high heat until the sauce is just shy of the consistency desired. Add the chicken mixture back to the pan, stir well, season to taste, and serve immediately over the waffles.

Serves 2

WINE:
An inexpensive California Chardonnay

Sweets

Here they are, folks, the rich and famous! Strawberry shortcake! Lemon meringue pie! Bread pudding with bourbon hard sauce! Butter pecan ice cream! You've heard about them before, but here are the best recipes. You may think there's nothing new here, but I tried dozens of recipes before choosing these superior ones.

I've also included a few newfangled sweets such as Poached Pears with Stilton Custard, Caramelized Pecan Tart, and Buttermilk Cheesecake to demonstrate the diverse skills and flavors of southern bakers.

We southerners do have a sweet tooth, but I think that most southerners today would forgo a piece of pie in the summer if they could have perfectly ripe melon instead—it might be sprinkled with a few turns of the pepper mill. Fresh fruit is often the only dessert—sliced ripe peaches are always welcome. And look at the surprising splash of vinegar on the strawberries in the first recipe. What delicious food!

Wines and Dessert

Some of the most extraordinary wines in the world are dessert wines—Banyuls, Sauternes, and Beaumes de Venise. However, rarely do I recommend that these wines accompany desserts. In most cases you should let these elegant, rich wines be the dessert themselves—or wait until *after* dessert to serve them.

I have recommended a beverage to accompany only a couple of these delicious desserts: a late-bottled vintage port is the one beverage that complements John's Poached Pears with Stilton Custard. And we always pour a little shot glass of sipping bourbon to have with his bourbon-drenched fruitcake. If there's some alcohol in the dessert, you might try a little glass of it to see how it goes with the dish.

Demi sec champagne seems to be more readily available these days. The excellent acidity coupled with a high dosage of sugar makes a fine complement to light desserts, but, in general, save Champagne for starters!

Debbie Marlowe

Fresh Strawberries and Sorbet

Strawberries have for decades come to the southern table nestled in shortcake and mounds of whipped cream, echoing the English traditions of antebellum plantations. I adore strawberry shortcake and have included a recipe in this book. But today's lighter palates will appreciate the following idea from northern Italy, where I ate the sweetest wild *white* strawberries barely sweetened with sugar.

The sorbet is meant to be used as an intermezzo between courses or as a cooling dessert when the first hot weather brings a wealth of berries and mint to southern gardens.

1 pint ripe fresh strawberries

1 teaspoon balsamic, berry, or red wine vinegar

1 teaspoon sugar

FOR THE SORBET:

¼ cup tightly packed fresh mint leaves

2 cups chilled semi-dry Champagne, Italian prosecco,
semi-seco cava, or another sparkling wine of your choice

At least an hour before you plan to eat them, hull the berries. Cut small berries in half, larger ones into a few pieces, dropping them into a nonreactive container. Sprinkle evenly with the vinegar, then the sugar, and toss well. Cover and refrigerate for an hour, then serve them for dessert or continue with the recipe for sorbet.

Place the prepared berries and mint leaves in a blender or food processor and blend until uniformly smooth. No large pieces of mint should be visible. Add the sparkling wine slowly so that it does not bubble over and continue to blend until uniformly smooth. Freeze according to the manufacturer's instructions for your ice cream freezer.

Makes about 3 cups or 6 servings

Fruit Salad Dressing

This recipe came to me from Cassandra McGee, who was raised in Anderson, in the "upcountry" of South Carolina. She calls it "Dorothy's mother's fruit salad dressing" because it came from her friend's mother, Minnie Payne Davis. She told me that she thinks that this is an old Payne family recipe.

This old-fashioned fruit custard is delightful over fresh fruit or as a garnish or dipping sauce for sweets such as fried bananas or angel food cake. I use strained fresh fruit juices in this recipe.

¼ cup fresh orange juice, strained
¼ cup fresh pineapple juice, strained
¼ cup fresh lemon juice, strained
2 eggs, lightly beaten
⅓ cup sugar
½ cup heavy cream, whipped

Put the strained fruit juice, eggs, and sugar in the top of a double boiler or in a stainless-steel bowl that will fit snugly over a simmering water bath. Mix well, then place over the simmering water. Cook until the mixture coats the back of a spoon, stirring constantly. Remove from the heat, cool, and refrigerate.

When cool, add the whipped cream. Store in the refrigerator; it will keep for about 2 weeks.
Makes about 1¹/₂ cups

Zesty Peach Compote with Ginger Ice Cream and Gingersnaps

JoAnn Yaeger is the best cook I know. She's one of those odd southerners who's as at home in New York City as she is in the West Virginia hinterlands where she was raised. With Hungarian and gypsy blood, she draws her often zaftig desserts more from Eastern Europe than from Appalachia.

JoAnn told me that this peach dish is her all-time favorite. It is unusual and exciting, though I do not recommend it for everyone: it *is* hot and spicy, qualities many people do not appreciate for dessert.

The recipe calls for freestone peaches in a tupelo honey glaze. It is served over candied ginger ice cream. JoAnn garnishes hers with a Tabasco spice cookie that I find impossible to make; instead I buy the best gingersnaps I can find and use them. JoAnn also uses, as a garnish, "fried strips of a good pie dough (which you can fold twice like feuilletées), chilled, rolled, cut into strips with a fluted cutter, tossed in sugar—vanilla sugar is best—and fried." I've stuck with my store-bought snaps.

FOR THE PEACHES AND SPICED SYRUP:

3 ripe unblemished freestone peaches

¾ cup tupelo or orange blossom honey

zest of ½ orange, cut into very thin slivers

2 tablespoons fresh orange juice

¾ teaspoon hot red pepper flakes

¾ teaspoon balsamic vinegar

2 teaspoons Grand Marnier

TO SERVE:

1 quart candied ginger ice cream (see variations with French Vanilla Ice Cream recipe)

gingersnaps

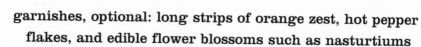

garnishes, optional: long strips of orange zest, hot pepper flakes, and edible flower blossoms such as nasturtiums

Submerge the peaches in boiling water for about 1 minute to loosen the skins. They should peel easily. Place the peeled peaches aside in the refrigerator.

Combine the remaining ingredients and steep in a saucepan over gentle heat until the flavors mingle thoroughly. You should have about 1 cup of syrup (6 servings) that will keep for several weeks at room temperature. Set aside to cool.

Divide the ice cream among 6 pasta bowls or plates, putting it in attractive mounds. Halve the peaches, remove the stones, and place a half on each plate or slice them and divide the slices among the plates, fanning out the slices on the plates.

Dribble the honey glaze over all, then stick a cookie or two in the mounds of ice cream. Garnish, if desired, with orange zest, 2 or 3 hot pepper flakes per plate, and edible flowers.

Serves 6

Fried Bananas

Banana fritters are a popular dessert throughout the tropical and subtropical regions of the world. I have banana trees growing in my Charleston courtyard; they produce a large banana that is never very sweet—perfect for this dish. I have always loved fried bananas, but chef JoAnn Yaeger's are simply the best. Her Hungarian roots show clearly in this one: She uses a rich palacsinta (Hungarian pancake) batter to dip the bananas in, then thoroughly coats them with dry bread crumbs. Purveyors to the restaurant trade sell bread crumbs that are for some reason called "Japanese"; they are very white (no crusts), large crumbs that are very dry. They produce the crispest crust. I keep stale baguettes in paper bags and allow them to dry rock hard; I grate them slowly through the large holes of a hand grater. The crumbs work just fine.

Fried bananas invite a host of garnishes: ice cream, chocolate sauce, fruit purees, or the fruit salad dressing earlier in this chapter. JoAnn makes a chocolate sauce like the icing for the chocolate cake here: divide the recipe in half, omit the walnuts, and add a little more honey or cream to make it more liquid. You can put a pool of the sauce on each plate or drizzle it all over the bananas. Everyone *loves* these bananas.

> **tasteless vegetable oil for frying**
> **½ cup soft southern or cake flour (see Ingredients**
> **　and Sources)**
> **pinch of salt**
> **pinch of sugar**
> **1 egg**
> **½ cup whipping cream**
> **1 tablespoon Grand Marnier**
> **4 firm ripe bananas, peeled and halved**
> **1 cup very dry bread crumbs**
> **sugar, ground cinnamon, and freshly grated nutmeg,**
> **　optional**

Heat at least 2 inches of oil in a pot over medium-high heat.

Stir the flour, salt, and sugar together in a bowl, then make a well in the center. Add the egg and a little of the cream and stir together with a wooden spoon, gradually adding a little more of the cream until it is all incorporated into the batter. Stir in the Grand Marnier.

When the oil has reached 365°, dip the bananas in the palacsinta batter, then in the bread crumbs. Pack the crumbs well onto the bananas, then fry in the oil. Do not crowd the bananas and keep the temperature at 365°. When golden brown all over—2 or 3 minutes—transfer the bananas to a rack to drain.

Just before serving, dust the bananas, if desired, with sugar flavored with a hint of cinnamon and/or nutmeg. Serve with the garnish of your choice.

Serves 4

Cakes

It is bewildering to me why people—even good cooks—shy away from cake baking. Everyone seems to have a fear of the cake falling or being too dry or of what is perceived as strict scientific method. I seldom refer to a recipe when I bake cakes, because I know one good, basic formula that is infinitely variable. It's a variation on a European sponge cake, and it relies on no artificial leavening, just air beaten into eggs.

Different flours, cocoa, bread or cake crumbs, or ground nuts can be used in this basic cake recipe. The coconut cake and Huguenot torte in my first book, *Hoppin' John's Lowcountry Cooking,* are both butterless variations of this recipe. The cake keeps as well as a classic genoise, can be drenched in fruit syrups or liqueurs, and is simplicity itself to make.

Basic Cake Recipe

For this simple cake, egg yolks, sugar, and butter are beaten until they have doubled in size. Beaten egg whites are folded into the yolk mixture, then a soft flour—one made from wheat that has little gluten, the tough molecules that give bread its structure—is added. Have all ingredients at room temperature. If you're pressed for time, warm mixing bowls and eggs by running hot water over them before using.

> **13 eggs at room temperature**
>
> **2 cups sugar**
>
> **1/2 cup butter, 1 stick, melted but not hot**
>
> **1 tablespoon vanilla extract**
>
> **2 cups sifted soft southern flour or cake flour (see Ingredients and Sources)**
>
> **pinch of salt**

Grease three 9-inch cake pans, line them with parchment or wax paper, and grease the paper. Dust the insides of the pans lightly with flour. Preheat the oven to 350° and set the oven rack in the lower third of the oven.

Separate the eggs, putting the yolks in a wide stainless-steel bowl that will fit snugly over a saucepan. Add 1 cup of the sugar to the yolks and beat well with a whisk, then place the pan over simmering water and continue beating until the yolks are thick and light colored, about 5 to 7 minutes. Add the butter a little at a time and continue beating until the mixture is very thick and has doubled in volume. Stir in the vanilla, turn off the heat, and proceed with the recipe, occasionally beating the yolk mixture to keep it fluffy and to prevent a skin from forming.

In the large bowl of an electric mixer, beat the egg whites until very foamy, then gradually add the remaining cup of sugar and continue beating until they form soft peaks. Remove the yolk mixture from the heat and fold in the beaten whites, using the wire whisk. Sift the flour and salt over the mixture and fold in swiftly, but gently, until just mixed. Scoop big batches of the batter up from the bottom of the bowl and pull the whisk straight up, allowing the flour to sift through the wires. You do not want to knock the air out of the mixture.

Divide the batter between the 3 cake pans and bake for about 25 minutes or until the cakes just begin to pull away from the pans and a toothpick stuck in the center of the cakes comes out clean. Transfer to racks to cool in the pans. As soon as they're cool enough to handle, remove the cakes from the pans, remove the paper lining, and set them to finish cooling on the racks before assembling the cake with fillings and icings.

FILLINGS AND ICINGS

The basic cake can be drenched in your favorite liquor or liqueur, covered with jam, and iced with buttercream. I once made a friend's wedding cake by stacking six large layers of this cake, shaved slightly to form a large cone. The layers were drenched in the sugar syrup from preserved figs. Between the layers, a layer of those preserves was topped with buttercream sweetened with the fig syrup. The entire cake was wrapped in rolled fondant, then covered with crystallized golden figs. It was the most delicious cake I have ever eaten, and the 80 servings were devoured by the 50 guests in a matter of minutes. But the easiest icing, made with whipped cream, is also one of the most delicious. Bolstered with beaten egg whites, it will hold up a little longer than plain whipped cream.

Lemon Curd Cake

Lemon curd is a popular cake filling in the South, and it combines nicely with the basic cake when the layers are doused with bourbon. A little can be beaten into the whipped cream icing as well. The recipes follow.

¼ cup bourbon
3 layers basic cake
1 recipe lemon curd, recipe follows

1 1/3 cups heavy cream

1 egg white

Sprinkle the bourbon evenly over the cakes and allow to sit while you make the lemon curd.

Place a dollop of lemon curd on a cake platter to keep the cake from slipping. Place a cake layer on the platter and coat it with one third of the lemon curd. Place a second layer on the cake and do the same. Place the third layer on the cake.

Beat the cream and egg white together until soft peaks form. Beat in the remaining lemon curd, then ice the cake. Serve as soon as possible at room temperature.

Serves 12

LEMON CURD

2 or 3 lemons as needed

5 egg yolks

3/4 cup sugar

1/2 cup butter, 1 stick, at room temperature, cut into pieces

Grate the zest from 2 lemons, then squeeze the juice into a measuring cup. If you do not have 1/3 cup, squeeze more juice from another lemon. In the top of a double boiler or in a wide stainless-steel mixing bowl that will fit snugly on top of a saucepan, beat the egg yolks with the sugar and the lemon juice and zest with a wire whisk. Put the bowl on top of a simmering water bath and continue to whisk until the mixture is very thick and light colored, about 7 minutes. Remove from the heat and gradually whisk in the butter, a little bit at a time. The mixture should be bright yellow and very silky. Covered in the refrigerator, it will keep for up to a month. It can be used to fill cookies and cakes or at tea or breakfast on toast.

Makes 1 2/3 cups

Half-Pound Cake

The traditional pound cake calls for a pound of flour, a pound of sugar, and a pound of eggs. I regularly use my kitchen scale and highly recommend that you do, too. *Mrs. Hill's New Cook Book* (1872) advised: "By all means be supplied with well-balanced scales, as in cake-making nothing should be done by guess-work, and measuring is much less exact than weighing." Recipes both old and new often call for a dozen large eggs, but I've found that the eggs not only weigh more than a pound, but also make a huge cake. I halve the cake. If the eggs are very fresh, I use four; if they aren't freshly laid, I use five (fresh eggs weigh more). This half-pound cake is true to the older recipes with no chemical leavening. It makes one cake in an average loaf pan.

Pound cake is a lily begging for gilding. In this version I've spiked the batter my way. Mary Randolph (1824) added grated lemon peel, nutmeg, and a gill (¹/₂ cup) of brandy, but no artificial leavening. Mrs. Hill added the juice of a lemon and "a good wineglass of brandy" but no chemicals (this is essentially her recipe). However, when she used a full dozen eggs, like most homemakers then and since, she added a teaspoon of soda and 2 teaspoons of cream of tartar as a matter of course. You can flavor the cake just about any way you like; most southern cooks prefer bourbon or sherry. I like to use Herbsaint, the New Orleans anisette, and a bit of almond extract; Mrs. Randolph's lemon peel is good, too.

Serve thick slices of this cake with ice cream for dessert or toasted and buttered for tea or breakfast.

¹/₂ **pound eggs, 4 if very fresh, 5 if not, at room temperature, separated**

¹/₂ **pound butter, 2 sticks, at room temperature**

¹/₂ **pound sugar, 1 cup**

¹/₂ **pound unbleached, all-purpose flour, about 2 cups**

3 tablespoons bourbon, rum, Herbsaint, or sherry

¹/₂ **teaspoon pure vanilla or almond extract**

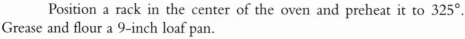

Position a rack in the center of the oven and preheat it to 325°. Grease and flour a 9-inch loaf pan.

With an electric mixer or a whisk, beat the egg whites until foamy and set aside.

With the electric mixer (using the same beaters—no need to wash), cream the butter and sugar together until the mixture is smooth and light. Lower the speed and add the egg yolks and flour a little at a time, alternating and mixing well after each addition before adding the next.

Beat in the remaining ingredients and mix until the batter is smooth.

Put a wire whisk down in the egg whites and finish beating them until they hold firm peaks but are not dry. Fold them gently but thoroughly into the batter with a rubber spatula.

Gently pour the batter into the prepared pan. Bake the cake for 1½ hours, then turn off the oven and crack the door open. The cake should be a deep golden brown, and a clean straw inserted deep into it should come out both clean and dry.

Savannah architect and food writer Damon Fowler warns that "the top will actually split, so don't be alarmed when this happens. Make sure the cake is completely done before taking it from the oven; it may look nice and puffy and brown, but if you take it out before the center is completely done, it will collapse and have what southerners call a 'sad streak.' "

After another 30 minutes, remove the cake from the oven and place on a rack on top of the stove, away from drafts and changes in temperature, to let it cool completely before taking it out of its pan or slicing.

Strawberry Shortcake

During the spring throughout the South, when strawberries come to the supermarkets by the truckload, huge displays of the berries, along with packaged ladyfingers, sponge cakes, and pound cakes, dominate the produce sections. The strawberry price wars fill the local newspapers with colorful ads, offering the berries for a song, with the baked goods thrown in as a bonus.

Why anyone would want those store-bought baked goods is beyond me—homemade shortcake and ladyfingers take about 15 minutes and are infinitely superior. Shortcake is nothing but a gussied-up biscuit, made with butter, cream, and a little sugar. And short they are—five times the normal amount of fat! Traditionally the recipe is made into one large cake, but in this recipe I make eight individual cakes. You can wrap them well in aluminum foil and reheat them and serve them later if you like.

> 4 cups ripe fresh strawberries
> ¼ cup sugar
> 3 cups soft southern flour (see Ingredients and Sources),
>   plus flour for dusting
> ⅓ cup sugar
> 2 teaspoons baking powder
> 1 teaspoon salt
> ¾ cup butter, 1½ sticks
> 1 egg
> 1 cup whipping cream
> whipped cream or crème fraîche (Chapter 6), sweetened
>   with a bit of confectioners' sugar

One or 2 hours before you plan to serve the shortcake, hull the berries and slice all but 8 of them (for garnish). Toss the berries with the sugar. Set aside at room temperature.

Preheat the oven to 425° and line a baking sheet with parchment paper.

Sift the flour, sugar, baking powder, and salt together into a large mixing bowl. Cut in the butter with a pastry blender or 2 knives until it is evenly incorporated.

Mix the egg with the cream and gradually add to the flour mixture, mixing it in with a rubber spatula. Avoid touching the dough with your hands.

Flour a counter and either your hands or a rolling pin and dump the dough out onto the counter. Pat it out or roll it to a thickness of ³/₄ inch in either a 6- by 12-inch rectangle or a 9-inch circle. Make the circle only if you have a 3-inch open biscuit cutter with high sides (a low cookie cutter will not do); otherwise, make the rectangle. Cut out eight 3-inch square (or circular if you're using the biscuit cutter) biscuits and place them close, but not touching, on the baking sheet.

Bake for 12 to 15 minutes or until lightly golden. Remove them from the oven and transfer them with a metal spatula to a platter or to individual plates. Split each one in half horizontally, using a fork or a large serrated knife. Split all the shortcakes, even those you want to serve later. (To save, wrap each split shortcake individually in aluminum foil.)

To serve, spoon a few berries and some juice onto the bottom half of each biscuit, then add a dollop of whipped cream or crème fraîche (I prefer the sweetened crème fraîche). Cap with the biscuit top and add another dollop of cream and a whole berry. Drizzle with juice and serve immediately.

To serve refrigerated biscuits later, preheat the oven to 250°. Open each wrapped biscuit carefully and put a little dab of cold butter in each one, then carefully rewrap and return to the oven for a few minutes to warm. You don't want to melt the butter totally, but simply warm the biscuit and butter through. Serve as directed.

Serves 8

Ladyfingers

As I've written before, most of the traditional southern desserts can be described as typically country French or English. Some are combinations of the two, such as the trifles using the French ladyfinger and the English custard (even the French call it *crème anglaise*). Many of these old-fashioned desserts have fallen out of favor as supermarkets offer dozens of flavors of ice cream and even small-town restaurants offer trendy bistro fare. Some of the old funny-sounding puddings, as the English call sweets, never really traveled much beyond the colonial port cities. Rarely since their mention in *The Kentucky Housewife,* published in Cincinnati in 1839, does a cookbook from Tennessee or Kentucky, for example, contain recipes for old Carolina and Virginia favorites like charlotte russe, tipsy pudding, blancmange, jumbles, or syllabub.

Homemade ladyfingers are so much more delicious than store-bought; they deserve to be rediscovered. They are made specifically for French charlottes and for southern variations on the English trifle such as the Gypsy later in this chapter. In England leftover cake is often used for the dessert. In the South, with our proverbial sweet tooth, there's rarely a leftover dessert. The recipe is a simple sponge cake batter baked in finger shapes.

4 eggs at room temperature, separated

½ cup sugar

½ teaspoon vanilla extract

¾ cup unbleached all-purpose flour

¼ teaspoon salt

confectioners' sugar

Preheat the oven to 325°. Grease and dust with flour a large baking sheet or 2 smaller ones.

Beat the egg whites with an electric mixer until they hold soft peaks, then beat in 2 tablespoons of the sugar and continue beating until the whites are very smooth, shiny, and stiff.

Using the same beaters, beat the egg yolks with the mixer until light colored and doubled in size. Gradually add the rest of the sugar and continue beating until very thick and tripled in size. Beat in the vanilla.

Sift the flour and salt together, then fold it and the egg whites into the egg yolk mixture, alternating the two. Work lightly to keep the mixture as voluminous as possible.

With a large spoon or spatula, carefully transfer the batter to a pastry bag if you have one or into a heavy-duty Ziploc plastic bag with a corner cut off. Spoon or pipe the batter out onto the baking sheet(s) in finger shapes about 4 inches long and ¹/₂ inch wide. You should have about 2 dozen ladyfingers. Dust lightly with confectioners' sugar.

Bake for about 20 minutes or until lightly browned around the edges. Remove from the oven and transfer the ladyfingers to a rack to cool. *Makes about 24*

Angel Food Cake

When you make ice cream, use the leftover egg whites to make this southern classic and serve the ice cream with the cake. Angel food is the easiest cake to make, and it is fat-free.

> 1 cup sifted soft southern or cake flour (see Ingredients and Sources)
>
> 1¹/₂ cups sugar
>
> 12 egg whites at room temperature
>
> ¹/₄ teaspoon salt
>
> 1 heaped teaspoon cream of tartar
>
> 1 teaspoon vanilla extract
>
> ¹/₂ teaspoon almond extract

Preheat the oven to 375°. Sift the flour with ½ cup sugar at least 3 times and set aside.

In the large bowl of an electric mixer, beat the egg whites, salt, cream of tartar, and extracts on the highest speed until the whites begin to turn opaque. Add the remaining sugar a little at a time and continue to beat until all the sugar is just blended in and the whites hold firm peaks. Turn off the mixer and sift about a fourth of the flour at a time over the whites and fold in, repeating with each fourth until all of the flour is folded evenly into the egg whites.

Use a perfectly clean and dry 10-inch tube pan that is 4 inches deep or a 10-inch springform pan at least 3 inches deep. With a large spatula, gently push the cake batter evenly into the pan, making one last stir through the center of the batter. Bake for 30 to 35 minutes or until a straw inserted in the center of the cake comes out clean. If you're using an angel food cake pan with a center tube, turn the cake over to cool for one hour before removing from the pan. (Most angel food cake pans have a center tube that protrudes above the top of the pan so that they can be inverted to cool the cake with air circulating underneath. If your tube pan has no extension to allow for circulation, place the inverted pan over the neck of a bottle or an inverted funnel.) If you're using a springform pan, put it on a rack to cool and, as soon as it's cool enough to handle, loosen the outer rim.

To remove the cake, slip a thin knife between the cake and the pan all around the outer edge and the tube. Invert the cake on a platter and lift off the pan. "Cut" pieces with two forks, placing the tines back to back and pulling the cake apart in opposite directions. Serve with ice cream or saturated with fresh fruit juices and topped with fruit and whipped cream.

American Chestnuts

In the rolling hills outside Gainesville, the terrain surprises the visitor to north Florida who expects palm trees and sand. More surprising, perhaps, is the 300-acre chestnut orchard that Bob Wallace owns with his partner and former University of Florida classmate Rick Queen. American chestnuts, once the pride of cooks and cabinetmakers, were virtually destroyed by an Asian blight that entered the United States at the turn of the century. By 1940 more than three billion trees had died (or had been cut down to stop the disease)—a fourth of the eastern American hardwood forests. The nut was larger, easier to peel, and sweeter than its famed European cousin.

Wallace's grandfather, Dr. Robert Dunstan, a well-known plant breeder in Greensboro, North Carolina, received a cutting from a single healthy, disease-resistant tree that a hunter had found near Salem, Ohio, in the 1950s. Through cross-breeding and grafting, Dunstan developed the tall and vigorous chestnuts that grace Wallace's Chestnut Hill Nursery in Florida. Though 60 mature, blight-free trees now produce about a ton of nuts each year, it will not be until the year 2000 that Wallace and Queen are able to harvest chestnuts instead of using them for seeds. Meanwhile, they import a line of high-quality, organically grown Italian chestnuts that have been steam-peeled and flash-frozen. Wallace's wife, Deborah, runs a test kitchen for Chestnut Hill Orchards, which distributes the nuts as well as chestnut flour and trees (see Ingredients and Sources, Nuts).

Mrs. Wallace's chestnut torte is sweetened naturally with Sucanat, another natural product that points to our young cooks' growing interest in unprocessed foods. Sucanat was developed by the eminent Swiss medical researcher Dr. Max-Henri Beguin. It is 100 percent evaporated sugar cane juice, made from organically grown cane. As a whole food it is rich in minerals, trace elements, and vitamins. It is substituted cup for cup for refined sugars, but it has a nuttier, fuller taste closer to molasses and a larger grain as well.

Chestnut Torte

Begin this recipe the day before you plan to serve it. It requires several hours for ingredients to chill.

FOR THE TORTE:

butter for greasing the pans

6 eggs, separated

1½ cups Sucanat or sugar

1½ teaspoons vanilla extract

2 cups unsweetened chestnut puree (see note)

FOR THE FILLING:

2 egg yolks

⅓ cup Sucanat or sugar

1 tablespoon strong brewed coffee

1½ ounces semisweet chocolate

6 tablespoons butter, softened

½ teaspoon vanilla extract

½ cup chestnut puree (see note)

TO SERVE:

2 cups whipping cream

1 egg white

confectioners' sugar, optional

Preheat the oven to 325°. Butter two 8-inch springform pans. In a mixing bowl, beat the egg yolks for the torte with the sweetener until thick, then beat in the vanilla. Fold in the chestnut puree. In a separate bowl, beat the egg whites until stiff but not dry, then fold them into the chestnut mixture gently but thoroughly. Turn the batter out into the prepared pans, dividing it evenly. Bake for 50 minutes or until the cakes begin to pull away from the pans.

Remove the cakes from the oven and allow to cool in the pans on racks. The layers will fall. Loosen the sides of the pan after they fall. When thoroughly cooled, remove the sides but not the bottoms of the pans. While the cakes are cooling, make the filling.

In the small bowl of an electric mixer, beat the egg yolks, sweetener, and coffee for the filling on medium speed until the sweetener is dissolved. Melt the chocolate, then slowly add to the egg mixture, beating constantly. Add the butter and continue to beat until the mixture is smooth, then add the vanilla and the puree, beating until smooth. Chill the mixture for several hours.

Several hours before serving, place one of the cake layers on the serving plate and spread with the filling. Carefully ease the second layer off its metal base and over the first layer. Return to the refrigerator to chill for another 2 hours.

Make an icing by whipping the cream and the egg white together until stiff, sweetening to taste, if desired, with confectioners' sugar. Spread it over the tops and sides of the torte, leaving it rough.

Serves 12

NOTE:

To puree chestnuts, boil peeled chestnuts in water or milk until tender, 5 to 10 minutes. Drain, then press through a sieve, pass through a food mill, or grind in a food processor or blender. Whip in 2 tablespoons butter per cup of pulp.

Canned chestnut puree will work, but most of it is sweetened. You will need about 1 pound. Look for purée de marrons au naturel, *which is only slightly sweetened. You can reduce the amount of Sucanat or sugar if need be.*

Orange Banana Nut Bread

This old favorite is always called "bread," but in fact it's a sweet. Some versions have no nuts, some have dried fruits such as raisins or dates, and some have fewer eggs or some added milk or fruit juice.

I always seem to have bananas on hand, and they often ripen before I use them. I just toss the bananas in their peels in the freezer and make banana bread with at least one of the defrosted, overripe bananas. Nutmeg is the traditional seasoning throughout the Caribbean; I've added some orange peel as well.

½ **cup butter, 1 stick**

¾ **cup sugar**

2 **eggs, lightly beaten**

1 **tablespoon grated orange zest**

freshly grated nutmeg to taste

3 **large ripe bananas, thoroughly mashed**

1½ **cups unbleached all-purpose flour**

1 **teaspoon baking soda**

1 **teaspoon salt**

½ **cup chopped walnuts, pecans, black walnuts, or**
  a combination

Preheat the oven to 350° and grease an 8- or 9-inch loaf pan.

Cream the butter and sugar together in a mixing bowl, then add the eggs and mix until light. Add the orange zest, nutmeg, and bananas and mix thoroughly.

Sift the flour, soda, and salt together and add to the liquid ingredients. Mix well, then add the nuts and mix well again. Fold into the greased pan and bake for 1 hour. Allow to cool before serving.

Serve cold or warm or toasted, with or without butter.

Makes 1 standard loaf, about 12 slices

Fresh Pineapple
Upside-Down Cake

Native to tropical America, pineapples have been favored in the South since colonial days. Most recipes for this American classic call for canned pineapple slices, but so many of today's modern supermarkets carry fresh, ripe pineapples, it seems silly to use canned. If your supermarket sells fresh pineapple already cored, by all means buy it that way, but be sure to save a little juice for the batter. If you must use canned, buy slices packed in unsweetened pineapple juice. If you use juicy fresh pineapple, be sure to cut and drain the slices before using them, saving the drained juice.

This is another of those dishes that call for the southerner's well-seasoned cast-iron pan. You can use a cake pan or casserole dish, but be sure to grease it well if you do.

> 4 tablespoons butter, ½ stick
>
> ½ cup tightly packed light brown sugar
>
> 5 slices of cored pineapple, fresh or canned, drained
>   if fresh
>
> 15 perfect pecan halves, optional
>
> 1 cup unbleached all-purpose flour
>
> ½ teaspoon baking powder
>
> ¼ teaspoon salt
>
> 4 eggs, separated
>
> ⅔ cup sugar
>
> 1 teaspoon vanilla extract
>
> 1 tablespoon dark rum
>
> ¼ cup pineapple juice

Preheat the oven to 350°. In a well-seasoned 10-inch cast-iron skillet or a greased 10-inch cake pan or casserole, melt the butter and sugar together over low heat. Turn off the heat.

Pat the pineapple slices dry, then cut all but one of them in half. Place the whole slice in the center of the skillet, then place the halves around the center slice, curved sides toward the middle of the pan. Place the pecan halves flat side down in the 15 spaces that fall in the center of the slices and between them.

Sift the flour, baking powder, and salt onto wax paper or a paper plate. Beat the egg yolks with the sugar in a mixing bowl until well mixed and light colored, then beat in the vanilla, rum, and pineapple juice. Add the sifted ingredients and mix well.

In a separate bowl, beat the egg whites until they form soft peaks, then fold them evenly into the batter. Pour the batter into the skillet and place on the middle rack of the preheated oven. Bake for about 30 minutes or until the top has browned.

Remove the skillet from the oven and immediately place a large platter with a lip over the skillet. Quickly but carefully invert the skillet and platter, using hot pads so as not to burn yourself. Wait a minute, then lift the skillet from the cake. Serve immediately or at room temperature.
Serves 8 to 10

Actually Delicious Fruitcake

Many people shy away from fruitcake because they're expecting the heinous commercial variety filled with rainbow-colored candied fruits and bitter rinds. Others resent the long ripening time so many recipes call for. This version is utterly delicious the day it is made—though you start the recipe the night before. It is chock-full of your favorite dried fruits (and you can vary them to suit your own palate).

> 1½ **pounds dried fruits such as cherries, pears, peaches, raisins, prunes, dates, and figs, about 3 cups**
> 1 **tablespoon grated orange or lemon zest**
> ¾ **cup bourbon**

1 cup chopped pecans, almonds, walnuts, or a mixture

¼ pound unbleached all-purpose flour, about 1 cup

½ cup unsalted butter, 1 stick, at room temperature, plus butter for greasing the pan

½ cup sugar

3 eggs at room temperature

pinch of salt

liquor of your choice

Dice the dried fruit and put it in a large mixing bowl. Add the grated zest and bourbon, toss well, cover the container, and leave at room temperature overnight.

The next day, grease a standard loaf pan or a 9-inch Bundt pan and set aside. Preheat the oven to 350°.

Add the nuts to the dried fruit and toss well. Sift ¼ cup of the flour over the mixture and toss again so that the fruits and nuts are coated lightly. In the bowl of an electric mixer, cream the butter and sugar together, then add the eggs one at a time, beating well after each egg, until the mixture is well blended and light. Sift the salt and remaining flour together over the fruit and nuts, tossing it all together. Add the butter and egg mixture and fold it all together.

Turn the batter into the prepared pan and bake for 1½ hours or until a straw inserted in the center of the cake comes out clean. The top should be browned and the edges just pulling away from the sides.

Set the cake in its pan on a rack and cool for 20 minutes. Turn the cake out on a plate and sprinkle liberally with the liquor of your choice. You can serve the cake immediately or wrap it in liquor-soaked cheesecloth and put aside in a tin for several months.

BEVERAGE:
Shot glasses of sipping whiskey neat

Chocolate Cake with Chocolate Icing

In the South a "chocolate" cake is usually a yellow cake iced with chocolate. "Devil's food" is a chocolate cake with any number of white icings; the cookbook sponsored by my South Carolina hometown's PTA in 1948 has five devil's food cake recipes (some calling for mashed potatoes as an ingredient), three fudge cakes, and several other chocolate cakes under the layer cake section. German chocolate cake is always iced with a coconut and pecan icing. The only way you'll get a chocolate cake with chocolate icing in the South is to call it just that.

Most versions of this popular dessert are in layers with a shiny nearly black icing made with boiling water. Some are light, others are very nearly brownies. The updated recipe here comes from George Wearn, a television producer from Atlanta and a fine cook. The cake is very rich, and the icing is poured on like a sauce.

FOR THE CAKE:

7 ounces bittersweet or semisweet chocolate or half sweet and half unsweetened chocolate

1 cup unsalted butter, 2 sticks, softened, plus butter for greasing the pan

1 cup sugar

6 eggs, separated

3 tablespoons cake, pastry, or soft southern flour (see Ingredients and Sources), plus flour for dusting the pan

3 tablespoons unsweetened cocoa powder, not Dutch process

1 cup finely ground walnuts

1 teaspoon vanilla extract

pinch of cream of tartar

FOR THE ICING:

¼ pound bittersweet or semisweet chocolate or half sweet and half unsweetened chocolate

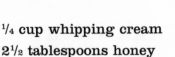

¼ **cup whipping cream**
2½ **tablespoons honey**
¼ **cup chopped walnuts**

Preheat the oven to 350°. Generously brush an 8- to 12-inch Bundt pan with melted butter and dust with flour.

Melt the chocolate in a double boiler over simmering water, then set aside to cool. In the large bowl of an electric mixer, cream the butter until it is perfectly smooth, then add the sugar and beat until the mixture is fluffy. Add the egg yolks one at a time, beating well after each addition.

Sift the flour and cocoa together, then add to the butter mixture, beating on medium-low speed. Continue beating and add the melted chocolate, nuts, and vanilla, blending all together well.

With clean, dry beaters, beat the egg whites and cream of tartar in a separate bowl until stiff but not dry. Fold a fourth of the whites into the batter, then gently fold in the rest of the whites. Turn out into the prepared pan and bake for about 50 minutes or until the cake forms a crust and cracks but the center remains moist. Set the pan on a rack to cool and run a thin sharp knife blade around the sides and center of the pan to loosen the cake. Allow to cool for 15 minutes while you make the icing.

In a heavy saucepan over low heat, melt the chocolate with the cream and the honey, stirring until smooth. Turn off the heat and allow the pan to cool somewhat. Turn the cake out of its pan onto a plate, then pour the icing over the top of the cake, allowing it to ooze over the sides. Sprinkle with the chopped nuts. Serve warm or cool.

Serves 10 to 12

WINE:
Sparkling Cabernet Franc from Saumur

German Chocolate Cake

When I was growing up, my mother's best friend, Cassandra McGee, would always make a German chocolate cake for birthdays. I loved the coconut-pecan icing and the wholesome chocolate cake layers. When I asked Cassandra for the recipe, she told me to buy some Baker's German Sweet Chocolate and follow the recipe on the inside of the box.

The current Baker's version assumes you have a microwave, which I don't. Its icing calls for evaporated milk and sweetened coconut, but I use whipping cream and unsweetened fresh or frozen grated coconut. This is really a wonderful cake and an American classic. According to *The Southern Heritage Cakes Cookbook,* the recipe first appeared in a Dallas newspaper in the 1950s. Whatever its origin, it is delicious.

FOR THE CAKE:

¼ pound sweet or bittersweet chocolate

½ cup boiling water

4 eggs at room temperature, separated

1 cup butter, 2 sticks, softened

2 cups sugar

1 teaspoon baking soda

1 cup buttermilk at room temperature

2 cups unbleached all-purpose flour or 2¼ cups soft
southern all-purpose flour (see Ingredients and Sources)

½ teaspoon salt

1 teaspoon vanilla extract

FOR THE ICING:

1 cup whipping cream

1 cup sugar

3 egg yolks

½ cup butter, 1 stick

1 teaspoon vanilla extract

6 ounces fresh or frozen grated coconut, 1¼ cups (see note)

1 cup chopped pecans

Grease three 9-inch cake pans, line the bottoms with wax paper, and grease again. Preheat the oven to 350°.

Combine the chocolate and boiling water, stirring until melted.

In the small bowl of an electric mixer, beat the egg whites until they form soft peaks, then set aside. With the same beaters (don't bother to wash them), cream the butter in a separate bowl, then gradually add the sugar, beating constantly. Add the egg yolks one at a time, beating well after each addition. Add the melted chocolate and beat in well.

Dissolve the soda in the buttermilk. Sift the flour and salt together, then add in thirds to the batter, alternating with the buttermilk and ending with the flour. Stir in the vanilla.

With a large whisk, reach down into the beaten egg whites and make sure they're still whipped throughout. If not, beat them until they are. Pick up a whiskful of the whites and mix into the batter, then fold in the remaining beaten whites.

Divide the batter among the prepared pans and bake for 30 minutes or until a wooden pick stuck into the center of the cakes comes out clean. Cool in the pans for 15 minutes, then transfer the cakes from the pans to wire racks and cool completely. While the cakes are cooling, make the icing.

Combine the cream, sugar, yolks, and butter in a saucepan over medium heat and cook, stirring often, until the mixture is very thick, about 20 minutes. Remove from the heat and stir in the vanilla, then fold in the coconut and nuts. Allow to cool completely before icing the cake.

To ice the cake, remove the wax paper from one of the layers and place it right side up on a cake platter. Spread a third of the icing on the layer, then repeat with the remaining 2 layers, stacking them. Do not ice the sides of the cake, but allow the cake layers to show through.

Serves 12

NOTE:
Unsweetened coconut is sold frozen in 6-ounce packages as "flaked." Don't worry if the coconut isn't completely thawed when you stir it in. You'll have to stir it more rigorously to get it to break up evenly, but the icing will cool off more quickly.

Black Walnut Brownies

While brownies may not be specifically southern, they are certainly offered at our bake sales, and every fund-raiser cookbook gives at least one recipe. Even the eighteenth-century Moravian village of Old Salem in North Carolina offers its recipe for "the best." Most recipes call for a stick of butter and anywhere from 2 to 6 ounces of unsweetened chocolate. In this version I use high-quality semisweet chocolate (see Ingredients and Sources) and gamy black walnuts for an intensely flavored, unforgettable brownie.

This recipe will produce either cakey or fudgey brownies.

½ cup butter, 1 stick, cut into 8 pieces

½ pound semisweet chocolate, broken up

2 eggs at room temperature

¾ cup sugar

1 teaspoon vanilla extract

¼ cup unbleached all-purpose flour

1 cup chopped black walnuts (see Ingredients and Sources)
confectioners' sugar, optional

Preheat the oven to 350°. Butter an 8-inch square pan with 1 tablespoon of the butter and set aside.

Melt the remaining butter with the chocolate in the top of a double boiler over simmering water. Set aside. While the chocolate is melting, beat the eggs in the bowl of an electric mixer at high speed until doubled in volume. Gradually add the sugar and continue beating until the mixture is very light and has tripled in volume. It may take as long as 10 minutes.

Lower the mixer speed to medium and beat in the chocolate mixture and the vanilla until everything is well blended. Turn off the motor and add the flour, then turn the mixer on to its lowest speed, scraping down the sides and mixing until the flour is absorbed. Fold the nuts into the batter, evenly distributing them, and spoon the batter into the greased pan.

Bake on the center rack of the oven until a wooden toothpick inserted in the center comes out clean, about 30 minutes. Place on a wire rack to cool completely before cutting into sixteen 2-inch squares. For a chewier texture, cover the brownies and allow to stand overnight. Dust with confectioners' sugar just before serving if desired.

Makes 16 brownies

Shortbread Lemon Squares

Lemon squares are the quintessential southern bar cookie, straight from England. The best are assembled from homemade shortbread and lemon curd. In this version I've used a traditional sandy shortbread recipe from Cheshire made with a little semolina. The shortbread is partially cooked in a slow oven, then the lemon curd is added as it finishes baking.

Follow the lemon curd recipe early in this chapter, but grate the lemon zest onto a piece of wax paper. You'll use the wax paper again to press the shortbread into place.

½ cup butter, 1 stick, at room temperature

¼ cup sugar

¼ teaspoon salt

1 cup unbleached all-purpose flour

¼ cup semolina

1 recipe lemon curd

confectioners' sugar (optional)

Preheat the oven to 325°. Cream the butter, sugar, and salt together in a mixing bowl. Add the flour and semolina and mix well. Turn the mixture out into an 8-inch square baking pan and cover with a piece of wax paper. Press evenly into the pan, then remove the wax paper.

Bake for 20 minutes, then remove from the oven. Add the lemon curd and bake for another 10 minutes. Remove from the oven and place on a rack to cool completely.

Dust with confectioners' sugar if desired and cut into sixteen 2-inch squares.

Makes 16 squares

Delicate Benne Seed Wafers

It is said that Italians are the only immigrants whose cooking has not influenced the traditional cuisine of the South. That may be true, but they have had a remarkable effect in this century, well beyond the obvious popularity of pasta, sun-dried tomatoes, and tiramisù. Clementa Annunciata Iamundo Florio was born in Charleston in 1913. Her recipe for the traditional Lowcountry benne (sesame) cookie yields the lightest, most delicate ones I've ever tasted. Her daughter Donna, who gave me the recipe, warns: "You can eat a dozen or more in one sitting!"

The recipe is time-consuming because you must carefully pat the dough (which is too short to roll) for each cookie. Be patient: The technique produces the crispiest cookie of this sort.

> ½ cup benne (sesame) seeds
>
> ½ cup butter, 1 stick, softened
>
> 1 cup sugar
>
> 1¾ cups unbleached all-purpose flour
>
> ½ teaspoon salt
>
> ½ teaspoon baking soda
>
> 2 teaspoons baking powder
>
> ½ teaspoon vanilla extract
>
> 1 egg

Parch the seeds in a heavy skillet over medium heat, shaking the pan occasionally, until evenly browned, about 15 minutes. Cream the butter and sugar together in a mixing bowl. Sift the flour with the salt, baking soda, and baking powder and set aside. Add the vanilla and egg to the butter and sugar and blend well. Add the dry ingredients and mix well. Refrigerate the dough for an hour.

Preheat the oven to 325°. Heavily grease a cookie sheet or two and set aside. Pinch small pieces of dough and roll them into little balls. Place the pieces one at a time on the cookie sheet and flatten each piece out by patting with the fingertips or the heel of your palm until it forms a circle as thin as possible—about 2½ inches in diameter.

Bake until brown, about 10 minutes. Cool for about 1 minute, but no more, on the cookie sheet before transferring them with a metal spatula to wire racks to cool. Scrape the cookie sheets clean and regrease before each batch. Store in airtight containers.
Makes about 6 dozen cookies

Summer Cobbler

I'm not about to say that one style of cobbler is better than another: I've yet to taste a bad one. Some have biscuit doughs like shortcake; others are deep-dish pies with very short crusts. One of my favorites, "campfire cobbler," is so named because it can be made with so little effort: a stick of butter is melted in a baking dish, then a batter made of equal parts of flour, sugar, and milk is added; juicy fruit is piled on top, and the cobbler is baked for an hour.

Lee Bailey is a southern gentleman, though he now lives for the most part in Manhattan. Nearly all of his dozen excellent books include a cobbler recipe. The technique in this recipe is Lee's; he learned it from Edna Lewis. I've replaced their vegetable shortening with 2 ounces (or 4 tablespoons) of frozen duck fat. If you don't have a kitchen scale, be sure to measure out the tablespoons before you freeze the fat. You can use vegetable shortening as in Lee's recipe, but the duck fat is more delicious.

I call this "summer cobbler" because I like to make it with the soft summer fruits such as blackberries, but you can use put-up fruits such as frozen blueberries or home-canned peaches, tropical fruits such as mangoes, or fall apples sautéed first with a little sugar. Sugar and season the fruits to your own liking; rum, spices, and lemon juice and zest are welcome additions.

1½ cups unbleached all-purpose flour, plus flour
  for dusting

pinch of salt

5 tablespoons frozen butter

4 tablespoons frozen duck fat or frozen solid vegetable
  shortening

4 to 5 tablespoons ice water as needed

6 cups soft summer fruit such as blackberries and/or
  peaches, peeled and sliced as for a pie, at
  room temperature

1 cup sugar

4 tablespoons butter, ½ stick, cut into small pieces

Pulse the flour and salt a couple of times in a food processor. Add the frozen butter and duck fat. Process until the mixture is uniform; with the motor running, add the water in a stream until the dough just holds together. Gather it up into a ball and place between 2 sheets of wax paper. Flatten into a disk, wrap well, and refrigerate for at least 30 minutes.

Preheat the oven to 450° and lightly grease a 1½- to 2-quart baking dish. I use a soufflé dish.

Dust a counter and a rolling pin with flour and roll the pastry out into a large ragged circle several inches bigger than the pan. Line the dish, allowing the excess to drape over the sides.

Toss the fruit with the sugar, then fill the pastry shell. Dot with the butter, then bring the loose edges of the pastry up and over the fruit. There won't be enough dough to cover the top completely, but be sure to add any little remaining scraps to the top of the cobbler.

Place in the oven, turn the heat down to 425°, and bake until bubbly and golden, about 45 minutes.

Serve warm or cooled either plain or with cream, crème fraîche, whipped cream, or ice cream.

Serves 6 to 8

Caramelized Pecan Tart

This recipe is inspired by one from Steve Jackson, who made a name for himself as chef to the South Carolina governor. In this variation of the classic southern pecan pie the sugar is allowed to cook to a candy stage. The tart is very sweet; serve small slices. It keeps very well.

PASTRY:

> 1 egg
> 1¼ cups unbleached all-purpose flour, plus flour
>   for dusting
> ¼ cup sugar
> 1 pinch salt
> ½ cup butter, 1 stick, cut into 8 pieces

PECAN FILLING:

> ½ cup butter, 1 stick
> ½ cup lightly packed light brown sugar
> ½ cup mild-flavored honey
> ¼ cup heavy cream
> 3 cups coarsely chopped pecans

For the pastry, beat the egg lightly and set aside. Put the flour, sugar, and salt in a food processor and pulse to mix. Add the butter pieces and process in quick bursts until the mixture looks like cornmeal.

Turn the processor on and immediately begin adding the beaten egg in a slow stream, stopping the processor when the dough just comes together. Remove from the processor and flatten into a disk about 6 inches in diameter and about 1 inch thick, then wrap in plastic and refrigerate for at least 1 hour.

Preheat the oven to 350°. Put all the filling ingredients in a heavy saucepan over low heat. When the butter and brown sugar have melted, increase the heat to medium and continue to cook until the mixture is bubbly and at the soft ball stage (about 235°). Remove from the heat.

Dust a counter and rolling pin lightly with flour. Remove the dough from the refrigerator and roll into a 12-inch circle. Lift into a 2-inch-deep, 8-inch tart pan and press into place. Prick the bottom with a fork and bake "blind"—line the crust with wax paper, then fill with beans, rice, coins, or pie weights—for 10 minutes. Remove from the oven, remove the weights, pour the pecan mixture into the tart shell, and return to the oven, baking for an additional 15 minutes.

Cool completely before serving. Jackson recommends serving the tart with a little whipped cream flavored with Frangelico (a hazelnut and herb liqueur).
Makes 10 to 12 servings

Lemon Meringue Pie

When we were discussing recipes to be included in this southern collection, my editor asked if I had a great recipe for lemon meringue pie. I had already decided *not* to include a key lime pie, not only because the Florida Keys are hardly southern but also because key limes are next to impossible to find. I do not care for cloyingly sweet lemon pies made with condensed milk, or the standard ones thickened with cornstarch or flour.

This is a very old recipe with none of those traditional thickeners. It's really just a lemon curd made with whole eggs, poured into a crumb crust, and baked with a meringue topping. It is not so sweet as other recipes, but it *is* rich: you can cut smaller slices of this one, but you can't reduce the sugar in the standard pies.

FOR THE CRUST:

> 1¼ cups graham cracker crumbs, about 10 crushed
>   crackers
> ¼ cup confectioners' sugar
> 5 tablespoons melted butter

FOR THE FILLING AND MERINGUE:

> 4 lemons
> 5 eggs plus 3 egg whites
> 1½ cups sugar
> ½ cup butter, 1 stick, cut into 8 pieces
> ¼ teaspoon cream of tartar
> pinch of salt

Grease a 9-inch pie plate, then dust it with flour.

For the crust, combine the crumbs, sugar, and melted butter in a bowl and mix thoroughly. The mixture will be in crumbs, not a dough. Dump the crumb mixture into the prepared pie plate and distribute it evenly with your fingertips, then press it into place firmly enough that it holds its shape. Be sure to come all the way up to the edge of the pan. Set the crust in the refrigerator to chill while you make the filling.

On a piece of wax paper, grate the zest of the lemons. You should have about 2 tablespoons plus 1 teaspoon. Put 2 tablespoons in the top of a double boiler or in a wide stainless-steel bowl that will fit snugly over a pot of simmering water. Put the extra teaspoon aside in a little bowl. Juice the lemons until you have ⅓ cup. Add that juice to the 2 tablespoons zest. Squeeze another teaspoon of juice and add it to the teaspoon of zest.

Add 4 whole eggs, 1 egg yolk, and 1 cup of the sugar to the 2 tablespoons lemon zest and juice. Mix well, then place over simmering water and cook, stirring constantly with a whisk, until it is very thick, about 7 minutes. Remove from the heat.

Whisk in the butter 1 or 2 pieces at a time. Set the custard aside to cool while you prepare the meringue.

Beat the 4 egg whites until foamy, then add the cream of tartar and salt and beat until they hold soft peaks. Gradually add the remaining ½ cup sugar and beat until it is all incorporated. Add the reserved teaspoon of zest and juice and beat once more until it is just mixed in.

Preheat the oven to 300°. Remove the crust from the refrigerator and put on a level counter. Pour the lemon filling into the crust. Fold the meringue out onto the pie and cover completely, being sure that the meringue goes from crust to crust so that it does not shrink away from the sides. Use the back of a large serving spoon to pull up the meringue in attractive peaks.

Bake the pie for about 20 minutes or until the meringue is lightly browned on the peaks. Remove to cool on a rack in a completely draft-free place. It should cool completely before it is served. It can be served at room temperature, but I prefer to refrigerate it after it has cooled down a bit and serve it chilled.

Serves 8 to 10

Abbeville Gypsy

Variations on the English trifle such as this one are all but forgotten in many areas of the South, but in Abbeville, South Carolina, this is still the traditional dessert on Christmas Day. No one knows for sure how a food so firmly rooted in English tradition came to be named after nomads who are otherwise rarely associated with the South, but I suspect that it's just a euphemistic variation of *tipsy* that was adopted during the temperance movement or Prohibition. Trifle, tipsy parson, tipsy squire, and Abbeville gypsy all vary in ingredients and garnishes, but they all *must* be tipsy, or flavored with spirits.

This recipe comes from Cassandra McGee ("Gee" to her grandchildren and many others). Gee hasn't lived in Abbeville in over fifty years, but she and her clan always make this old family recipe at Christmas. Many southern homes have a special clear glass trifle dish made to show off the dessert, but you can use a deep bowl or soufflé dish just as easily. You should start this recipe several hours or a day ahead.

1 quart milk

4 eggs

1 cup sugar

4 teaspoons sherry or bourbon or to taste, plus more for
  the whipped cream

1 pint whipping cream

1 recipe homemade ladyfingers or 2 packages
  store-bought (see note)

¼ pound blanched almonds, chopped or
  slivered

about ⅔ cup sugar

sherry or bourbon

Heat the milk to a simmer in a saucepan over low heat or in a double boiler. Beat the eggs and sugar together in a mixing bowl, then add a little of the hot milk and stir. Add the egg mixture to the milk, stirring constantly until it coats the spoon. The custard will thicken more as it cools. Add the sherry or bourbon, then cool the custard completely.

Whip the cream, then flavor it with a little sugar and with sherry or bourbon.

Line the bottom of a deep bowl or soufflé dish with ladyfingers flat sides down. Pour in about 1 inch of custard, then line the walls of the dish with ladyfingers, flat sides out. Sprinkle with a layer of the almonds, then add a layer of whipped cream. Make another layer of custard, followed by the almonds and whipped cream. Put the gypsy in the refrigerator to chill for several hours or preferably overnight.

Serve in clear glass stemware.

Serves 6

NOTE:
Store-bought ladyfingers are filled with chemicals and artificial flavorings. The recipe in this book makes 6 ounces of ladyfingers, the same amount you get in 2 typical store-bought packages.

Old-Fashioned Pearl Tapioca Pudding

This recipe comes from Virginia chef Jimmy Sneed. It has often taken talented young chefs like Sneed to revive and refine some grand old American favorites, such as this simple custardy dessert. Do not serve the dish ice-cold; room temperature is perfect. And start a day ahead.

> ½ cup medium or large tapioca pearls
> 1 vanilla bean
> 1½ cups milk
> 1½ cups heavy cream
> ½ cup sugar
> pinch of salt
> 2 egg yolks

Cover the pearls with water and soak overnight or for at least 6 hours. Drain. Split the vanilla bean and scrape the seeds into the milk, cream, and drained tapioca in a heavy pot. Cook very slowly for an hour, stirring often. Add the sugar and salt, then bring to a simmer, stirring constantly and being careful not to let the tapioca stick to the bottom of the pan.

Beat the yolks in a bowl and stir in a little of the tapioca mixture to equalize the temperature. Add to the pan while stirring and stir it all well together. Pour into a bowl and cool before serving.

Serves 6

Karen's Buttermilk Cheesecake

When I asked Karen Barker, the pastry chef and co-owner with her husband Ben of Durham, North Carolina's Magnolia Grill, if she makes a good version of a traditional southern chess or buttermilk pie—or something with berries—she sent me this recipe, explaining, "This combines the best aspects of traditional New York–style cheesecake and good ol' traditional buttermilk pie. Given the fact that I'm originally from Brooklyn and now reside in the Southern Part of Heaven, it's very indicative of both my personal history and baking style. . . . This would work as a molded, baked custard in a water bath: chill, turn out, and serve with peach compote, fresh berries, blackberry sauce . . . or turn this into bar-type cookies by baking them in brownie pans and cutting them into squares, which are also nice garnished with berries."

Karen uses Bergey Buttermilk, which "comes from just over the Virginia border and is possibly the world's best." Mass-produced cultured buttermilk from your grocer's won't taste exactly the same, but the recipe works like a charm anyway and the cheesecake is delicious. The cornmeal in the crust recalls a classic southern chess pie. Serve with a mixture of fresh berries in season or a berry puree.

1 cup butter, 2 sticks, at room temperature

1½ cups graham cracker crumbs

½ cup cornmeal

1 cup plus 2 tablespoons sugar

1½ pounds cream cheese, 3 large packages, at room temperature

grated zest of 2 lemons

¾ cup buttermilk

1 teaspoon pure vanilla extract

4 eggs

Preheat the oven to 350°. Set half the butter aside. Melt three quarters of the remaining butter and use the extra 2 tablespoons to grease a 10-inch springform pan.

Combine the cracker crumbs, cornmeal, 2 tablespoons of the sugar, and the melted butter in a bowl and mix thoroughly. The mixture will be in crumbs, not a dough. Dump it out into the prepared pan and press it into the bottom and 1 inch up the sides. Bake for about 10 minutes or until light golden. Remove from the oven and set aside.

Cream the remaining room-temperature butter, remaining cup of sugar, and the cream cheese with the lemon zest in the large bowl of an electric mixer until smooth. Add the buttermilk and vanilla and beat, occasionally scraping down the sides, until well mixed. Add the eggs and beat slowly until just combined. Do not overbeat.

Pour the batter into the reserved crust and bake for 25 minutes. Turn the heat down to 300° and bake for an additional 25 minutes. Turn the oven to low and bake until done—approximately 20 minutes more or until the cake is set around the edges and barely jiggly in the very center. Cool and chill for several hours before serving.

Serves 10 to 12

Apple Bread Pudding and Bourbon Hard Sauce

For years I tried unsuccessfully to get the recipe for this bread pudding from Scott and Ruth Fales, who own Charleston's Pinckney Cafe. It took Jeffrey Steingarten, *Vogue*'s tireless food editor, to make their sous-chef Roger Cooper finally give in. This is the version that Jeff ran in his *Vogue* article on bread puddings. It is truly one of the best you will ever eat.

½ cup butter, 1 stick, melted
2 Granny Smith apples, peeled, cored, and sliced ¼ inch
   thick, about 3 cups

½ cup raisins

¼ cup bourbon

3 cups milk

1½ cups sugar

2 tablespoons ground cinnamon, plus ½ teaspoon for
sprinkling on top

¼ whole nutmeg, grated, about ⅜ teaspoon

3 eggs

1 day-old French baguette or long Italian loaf, about ½
pound, cut into slices ¾ inch thick, scant 2 quarts

Bourbon Hard Sauce (recipe follows)

Preheat the oven to 350°. Put 3 tablespoons of the butter into a
10- to 12-inch skillet and over medium-high heat sauté the apples and raisins
for about 5 minutes, until the apples begin to color. Add the bourbon, carefully
set aflame, and continue cooking for another minute or two.

Meanwhile, bring the milk to a bare simmer and remove from the
heat. In a large bowl, mix 1 cup of the sugar with the 2 tablespoons cinnamon
and the nutmeg. Thoroughly whisk in the eggs, followed by the scalded milk.

Cover the bottom of a 2-quart soufflé dish (3 to 4 inches deep and
7 to 8 inches in diameter) with a third of the bread, followed by half of the
apples. Repeat and finish with the final third of the bread. Pour about half
the egg and milk mixture over the bread, wait a minute or two while it is
absorbed, and then pour on the rest. Push down any bread that bobs above
the surface reasonably flat; the mixture should come up to the very top of
the baking dish. Sprinkle the remaining ½ cup sugar over the surface and
then the ½ teaspoon cinnamon. Drizzle the remaining 5 tablespoons of
butter over the sugar.

Place the soufflé dish in a large pan filled with very hot water and
bake for 1½ to 2 hours; a sugar crust should have formed on the top of the
pudding, and its internal temperature should rise to between 160° and 180°.
Remove from the oven and allow to settle for at least 10 minutes. Scoop out
the bread pudding with a large serving spoon; each serving should include
the crisp sugar crust on top and the soft, eggy part at the bottom of the pan.
Generously top each portion with Bourbon Hard Sauce.

Serves 8 to 12

BOURBON HARD SAUCE

½ cup butter, 1 stick, cut into 1-inch pieces
1 pound confectioners' sugar
1 egg
¼ cup heavy cream
¼ cup bourbon

Cream together the butter and sugar in the bowl of an electric mixer, beginning with the slow speed and increasing to high. (If your mixer has a paddle attachment, use it instead of the whisk.) When the butter has disappeared into grains the size of rice, reduce the speed to medium and add the egg. Then beat in the cream by dribbles, followed by the bourbon. Refrigerate the hard sauce until you're ready to spoon it over the warm bread pudding.

French Vanilla Ice Cream

This luscious ice cream is the classic recipe that spread across the South as early as fifty years before the invention of commercial ice-making machinery. By the time Mary Randolph, for example, published *The Virginia House-Wife* in 1824, she was well enough versed in the fine art of ice cream making to chastise those "indolent cooks" who would not properly churn the custard. In the 1825 edition of her classic cookbook, she included a design for a home refrigerator, though mechanical refrigeration was yet to be invented. Ice, however, was widely available in the larger cities of the South in the late eighteenth century. From this basic, rich recipe followed dozens of variations. Some suggestions follow the recipe. Save the egg whites, which can be frozen, to make angel food cake—a perfect foil for any ice cream.

1 vanilla bean

2 cups milk

6 egg yolks

¾ cup sugar

1 cup whipping cream or crème fraîche (Chapter 6)

Scrape the seeds from inside the vanilla bean into the milk. Add the pod to the milk and scald in a heavy saucepan, then remove from the heat. Beat the yolks in a bowl by hand or with a mixer until very light colored. Add the sugar and continue beating until doubled in volume. Remove the vanilla pod from the scalded milk and gradually add some of the milk to the egg mixture, then pour the eggs into the milk in the saucepan and cook over medium-low heat, stirring constantly, until the custard coats the back of a spoon, about 8 to 10 minutes.

Add the cream to the custard, cool, and chill. When thoroughly chilled, freeze in an ice cream maker according to the manufacturer's instructions.

Makes 1 quart to serve about 6

Variations

Butter pecan ice cream:

Salty nuts play off the rich cream base in this southern favorite. Simply fold the salted nuts into the ice cream recipe or into your favorite commercial brand. For the nuts, sauté 1 cup pecans with ½ teaspoon salt in 2 tablespoons butter for a few minutes, then roast in a 300° oven for 20 minutes or until brown.

Peach ice cream:

Omit the vanilla (add a little almond extract if you wish) and add 8 to 10 peaches, peeled, stoned, crushed, and chilled, to the custard before freezing.

Coconut ice cream:

Omit the vanilla and add 1 cup freshly grated coconut to the milk before scalding.

Praline ice cream:

Using your favorite brittle recipe, grind 1 cup praline powder from the candy. Fold into the custard before freezing.

Banana rum raisin:

Add 1 cup mashed ripe bananas and ¹/₂ cup golden raisins soaked in rum to the custard before freezing.

Candied ginger ice cream:

Add ¹/₂ cup chopped candied (crystallized) ginger to the scalded milk and continue with the recipe. When softly frozen, whip an additional 1¹/₂ cups cream to soft peaks and add to the ice cream freezer, then continue churning until evenly frozen.

Pumpkin Ice Cream

This is a very easy ice cream recipe that I like to serve on Thanksgiving, when it is often still warm in the South.

>   1¹/₂ cups milk
>   ¹/₂ cup sugar
>   2 eggs
>   1 cup heavy cream or crème fraîche (Chapter 6)
>   1 cup fresh or canned pumpkin puree
>   ¹/₄ teaspoon ground cinnamon
>   ¹/₂ teaspoon ground nutmeg
>   1 tablespoon bourbon

Mix the milk, sugar, and eggs together well, then heat them in a heavy pot over medium heat, stirring constantly, until slightly thick, about 10 minutes. Place the custard in the refrigerator until you're ready to churn the ice cream.

Add the cream to the custard, then mix in the pumpkin, spices, and bourbon. Chill according to the manufacturer's directions for your ice cream maker.

Makes 1 quart to serve about 6

Poached Pears with Stilton Custard

Fruits, cheese, and custard have come to the English table after dinner since Jacobean days; the tradition was brought early on to the southern colonies. Here I have paired the cheese with the custard. Rather than baking a caramel coating along with the flan, I reduce the pear-poaching liquid to a syrup to top it all.

This is an unusual and entertaining way to end a meal. I like to make it with the hard local Kieffer pears that grow all over the South. If you can't find a hard "cooking" pear, buy underripe ones.

FOR THE CUSTARD:

2 tablespoons butter, melted

3 eggs plus 2 egg yolks

1 14-ounce can sweetened condensed milk

1³/₈ cups milk (use the condensed milk can to measure)

5 ounces Stilton cheese

FOR THE PEARS:

4 hard Kieffer or underripe pears

1 cup Gewürztraminer wine

²/₃ **cup sugar**

1 lemon

4 or 5 black peppercorns to taste

2 tablespoons butter

Preheat the oven to 350° and put a kettle of water on to boil.

Paint the insides of eight ¹/₂-cup ramekins with butter and place them in a baking dish. Place in the refrigerator to chill for a few minutes, then remove them and grease them again.

Put the remaining ingredients in a blender and mix well. Strain into the 8 ramekins, then pour boiling water into the baking dish about halfway up the sides of the custards. Place in the oven and bake for about 40 minutes or until a knife poked in the center comes out clean. The tops will be golden brown.

Remove from the oven, then immediately transfer the custards to an empty baking dish. Put in the refrigerator to chill.

Meanwhile, peel the pears, cut them in half, and core them. I use a melon baller to cut out the center and a small paring knife to remove the stem and any tough parts through the center. In a heavy sauté pan, combine the Gewürztraminer and sugar and stir to dissolve. Place over moderate heat.

Cut several zests of lemon to use as garnish and set aside. Quarter the lemon and add it and the remaining ingredients to the pan. Place the pear halves centers down into the pan. Cover the pan and simmer until the edges of the pears are just beginning to soften. The time will vary according to the variety and ripeness of the pear, 20 to 45 minutes. Carefully turn the pear halves over, cover the pan again, and cook until the pears are just tender and translucent. Transfer the pears with a slotted spoon to a shallow dish such as a glass pie plate.

Increase the heat and reduce the poaching liquid until it begins to thicken. A thermometer will read about 212°. Remove from the heat and pour over the pears, straining out the solids. Refrigerate to chill.

To serve, slip a thin knife blade around the outer edge of the custards and invert them onto dessert plates. Transfer the pear halves with a slotted spoon from the syrup to a cutting surface and slice each lengthwise into about 6 slices. Place the slices around the custards and drizzle the sauce over all. Garnish with lemon zests.

Serves 8

WINE:
Late-bottled vintage port

Ingredients and Sources

I have tried to include a source for any ingredient that may not be available where you live, but I urge you to use common sense and to make substitutions if you cannot find the exact ingredient. This book is meant to be a guide to a *style* of cooking; use the recipes as inspiration. Substituting a little prosciutto for country ham or scallions for shallots or Cornish hens for poussins may alter the flavor a little, but it will not change that style.

I also highly recommend Joni Miller's excellent book *True Grits: The Southern Foods Mail-Order Catalog* (see Select Bibliography), available through my bookstore (see Corn Products entry).

Mail- and phone-order shopping, however, should never replace the process of building a rapport with your local farmers, butchers, fishmongers, wine merchants, grocers, and gourmet shops. If your city has a farmers' market, patronize it; if it doesn't, write city hall and plead. As Debbie Marlowe so wisely advised in her introductory note about wine, I, too, urge you to find merchants whom you trust and to stick with them. Encourage them to carry fresh ducks and mushrooms, local greens, and wines from outside Napa and Bordeaux. If you can't find parchment paper on the shelves of your grocery store and it has a bakery, ask the baker to sell you some of its supply. More than once I've bought items from the supermarket deli that the store itself doesn't stock.

Befriend your local restaurateurs and chefs, who have access to every ingredient imaginable. Don't hesitate to ask them to order special items for you; your request may add just enough to their order to help them meet distributors' minimums. And, no matter how small your home, you should at least grow a few herbs in pots: Nothing can replace the fleeting flavor of fresh picked.

Baking Powder.

Use a double-acting, aluminum-free brand such as Rumford, available at natural foods stores.

Blenheim Ginger Ale.

is in a class all by itself. Specify #3 Hot, #5 Not as Hot, or #9 Diet when you order: Blenheim Brothers, Box 452, Hamer, SC 29547; (800) 270-9344.

Butter.

The butter used in these recipes is unsalted. *Clarified butter* is the pure butterfat without any water or milk solids. To make it, simply melt some butter over very low heat. Skim off any foam on the surface and pour off the clear yellow fat. You can discard the milky white substance in the bottom of the pot or add it to the grits pot or any other buttery dish that will not be cooked over high heat.

Charcoal.

The only charcoal you should consider cooking food over is natural, lump charcoal made from 100 percent hardwood. (Briquettes contain 20 to 25 percent pulverized charcoal with added sawdust, lime, anthracite coal, sand and/or common dirt, glue, and sodium nitrate.) You should also never use lighter fluid. Aaron Schlabach Gourmet Charcoal has been made by the same family for three generations. Contact Lederman Rupp, Schlabach's grandson, to find a distributor in your area: (800) 253-9347.

Cheeses.

Specialty and farmstead cheeses are produced throughout the country now; try to find fresh local ones. Paula Lambert's Mozzarella Company—2944 Elm St., Dallas, TX 75226; (800) 798-2954—has produced both fresh and aged cheeses from cow's and goat's milk since 1982.

Ervin Evans and Pamela Morse produce award-winning goat cheeses at their Split Creek Farm: 3806 Centerville Rd., Anderson, SC 29625; (803) 287-3921.

Chocolate.

Merckens Chocolate is a superior American product that is available in bulk through retail outlets and cake-decorating supply houses throughout the country. For a supplier in your area, call (800) MERCKEN, or write to Rory Merckens, c/o Southern Chocolate Supply Company, 5619 Lamar Rd., Bethesda MD 20816.

Corn Products.

I have 2-pound bags of grits, cornmeal, and corn flour (the finest grind) ground to my specifications in the mountains of Georgia. They are available from Hoppin' John's, 30 Pinckney St., Charleston, SC 29401; (803) 577-6404.

Masa harina is ground posole, the Southwest's version of hominy or corn that is treated with slaked lime. It is widely available in supermarkets.

Dried Beans.

The best selection of the highest-quality beans are available from Phipps Ranch, PO Box 349, Pescadero, CA 94060; (415) 879-0787. All of its beans are organically grown and are harvested and sorted by hand.

Eggs.

All eggs used in these recipes should be large. Bring them to room temperature before using them. A few recipes call for uncooked eggs. Rather than fear salmonella, you will find it prudent to know the provenance of the eggs that you eat. If you can find fresh local eggs from small farmers, by all means use them, but don't be afraid of supermarket eggs. Nearly every box of the millions of eggs sold in the United States has a toll-free number on it as well as the batch number and expiration date. You can easily find out if the supplier has had an outbreak of salmonella. In reality few have. One egg in 10,000 is contaminated, and virtually all of the salmonella outbreaks have been institutional.

Flour and Wheat.

All flour is unbleached all-purpose unless otherwise stated. Soft, low-gluten wheat is ground into the soft southern flour I call for in biscuits and cakes. White Lily is a reliable brand. If you cannot find it in your area, you can make a softer flour by combining an all-purpose flour with cake or pastry flour, or you can write to White Lily at PO Box 871, Knoxville, TN 37901, and ask for its unbleached flour.

Cracked wheat and other whole grains are available from The Baker's Catalogue, RR2 Box 56, Norwich, VT 05055; (800) 827-6836.

Bulgur is cracked wheat that has been precooked. It is used to make tabbouleh. It is widely available in supermarkets and natural foods stores.

Garden Vegetables.

If you have a kitchen garden, you should grow your own okra, tomatoes, and other fruits and vegetables that don't do well in shipping. Kent Whealy's Seed Savers Exchange is a grassroots organization of amateur gardeners devoted to guarding our genetic resources. His *Garden Seed Inventory: An Inventory of Seed Catalogs Listing All Non-Hybrid Vegetable Seeds Still Available in the United States and Canada* is an invaluable resource. Seed Savers publishes three yearbooks a year for its members, offering 5,000 varieties of rare vegetable seeds: RR3, Box 239, Decorah, IA 52101; (319) 382-5990.

Meats.

Squab (young pigeon) has been raised on pure spring water and whole grains at the Palmetto Pigeon Plant (PO Drawer 3060, Sumter, SC 29151) since 1923. Palmetto also sells poussin and pheasant. Available fresh or frozen via air freight. Call (803) 775-1204 for a distributor in your area; the products are also available through D'Artagnan (800) 327-8246.

Quail is grown at Manchester Farms in Dalzell, SC; (800) 845-0421. It is also available through D'Artagnan.

The finest country hams are available from S. Wallace Edwards and Sons, PO Box 25, Surry, VA 23883; (800) 222-4267. I sell its old-fashioned, older-cure hams during the fall holidays in my bookstore (see Corn Products entry); place your Thanksgiving orders by Halloween; Christmas orders by Thanksgiving. Throughout the South grocers sell small packs of country ham slices. Edwards sells a box of eight 12-ounce vacuum-packed boneless slices (6 pounds), or you can order its 2- to 3-pound precooked "petite" ham. Clifty Farm in Paris, Tennessee, sells a $2^1/2$-pound package of center slices; (800) 238-8239.

Naturally raised, free-ranging veal, lamb, poultry, and venison are available from Jamie and Rachel Nicoll's Summerfield Farm Products and Gourmet Country Market, 10044 James Monroe Highway, Culpeper, VA 22701; (703) 547-9600.

The International Home Cooking Catalog includes exotic game and meats fresh from around the world; (800) 237-7423.

Preferred Meats is a wholesaler in Dallas with offices in San Francisco as well. It distributes many of these meats and poultry and can put you in touch with a retailer in your area; (214) 565-0243 in Dallas; (415) 285-9299 in San Francisco.

Maple Leaf Farms produces excellent ducks: PO Box 308, Milford, IN 46542; (219) 658-4121.

Mushrooms.

I've found at least one mushroom grower near every metropolitan area I've visited. Encourage your local grocer to carry an assortment of fresh mushrooms. Ben Cramer grows several varieties at his LowCountry Exotic Mushroom Farm, PO Box 867, John's Island, SC 29457; (803) 559-9200.

Nuts.

Fresh mammoth pecan halves, toasted pecans, and pecan meal are available from Orangeburg Pecan Co., Inc., PO Box 38, Orangeburg, SC 29116; (800) 845-6970. Also try San Saba Pecan, 2803 W. Wallace, San Saba, TX 76877; (800) 683-2101.

Organically grown steam-peeled chestnuts, chestnut flour, and blight-resistant chestnut and persimmon trees are available from Chestnut Hill Nursery, Rte. 1, Box 341, Alachua, FL 32615; (800) 669-2067.

Black walnuts are sold by Missouri Dandy Pantry, 212 Hammons Dr. E., Stockton, MO; (800) 872-6879.

Peanuts—raw, water-blanched, roasted, butter-toasted, salted, unsalted, shelled or unshelled—are available from The Virginia Diner in the Peanut Capital of the World, PO Box 310, Wakefield, VA 23888; (800) 642-NUTS.

Rice.

Most grocers carry several kinds of rice. For traditional southern cooking you'll need long-grain white rice. Basmati is a very aromatic long-grain rice from India. It is available at natural foods stores. Texmati is a fluffy aromatic rice that has fooled even some Indian rice experts; it is grown in Texas by RiceTec, Inc., which also grows Jasmati, a soft aromatic rice similar to Thai jasmine rice. More than 15,000 supermarkets now carry these excellent rices. Call (800) 232-RICE for more information or to find the nearest dealer.

Salt.

Salt should be pure, with no additives. I usually use a high-quality sea salt, though I worry about impurities in the Mediterranean brands.

Smoked Fish, Caviar, and Seafood.

Kyle Strohman and Richard Pla-Silva's trademark is their excellent Applewood Smoked Virginia Trout and Atlantic Salmon. They also have smoked salmon and trout mousses and trout caviar in season. Contact The Farm at Mt. Walden, Main St. 515, The Plains, VA 22171; (703) 253-9800.

Walter's Caviar is made the Russian way with eggs from Atlantic sturgeon. It's available from February to May from PO Box 263, Darien, GA 31305; (912) 437-6560.

SeaPerfect Clams by Atlantic LittleNeck ClamFarms are better than clams from the wild. They come in several grades. Call (800) 728-0099 for a distributor in your area.

Joe's Stone Crab Restaurant on Miami Beach is the best source for stone crab claws: (800) 780-CRAB.

Sun-Dried Tomatoes and Fruits

are produced in the Shenandoah Valley and sold by L'Esprit de Campagne, PO Box 3130, Winchester, VA 22604; (703) 955-1014.

Sweet Onions.

Texas, Georgia, South Carolina, Hawaii, and Washington all grow sweet onions. Check your local markets first. Wadmalaw Sweets are available from Planters Three, PO Box 92, Wadmalaw Island, SC 29412; (800) 772-6732.

Bland Farms Sweet Vidalia Onions can be ordered from PO Box 506, Glennville, GA 30427; (800) VIDALIA.

Texas 1015s are available from Sunblest Farms at PO Box 547, Donna, TX 78357; (800) 633-0572.

Wine Index

T his index lists the wines that Debbie Marlowe has recommended to accompany the foods in this book. It is meant to be used as a cross-reference when you already have the wine and are looking for something to complement it. Perhaps it's a bottle you already have in your cellar, or perhaps it's something you've never tried before that your wine merchant suggested. Or maybe you're just in the mood for some Gigondas and aren't sure what to fix.

The index is utter simplicity to use. The wines are divided into reds, whites, and rosés, then further by specific place of origin and/or type of grape or wine style. Say your boss gave you a bottle of Domaine de la Pousse d'Or, a Volnay that's ready to drink. Look under "Red Wines—France." Under "Burgundy" you'll find the Volnay suggested to accompany the standing rib roast, certainly a dish worthy of the wine. Or perhaps you have a bottle of California Sauvignon Blanc and are tired of the same old fish dishes with it. The index indicates several dishes where California Sauvignon Blancs are recommended, including an unusual Peach Soup and Green Tomato Soup. Several of the wines are cross-referenced to more than one recipe.

RED WINES

France:

Bordeaux: **Médoc,** veal Edistonian (74); **earthy red,** duck soup with turnips and parsnips (8); **St-Estèphe,** grilled lamb chops (94);

Burgundy/Beaujolais: **young, inexpensive,** grilled flank steak (77); **Savigny-lès-Beaunes,** sliced tenderloin with three sauces (78); **Volnay,** standing rib roast (81); **Cru Beaujolais,** grilled rabbit (95) and grilled quail (118); **Fleurie,** grilled quail with raspberry vinaigrette (118); **Beaujolais Nouveau,** blue cheese burgers (84);

Rhône: **Côtes-du-Rhône,** grilled veal chops (71); pan-seared steaks with mushrooms (82); **Gigondas,** marinated grilled pork chops (88); **Vacqueyras,** grilled rabbit (95)

Provence: **rouge,** duck sausage (121)

California:

Cabernet: Napa, grilled lamb chops (94); **other,** grilled flank steak (77)

Zinfandel: anchovy puffs (234)

Gamay: blue cheese burgers (84)

Grignolino: duck breasts with cabbage and apples (120)

Sangiovese: goat cheese strata (140)

Merlot: sliced tenderloin with three sauces (78)

Saumur, chocolate cake (265); **Provence,** fresh tuna salad (39), duck sausage (121), crab with country ham and sherry vinaigrette (61)

Italy:

Tuscany: **Chianti,** seared tuna with tomato-basil vinaigrette (41); **Sangiovese,** goat cheese strata (140)

Piedmont: **Barbera d'Alba,** shrimp creole (54); **Barbera d'Asti,** duck étouffée (126), **Grignolino,** duck breasts with cabbage and apples (120); **other,** braised veal shanks (72)

Spain:

Rioja, corn pasta lasagne (174); **Sangre de Toro,** chicken liver pâté (113); **full-flavored red,** onions stuffed with lamb and rice (92)

Other:

Non-oaky Pinot Noir, crispy steamed fish (46)
Good red table wine, country fried steak (76)

WHITE WINES

France:

Bordeaux: **Appellation Contrôlée Blanc,** light tomato soup (31); **Caillou Blanc de Château Talbot,** lamb shanks with celeriac (91); **Graves,** peanut soup (9); **medium-bodied,** grilled fish with sorrel (32); **other,** rustic omelet of potherbs and potatoes (132); fried chicken (104).

Loire: **Muscadet,** pasta with oysters, leeks, and country ham (57), oyster pie (58); **Chenin Blanc,** fried flounder (42); sweet onion tart (130); tomato, sweet corn, fried okra, and smoked bacon salad (213); **Vouvray,** scallops with fennel, orange, and red onion (59); tomato, sweet corn, fried okra, and smoked bacon salad (213); **Pouilly-Fumé,** oyster stew (22), benne fried sea bass (37); **Fumé Blanc,** goat cheese strata (140)

Burgundy: **Appellation Contrôlée Chablis,** sautéed oysters (55); **St-Véran and Meursault,** cream of shiitake mushrooms (12); **Chassagne-Montrachet,** potato pie with caramelized onions and shiitake sauce (152); **Pouilly-Fuissé,** rabbit compote (97), grilled poussins (116); **Rully (Côte Chalonnaise),** frittata of grilled vegetables (134), soft-shell crab and oyster po' boy (64); **big white,** grilled poussins (116); **Bourgogne Blanc,** chicken liver pizza (110)

Rhône: **Côtes-du-Rhône,** braised veal shanks (72); **southern Rhône,** deep-fried turkey breast (105); **fruity white Côtes du Lubéron,** Vidalia onion tarte tatin (160)

Alsace: **Pinot Blanc,** hearty fish stew (23), oyster pie (58); **Riesling,** smoked tomato soup (6); **Gewürztraminer,** hoppin' john salad (216)

Coteaux de l'Ardèche: **Grand Ardèche from Louis Latour,** baked grits with mushrooms and country ham (172)

Provence and other: **Marsanne Blanc,** shrimp gumbo (28); **Gascony,** rustic omelet of potherbs and potatoes (132)

California:

Chardonnay: **Napa,** chicken pie (106); chicken and vegetable curry (15); **Monterey,** chicken pie (106), oyster stew (22), corn and crab pudding (66); **Sonoma,** oyster stew (22); corn and crab pudding (66), shark en brochette (48) veal Edistonian (74), fried flounder (42); **Santa Barbara,** oyster stew (22); **North Coast,** shrimp Awendaw with kiwi (53), shark en brochette (66); **tropical fruit style,** chicken and vegetable curry (15); **inexpensive,** waffles with creamed chicken (237)

Sauvignon Blanc: **melony, herbaceous style,** peach soup (11); **Sonoma,** corn and crab pudding (66); **Fumé Blanc,** celeriac and fennel soup (14), goat cheese strata (140); **any,** fish with tropical fruit (33)

Pinot Blanc: fish stew (23), oyster pie (58), crab cakes (62)

Chenin Blanc: Vidalia onion tarte tatin (160), fried chicken (104), fried flounder (42); **Wente Brothers Le Blanc de Blanc,** scallops with fennel, orange, and red onion (59)

Riesling: smoked tomato soup (6), chili (19)

Gewürztraminer: hoppin' john salad (216)

Oregon:

Chenin Blanc: tomato, sweet corn, fried okra, and smoked bacon salad (213)

Washington State:

Fumé Blanc: fish with a potato crust (43)

Italy:

Pinot Grigio: grilled squid (49)

Chardonnay/Pinot Grigio: clams in fennel and tomato court bouillon (67)

Frascati: summer pasta (177)

Orvieto: scallops with fennel, orange, and red onion (59)

Spain:

Rioja, corn pasta lasagne (174), poached fish (35); **Viña Sol,** poached fish (35)

Germany:

Riesling, duck and oyster jambalaya (123), smoked tomato soup (6), Thai chicken salad (115); **Gewürztraminer,** hoppin' john salad (216)

Australia:

Chardonnay, sweet potato ravioli (148)

Portugal:

Dry Muscat, shrimp creole (54)

Rosé Wines

France:

Bandol, fresh tuna salad (39); **Sparkling Cabernet Franc from Saumur,**

chocolate cake (265); **Provence,** fresh tuna salad (39), duck sausage (121), crab with country ham and sherry vinaigrette (61)

California:

Rosé of Cabernet, fresh tuna salad (39)

OTHER WINES

Port, poached pears (286); **Madeira,** sweetbreads and chicken (109), oeufs en gelée (139)

Select Bibliography

These are the published works that I used most often while working on this book. I sell the ones that are still in print in my bookstore in Charleston (see Ingredients and Sources, Corn Products); I'll gladly search for the out-of-print titles for you.

Americus Recipes. Americus, GA: Junior Welfare League, 1961.

Bailey, Lee. *Lee Bailey's Country Desserts.* New York: Clarkson N. Potter, Inc., 1988.

———. *Lee Bailey's Long Weekends.* New York: Clarkson N. Potter, Inc., 1994.

———. *Lee Bailey's New Orleans.* New York: Clarkson N. Potter, Inc., 1993.

———. *Lee Bailey's Southern Food and Plantation Houses.* New York: Clarkson N. Potter, Inc., 1990.

Berry, Mrs. Willie S. *"Don't Forget the Parsley. . . ."* Orangeburg, SC: Orangeburg-Calhoun Technical College Foundation, Inc., 1982.

Bronz, Ruth Adams. *Miss Ruby's American Cooking.* New York: Harper & Row, 1989.

Bryan, Lettice. *The Kentucky Housewife.* With a New Introduction by Bill Neal. Columbia: University of South Carolina Press, 1990.

Burn, Billie. *Stirrin' the Pots on Daufuskie.* Daufuskie Island, SC: Burn Books, 1985.

Cason, Clarence. *90° in the Shade.* Chapel Hill: University of North Carolina Press, 1935.

Colquitt, Harriet Ross. *The Savannah Cook Book.* Charleston: Walker, Evans, & Cogswell Co., 1933.

Conway, Linda Glick, ed. *Party Receipts from the Charleston Junior League.* Chapel Hill: Algonquin Books, 1993.

Cooking in Old Salem. Williamsburg: Williamsburg Publishing Co., 1981.

Darden, Norma Jean and Carole. *Spoonbread and Strawberry Wine.* New York: Doubleday, 1978.

David, Elizabeth. *English Bread and Yeast Cookery.* New York: Viking, 1980.

Davidson, Alan. *North Atlantic Seafood.* New York: Viking, 1979.

Dull, Mrs. D. R. *Southern Cooking.* Atlanta: Cherokee Publishing Co., 1989.

Egerton, John. *Southern Food.* New York: Alfred A. Knopf, Inc., 1987.

Elverson, Virginia. *Gulf Coast Cooking: Seafood from the Florida Keys to the Yucatan Peninsula.* Fredericksburg, TX: Shearer Publishing, 1991.

Escott, Paul D., and David R. Goldfield, eds. *The South for New Southerners.* Chapel Hill: University of North Carolina Press, 1991.

Feibleman, Peter, and the Editors of Time-Life Books. *American Cooking: Creole and Acadian.* New York: Time, Inc., 1971.

Fitch, Jenny. *The Fearrington House Cookbook: A Celebration of Food, Flowers, and Herbs.* Chapel Hill: Ventana Press, 1987.

Four Great Southern Cooks. Atlanta: Dubose Publishing, 1980.

Fowler, Damon Lee. *Classical Southern Cooking.* New York: Crown Publishers, Inc., 1995.

Garden Seed Inventory, Third Edition. With an Introduction by Kent Whealy. Decorah, IA: Seed Saver Publications, 1992.

Glenn, Camille. *The Heritage of Southern Cooking.* New York: Workman Publishing Co., Inc., 1986.

Harris, Jessica B. *Iron Pots and Wooden Spoons: Africa's Gifts to New World Cookery.* New York: Macmillan Publishing Co., 1989.

Hedrick, U. P., ed. *Sturtevant's Edible Plants of the World.* New York: Dover, 1919.

Herbst, Sharon Tyler. *Food Lover's Companion.* Hauppauge, NY: Barron's Educational Series, Inc., 1990.

Hess, Karen. "The American Loaf: A Historical View," *The Journal of Gastronomy,* Volume 3, Number 4, Winter 1987/1988.

————. *The Carolina Rice Kitchen: The African Connection.* Columbia: University of South Carolina Press, 1992.

————, ed. *Martha Washington's Booke of Cookery.* New York: Columbia University Press, 1981.

Hess, John L., and Karen Hess. *The Taste of America.* New York: Grossman Publishers, 1977.

Hill, Mrs. A. P. *Mrs. Hill's New Cook Book.* New York: Carleston, Publisher, 1872.

Huguenin, Mary V., and Anne M. Stoney, eds. *Charleston Receipts.* Charleston: Walker, Evans, & Cogswell Co., 1950.

Junior League of New Orleans. *The Plantation Cookbook.* Garden City, NY: Doubleday & Co., Inc., 1972.

Lambert, Walter N. *Kinfolks and Custard Pie: Recollections and Recipes from an East Tennesseean.* Knoxville: University of Tennessee Press, 1988.

Ledford, Ibbie. *Hill Country Cookin' and Memories.* Gretna, LA: Pelican Publishing Co., 1991.

Leslie, Eliza. *Directions for Cookery in Its Various Branches.* Philadelphia: Carey & Hart, 1837.

Lewis, Edna. *In Pursuit of Flavor.* New York: Alfred A. Knopf, Inc., 1988.

———. *The Taste of Country Cooking.* New York: Alfred A. Knopf, Inc., 1976.

Lundy, Ronni. *Shuck Beans, Stack Cakes, and Honest Fried Chicken.* New York: Atlantic Monthly Press, 1991.

Maryland's Way. Annapolis: The Hammond-Harwood House Association, 1963.

McClane, A. J. *The Encyclopedia of Fish Cookery.* New York: Henry Holt and Co., 1977.

McCracken, Mary Lou: *The Deep South Natural Foods Cookbook.* New York: Pyramid Publications, 1975.

McCulloch-Williams, Martha. *Dishes and Beverages of the Old South.* Knoxville: University of Tennessee Press, 1988.

McKee, Gwen. *The Little Gumbo Book.* Baton Rouge: Quail Ridge Press, 1986.

Miller, Joni. *True Grits: The Southern Foods Mail-Order Catalog.* New York: Workman Publishing Co., Inc., 1990.

Montagné, Prosper. *Larousse Gastronomique.* New York: Crown Publishers, Inc., 1961.

Neal, Bill. *Biscuits, Spoonbread, and Sweet Potato Pie.* New York: Alfred A. Knopf, Inc., 1990.

Neal, William F. *Bill Neal's Southern Cooking.* Chapel Hill: University of North Carolina Press, 1985.

Orangeburg's Choice Recipes. Orangeburg, SC: Walter D. Berry, 1948.

Picayune Creole Cook Book, The. New Orleans: Picayune Publishing Co., 1900.

Pyles, Stephan. *The New Texas Cuisine.* New York: Doubleday, 1993.

Randolph, Mary. *The Virginia House-Wife.* With Historical Notes and Commentaries by Karen Hess. Columbia: University of South Carolina Press, 1984.

Rutledge, Sarah. *The Carolina Housewife.* Charleston: W. R. Babcock & Co., 1847.

Sahtein: Middle East Cookbook. Detroit: The Arab Women Union, 1979.

Schneider, Elizabeth. *Uncommon Fruits and Vegetables: A Commonsense Guide.* New York: Harper & Row, 1986.

Sea Island Seasons. Beaufort, SC: Beaufort County Open Land Trust, 1980.

Southern Country Cookbook. Birmingham: The Progressive Farmer Co., 1972.

Southern Heritage Cakes Cookbook, The. Birmingham: Oxmoor House, Inc., 1983.

Tartan, Beth. *North Carolina and Old Salem Cookery,* new and revised. Chapel Hill: University of North Carolina Press, 1955 and 1992.

Taylor, John Martin. *Hoppin' John's Lowcountry Cooking: Recipes and Ruminations from Charleston and the Carolina Coastal Plain.* New York: Bantam Books, 1992.

Tolley, Lynne, and Pat Mitchamore. *Jack Daniel's The Spirit of Tennessee Cookbook.* Nashville: Rutledge Hill, 1988.

Vegetables. Alexandria, VA: Time-Life Books, 1979.

Voltz, Jeanne, and Caroline Stuart. *The Florida Cookbook.* New York: Alfred A. Knopf, Inc., 1993.

Walter, Eugene, and the Editors of Time-Life Books. *American Cooking: Southern Style.* New York: Time, Inc., 1971.

Wilcox, Estelle Woods. *The Dixie Cook-Book.* Atlanta: L. A. Clarkson & Co, 1883.

Willan, Anne. *La Varenne Pratique.* London: Dorling Kindersley, Ltd., 1989.

Wolfert, Paula. *The Cooking of South-West France.* Garden City, NY: The Dial Press, 1983.

Index